EMOTIONAL ABUSE RECOVERY

3 Books In 1:

Divorce from A Narcissist, Healing Racial Trauma, Complex PTSD Trauma and Recovery, The Ultimate Guide for Overcome Anxiety and Developing Personal

BETHANY KEY

© Copyright 2020 - All rights reserved.

The content contained within this book may not be reproduced, duplicated or transmitted without direct written permission from the author or the publisher.

Under no circumstances will any blame or legal responsibility be held against the publisher, or author, for any damages, reparation, or monetary loss due to the information contained within this book. Either directly or indirectly.

Legal Notice: This book is copyright protected. This book is only for personal use. You cannot amend, distribute, sell, use, quote or paraphrase any part, or the content within this book, without the consent of the author or publisher.

Disclaimer Notice: Please note the information contained within this document is for educational and entertainment purposes only. All effort has been executed to present accurate, up to date, and reliable, complete information. No warranties of any kind are declared or implied. Readers acknowledge that the author is not engaging in the rendering of legal, financial, medical or professional advice. The content within this book has been derived from various sources. Please consult a licensed professional before attempting any techniques outlined in this book.

By reading this document, the reader agrees that under no circumstances is the author responsible for any losses, direct or indirect, which are incurred as a result of the use of information contained within this document, including, but not limited to, — errors, omissions, or inaccuracies.

DIVORCE FROM A NARCISSIST

Table of Content

Introduction 10
Chapter 1: Understanding And Defining Narcissism 14
Chapter 2: Types Of Narcissism 22
Chapter 3: What Is Narcissistic Abuse? 28
Chapter 4: Narcissistic Tactics 36
Chapter 5: How To Protect Yourself When Divorcing A Narcissist 42
Chapter 6: The Path To Recovery Freedom 50
Chapter 7: Tactics To Help You Deal With The Divorce 58
Chapter 8: Divorce And Your Children 66
Chapter 9: The Aftermath 72
Chapter 10: The Path To Recovery Freedom 78
Chapter 11: Redefining Yourself After Abuse 86
Chapter 12: Discover Your True Worth 94
Chapter 13: When The Healing Gets Tough 102
Chapter 14: How To Learn To Live And Love After Being With A Narcissist 108
Chapter 15: Transforming Your Future Interactions 116
Conclusion 122

HEALING RACIAL TRAUMA

Table of Content

Introduction 130
Chapter 1: Feelings Of Shame, Guilt, And Anxiety 134
Chapter 2: Forms Of Racial Trauma 140
Chapter 3: Types Of Racism 144
Chapter 4: Keys To Education Against Racial Trauma 152
Chapter 5: Learning From The History Of Racial Trauma 156
Chapter 6: Understanding Your Racial-Ethnic Identity 164
Chapter 7: Footprints And Symptoms Of Racial Trauma -Physiological Changes 170
Chapter 8: Stepping Into Freedom-Identify 180
Chapter 9: How To Support Your Own Healing? 186
Chapter 10: Contributing Factors To Ethnicity And Racial Trauma ... 192
Chapter 11: How To Stomp Out Racial Trauma 196
Chapter 12: Causes And Effects Of Racial Trauma 206
Chapter 13: Identifying The Problem 214
Chapter 14: What Is Anti-Racial Trauma? 224
Chapter 15: Solidarity Against Racial Trauma 230
Chapter 16: Hypocrisy Within Us 238
Chapter 17: Racial Trauma Theories In The Modern Age 246
Chapter 18: What Is Social Justice? 254
Chapter 19: Fighting Racial Trauma 260
Conclusion 266

COMPLEX PTSD FROM SURVIVING TO HEALING

Table of Content

Introduction ... 274
Chapter 1: Understanding PTSD ... 276
Chapter 2: Symptoms Of Cptsd ... 282
Chapter 3: PTSD Symptoms Differential Diagnosis ... 290
Chapter 4: Strategies To Recovery ... 298
Chapter 5: Dialectal Behavior Therapy ... 308
Chapter 6: PTSD And Relaxation ... 316
Chapter 7: What Is Psychotherapy? ... 326
Chapter 8: What Is Talk Cure Therapy? ... 330
Chapter 9: What Is Cognitive Behavioral Therapy? ... 334
Chapter 10: What Is Cognitive Processing Therapy? ... 342
Chapter 11: Somatic Or "Right-Brain" Psychotherapy ... 348
Chapter 12: What Is Emdr? ... 354
Chapter 13: Trauma And PSTD— PTSD Treatment With Hypnotherapy ... 364
Chapter 14: Can Medication Help? ... 374
Chapter 15: PSTD Methods ... 382
Chapter 16: About PTSD & Triggers ... 388
Chapter 17: Recovery And Daily Home Life Demands ... 398
Chapter 18: To Family And Friends ... 404
Chapter 19: Curing Ptsd With Eft, Meditation And Energy ... 410
Chapter 20: Trauma Treatment And Mental Health ... 416
Conclusion ... 418

DIVORCE FROM A

NARCISSIST

A Journey Through The Stages Of Recovery From A Narcissist And Rediscovering Your True Self

BETHANY KEY

Introduction

The narcissist needs people to constantly provide them with love and adoration. This supply of energy is what helps them maintain their false ego. One single person is not going to be able to give them all of the attention that they need, so they will include a variety of different people in their toxic lives to find the supply that they feel is required. You must always remember that the people the narcissist chooses are always replaceable, and their roles in the life of the narcissist can change very quickly. Each person that is in the web of the narcissist will constantly be battling to prove their value.

There are a lot of people that feel as if narcissists are drawn to them like magnets. It may not be that narcissists are more drawn to you, but you may be more at holding on to them. For instance, many people that can easily see the negative attributes of a narcissist such as their need to be the center of attention, the constant reassurance they are seeking, or the sensitivity they have to be slighted. When they see these things, they may not recognize them as narcissistic traits, but they are still unfavorable. Due to the fact that these are unfavorable traits, most people will not go any further with the relationship.

People are often disturbed by the types of behaviors that the narcissist displays. They will disengage themselves from the situation because it is easier than trying to deal with someone who is difficult from the very beginning. The people that tend to stick around the narcissist will handle this type of situation in a very different way.

If you are a person that feels like narcissists are constantly drawn to you, you might need to take a look at your standards for relationships and what behaviors you will and will not tolerate.

To understand whether or not your standards are healthy and will keep you protected, you can ask yourself the following questions:

- At any point in time, have you ended a relationship because of selfishness on your partner's behalf?
- Are you able to set clear boundaries and stick to them?
- Do you know what behaviors in a relationship you will tolerate, and which ones are totally unacceptable?
- Do you rationalize staying in a bad relationship because you believe it can get better? Is this because of the way things started out in your relationship?
- Do you allow your partners to devalue you?
- Is making excuses for your partner's bad behavior commonplace?
- Have you put up with mental, physical, or emotional abuse without leaving?

If you do find that these questions relate to you, it is time to sit back and really look over your standards. You need to find strategies that will help weed out people with bad behaviors before they sink their claws into you.

Exiting a relationship because you feel that someone is taking advantage of you or that they have nefarious intent is not wrong. It may seem difficult to weed out the narcissists, but when you give people too many chances, you are simply giving them more time to manipulate and take advantage of you.

There are also a few different personality traits that narcissists will pick up on and try to take advantage of. Certain traits are found to be more useful to narcissists than others. So, if you are extremely empathetic, have a desire to help others, you are willing to try harder than most to make relationships work, or your sense of responsibility is strong, and you are likely the perfect target for a narcissist.

All of these traits fall into the desires of a narcissist. Most people don't try and hide these positive attributes that they hold. Unfortunately, with this, the narcissist is able to pick their target quite easily.

Narcissists also genuinely enjoy taking advantage of truly intelligent people. Everything in their lives is a game, and roping someone into their game that is smart feels like a major win for the narcissist. The high they get from besting an intelligent person is better than many others.

It's unfortunate because many intelligent people end up being taken advantage of without realizing what is going on before it is way too late, and they have suffered at the hands of the narcissist for far too long.

People that have lived through narcissistic abuse will oftentimes question themselves. The narcissist has made them believe that everything they have gotten they have deserved. Even though this is utterly untrue, it is hard to make someone who has suffered from narcissistic abuse realize that none of it is their fault. At the end of the day, pretty much anyone can become the target of a narcissist. The most important thing that you can do is to pay attention to the new partners you are bringing into your life to make sure it does not end with the abuse and toxicity that comes along with a narcissist.

CHAPTER 1:

Understanding and Defining Narcissism

Narcissism is a character trait in which someone displays a heightened over-confidence due to their admiration of themselves; they can simply do no wrong. This is an exaggerated behavior that breathes and exudes arrogance, pretentiousness, and a deep-rooted ideology of false superiority. "I am special. Everyone else in the world is below me because they are not me." A person who exhibits narcissistic characteristics is often described as being cocky, self-centered, self-absorbed, and rude. They view life as a playground for manipulating emotion, as an untapped market in which to exploit and to bend the truth at will. They can be viewed as "winners," but they are crude people to be involved with due to their self-described perfection. So, too, are they, liars. Their success—in most cases—is because of their total and complete disregard for other people and their feelings. Or rather, narcissists will push past people no matter what those people are feeling. They view other people as obstacles. We are, basically, their next hurdle to get over. They would most likely push us off the edge of a top-floor balcony if it meant that they would get just a little more ahead of everyone else.

Narcissists are the perennial interrupters of conversation. They constantly crave the limelight; they feel as if they deserve everyone's attention at each and every single turn. They want to be seen. They want to be heard. They want to be the leading figure in any small gathering, work circles, friendship circles, and among the large crowds. They are the people who ooze confidence in every moment. They are very charming people and more often than not, they are quite funny, very sarcastic. They are good company in public, but once at home and in their own respective comfort zones, they shed their charming skins for the emotionally deprived, ostentatious colors that they don when returned to their private and intimate places. They use manipulation and excessive, yet believable, lies as a tool to such an extent that narcissists are almost fanatical individuals in regard to their use of such methods.

Narcissists have such a deep self-belief burning within them. But beneath all of that lies a person who has been deeply affected by life. Narcissists are people, though pretty hardcore ones, who have been shaped by past trauma, past experiences, or past abuse, which, in turn, has crafted them into a person with such anxiety that the line between nervousness and abandonment has morphed and blurred into a singularly, individualistic focus that the adulation that they are constantly seeking is due to their inner mental conflicts that were borne from a lonely and possibly unloved childhood. This has made them develop what we could call external spotlighted arrogance. The definition of this is, simply, a spotlight. Some form of an inner spotlight that externalizes itself—or switches on when it feels like it needs to be seen. It burns so bright that it forces people to shift and focus all undivided attention on the narcissist. This trait or behavioral characteristic, if looked at from a psychological perspective, is most common in children below the age of 10. It is that need to stand out from the rest, to get attention, whether that is from your parents, your family, your friends; it's a phase our brains go through during early childhood development that can be best linked to the behavior-type of being boastful or to brag about something. In a narcissist's case, what they are essentially bragging about is themselves.

We all know a narcissist. They could be our mother or our father; they could have been this way for as long as we can remember and have left us, now in adulthood, shattered, confused, exhausted. They could be our brother or our sister; they were always showered with praise, always told that they were the star—they were serial winners and developed an egotism that has become the prospective difficulties in our lives, still affecting us at this very moment. They could be a work colleague or an employee. But what are the roots of narcissism?

Narcissists tend to view themselves quite differently when compared to others, and they often make those around them feel inadequate and devalued. Here's the kicker—a narcissist always wants everything to be about themselves. You might not mind showering a one-year-old infant with all your attention, but you will start to mind when a 35-year-old demands the same level of attention and achieves it at your expense.

Narcissists easily victimize others by just being who they are, and it is unlikely they will ever change. This might seem rather severe, but until you deal with a narcissist, you will not realize how toxic such individuals can be. To understand NPD, you must first understand the way narcissists think about themselves.

Where Does Narcissism Come From?

Narcissism usually develops in early childhood. I have heard people say many times that narcissistic behavior reminds them of a toddler throwing a tantrum. I tend to agree with this statement based on personal experience. It seems the emotional trauma responsible for narcissism occurs around the age of a toddler, hence the narcissist's ability to handle emotions gets stuck at that level of mental development. That explains their dangerous emotional immaturity, doesn't it?

We all get exposed to trauma during the early stages of our development. It's simply inevitable. Trauma can result from something as simple as not being picked up by our parent as a baby or being fed against our will. It could also result from something more severe like our mother leaving us at the kindergarten for the first time, which can cause a long-lasting fear of separation. Our parents fighting and screaming at each other in our presence can leave their imprints on our subconscious mind, too. So, what kind of trauma produces a narcissist?

Growing up with an either overbearing and/or completely neglectful parent can warp a child's mind and cause them to be narcissistic adults later in life. A parent can be overbearing when it comes a child's performance in school and neglectful when it comes to the child's emotional needs.

The trauma of a narcissist is the perceived lack of control. The inability to acknowledge their own emotions makes a narcissist extremely uncomfortable. Admitting one "wrong" thing about themselves would make them feel as though everything is wrong. So, every abusive and manipulative action they take only serves one purpose: to feel in control. The root of their toxic behavior towards you has nothing to with you, it has everything to do with them. If you play close attention to their accusations, you will see that they, in fact, project their behavior, fears, and doubts on you. A narcissist may often lie, yet accuse you of lying all the time, no matter how much proof you present that they are wrong. They may feel as if everyone is out to get them and that they always get the short end of the stick, so they project their subconscious beliefs on you by accusing you of plotting schemes against them every time there is a simple misunderstanding.

You must keep in mind that narcissists never truly learned how to express and process their emotions. Their parents may have been overly protective and proud of them—but only when they fulfilled their parents' expectations. One could try to do some research about the past of the narcissist in question. Though it usually is difficult to get a clear picture. It's very difficult to find the truth about a narcissist, especially when their parents admit to not having been able to handle their child.

In many cases, one or both of their parents may display some narcissistic traits, too. That does not mean, however, that the children of a narcissist are bound to become narcissistic as well.

At the end of the day, it's not up to you to determine why the person that treated you so badly has become who they are today and it also not necessary for your recovery process. However, what is necessary for your recovery process is that you are aware that it's definitely not your fault in any way that they are a narcissist, and with that, you are not responsible for their chronic toxicity.

This can be an environmental cause that can lead to a forced image of perfection later in life. Another aspect is early childhood abuse. One way to deal with abuse is to see yourself as above it, too clean for it. Taking an abusive history into account, narcissism acts as a wall to prevent being hurt further in the future. Despite the several ways the disorder can be environmental, there is also some belief that the trait can in fact be hereditary. With genetics, though, seeing a specific behavioral trait can be difficult. Often, though it may seem genetic, it is moreover the way that parent or grandparent was raised that gives them the condition. This brings up the question of actual genetics. Science has yet to come to a clear conclusion on that though. Studies have not been able to come to a solid conclusion, and with many different conditions, it is hard to see which is environmental and which is genetic.

Majority of the cases of Narcissistic Personality Disorder, though, always point back to the parents who raised the child. Whether it is neglect, abuse, overprotection, rewarding for insignificance, Munchausen, or even the parent giving the child a hypochondriac disorder or a sense that they are superior, the child's behavior is usually created at an early age. With such a deep-seated basis and such a long time for growth, this makes the disorder even harder to overcome later in life. Changing someone's perspective of how they should see the world when they were raised and to see it differently can be a nearly impossible task. This also can cause more behavioral and personality issues. Taking away the one or only, defense someone has constructed in order to deal with trauma can then lead to an exposed and vulnerable feeling that can cause depression and/or anxiety. What happens then is the person goes from being narcissistic to high-risk Avoidant Personality Disorder, agoraphobia, social anxiety, self-harm, and even suicidal, or an intention of hurting others. People using narcissism to cover an abusive or traumatic childhood would have to be approached with the utmost care.

Even if the issues are genetic, there is really no direct way to treat genetics over a learned behavior cycle. Hereditary behavior issues are something a species line has evolved to. Somehow that series of genetics has evolved to see itself as more significant than others. Whether this has to do with the biological mating habits or some kind of protective reaction of the line, it is part of who the person is. Just as someone is likely to have a stronger inclination to be a leader or one who helps people for a living, being someone who sees themselves as above others will already be in their head from early childhood. As with learned behavior, this comes from one or both parents.

CHAPTER 2:

Types of Narcissism

There are many shades of narcissists that exist. If you're dealing with one, then you need to know exactly what kind they are. This is the only way you can figure out how to handle yourself, whenever you're forced to have interactions with them.

So let's get into the various kinds of narcissists that exist. There are three kinds of narcissists that you're likely to encounter if you haven't met them already. Under these, there are also subtypes. First, let's look at the main three: the classic narcissist, the vulnerable narcissist, and the malignant narcissist.

The Classic Narcissist

This kind of narcissist is what first springs to most people's minds when they think of a narcissist. They're the exhibitionists. The grandiose ones. The high-functioning narcissists. The classic narcissist is the guy who's a braggart, always going on and on about their achievements. She's the gal who feels entitled to special treatment, praise, and a statue in her honor, while you're at it. If you're not delicately and consistently placing your lips on their derriere, then you're uninteresting, at best, or in trouble, at worst. They hate it when the spotlight moves from them to someone else. They hate it when you share the spotlight with them. They're going to crop you out of pictures, because you looked better, or they perceive somehow you've dulled their glory. For the classic narcissist, even though they already feel superior to the rest of the human race, they have an obsessive need to be perceived as important by others.

The Vulnerable Narcissist

This guy is fragile. He's always "the victim." He's also called a closet narcissist. Compensatory. The vulnerable narcissist is—as far as he's concerned—better than everyone else they meet. What's the difference between him and the classic narcissist? He isn't a huge fan of being the center of attention. This narcissist is a leech, of sorts. She'll attach herself to people others think of as important, or special. No, she's not going to look for special treatment for herself—but what she will do is try to get people to feel bad for her. She'll suck up to you by being extremely generous with the gifts and compliments. This is how she'll get the attention she wants from you, and get her much needed ego boost.

The Malignant Narcissist

This guy is the stuff of nightmares. You may have heard of him referred to as a "toxic narcissist. They're the worst of the lot, being extremely manipulative. They will exploit everyone around them to no end.

The toxic, malignant narcissist is also antisocial. Not unlike sadistic psychopaths, and their sociopath counterparts, they've got quite a mean streak.

For the malignant narcissist, her goal is to control. Complete domination. She will do and say whatever she needs to, to feel all-powerful. She will lie. She will use violence. Nothing is beyond her. The worst part? She has absolutely no regrets. She is not riddled with remorse. She doesn't understand what it's like to feel guilty. She does enjoy watching other people in pain, though.

The malignant narcissist is the worst of the lot because they can be serial killers with no remorse. They're the kind who become dictators ad don't mind wiping off an entire race from the face of the earth.

Now that we have covered the three major types of narcissists, let's get into the subtypes.

- **Overt versus Covert Narcissist**

Overt and covert narcissists both enjoy making others feel like crap, bragging and looking for the chance to put one over you. The difference between both sub-types of narcissists though, is that while the overt narcissist is very obvious about all this, the covert narcissist is less likely to be noticed.

Usually, covert narcissists are heavy on passive aggression. In fact, it's possible for you to engage with a covert narcissist, and not have a single clue that they just manipulated you. They're quite stealthy in their methods. This stealth is just enough to give them plausible deniability if you find out they just played you like an upright bass.

You need to understand that while the classic narcissist is an overt narcissist, and the vulnerable narcissist is a covert narcissist, the malignant narcissist can be either.

- **Somatic versus Cerebral Narcissist**

Under this sub-type of narcissism, we're clarifying what the narcissist thinks is most important about himself, and others around him. True, the narcissist is always about hogging the spotlight, while everyone else remains in the faceless audience, applauding them.

However, the narcissists under this sub-type still want to be around people who complement them nicely or would be an added boost to their carefully, intricately woven persona. In other words, these narcissists like to show you off—as their property. "Look how smart or beautiful this person is! Aren't I awesome for being friends with them? But forget about them though—look at me! Look how good I look! Look at me big, big brain! Plenty of smarts!"

The somatic narcissist is crazy about her body. She wants to look hot, all the time. She's got to look good. She's got to retain her youth. She'd become a vampire if those existed, so she could stay young forever. She hits the gym hard. She loves mirrors—or more to the point, she loves what she sees in the mirror. She's taken with her reflection. Her wallpaper is her own selfie. Always.

On the other hand, the cerebral narcissist knows everything. Everything! As far as they are concerned, they are more intelligent than anyone in the room. For them, it's important people realize how smart they are, how much they've accomplished, and how much power they wield.

These subtypes can apply to any of the malignant, vulnerable, and classic types of narcissists. There are some who argue that cerebral narcissists are only ever vulnerable narcissists and that somatic narcissists are classic narcissists, always.

On the flip side, there are arguments that this sort of thinking is stereotypical. It is argued that the view is held only because the body is an external thing, so it would make sense that the classic narcissist is also a somatic narcissist; and since the mind is an internal, hidden thing, then the cerebral narcissist must be a vulnerable narcissist.

The trouble with these stereotypical deductions is evident when you think of the average hypochondriac. The vulnerable narcissist can also get the attention they need with their bodies—through either feigning or exploiting an illness they have. Also, it's possible to have a classic narcissist who's also a cerebral one, seeking admiration because of all they've learned or achieved academically speaking.

Unique Sub-Types of Narcissists

Besides the sub-types we've already covered, we have a couple more, which studies have discovered and labeled as special. These subtypes are the inverted narcissist and the sadistic narcissist.

- **The Inverted Narcissist**

This narcissist is both covert and vulnerable and, codependent. They get into relationships with other narcissists, so they can feel good about themselves. In fact, if their significant other is not a narcissist, then there's a huge chance they will get absolutely no satisfaction from their relationship. The inverted narcissist is a victim of childhood abandonment.

- **The Sadistic Narcissist**

This sort of narcissist is malignant and has a striking similarity to psychopaths, and sociopaths alike. They love hurting others. They're like demons wearing a human meat suit. All their interactions are only ever about one thing: control. They get off on making others feel like crap by utterly humiliating them. They also have some really out-there sexual kinks.

CHAPTER 3:

What Is Narcissistic Abuse?

Narcissists may demonstrate traits that allow them to be characterized and understood by psychiatrists, but this does not mean that all narcissists are the same. Some narcissists have a more seductive pattern to their manipulation, while others are especially virulent and vindictive in their behavior. A similar statement can be made about narcissistic abuse. Narcissistic abuse is an umbrella term that refers to a spectrum of abusive practices. People with narcissistic personality behavior may all be involved in the abuse of one type or another, but some are apt to be more dangerous abusers than others.

Narcissistic abuse is a subject worthy of discussion because of the trauma it causes to the victims. Narcissistic abuse generally does not leave a scar or a bruise.

This type of abuse can drive a person to a nervous breakdown or suicide. It can render people so depressed and isolated that they are unable to leave the house or maintain employment. Narcissistic abuse is traumatic enough that there are clinicians that specialize in treating it. And much has been written on the subject to provide guidance to those interested in contributing to this effort.

Narcissistic abuse us a difficult quantity to handle and describe because many people do not realize that they are being abused.

Definition of Narcissistic Abuse

Narcissistic abuse can be thought of as any abuse that a narcissistic person commits against another person. That being said, narcissistic abuse historically referred to the manner of emotional abuse that narcissistic parents committed against their children. Today, we think of narcissistic abuse as the spectrum of damaging words and behaviors that are done by people with a narcissistic personality disorder.

This type of abuse is generally emotional abuse, although narcissistic people can become physical if in a rage. Emotional abuse itself refers to the gamut of words and deeds that can be traumatic to the other person. As we have seen, the narcissistic person is prone to belittle, demean, and bully others as a part of establishing the dysfunctional dynamic of the narcissistic relationship.

Types of Narcissistic Abuse

Those readers familiar with the literature on narcissism may be familiar with the terms gaslighting and love-bombing, which describe types of behavior associated with narcissists. In particular, it is a particularly effective tactic that these individuals engage in, which serves the purpose of weakening and isolating their target. Gaslighting is essentially a specific type of manipulation. Many different types of narcissistic abuse involve manipulation, a behavior the narcissist is particularly adept at.

The most common type of narcissistic abuse is emotional abuse, as the narcissist typically uses the emotions of the target against them. The narcissist is sensitive to the emotional cues that other people send, and they learn how to use those cues against them. Something as simple as an unconscious gesture that you make when you are happy or when you are sad serves as a clue to the manipulator of what you are feeling. In truth, the manipulator does not sincerely care how you feel because they lack empathy. They use these gestures as sources of intelligence that can be used against you either for manipulation or abuse. In fact, the distinction between manipulation and emotional abuse is not always clear. Many books have been written that attempt to sanitize manipulation, seeing this as a tactic that people can (and often do) use for good. For example, a parent can manipulate their children into doing their schoolwork. A wife can also manipulate her husband into applying for that job he was recommended for. These types of manipulation are regarded by some as "normal" and not harmful. This leads these advocates for manipulation to see it as a form of persuasion rather than an art that is always used for harm.

Emotional abuse can be simply defined as using the feelings of others as a tool to wound them

Emotional abuse frequently happens in narcissistic relationships because the partner of the narcissist is often a sensitive person—an empath—who is particularly sensitive and responsive to emotional cues. The narcissist in the relationship with the empath, therefore, has not only amply information on what they are feeling but plentiful opportunities to wound them.

In spite of the supporters of manipulation, we can think of both emotional abuse and manipulation as types of abuse that occur in narcissistic relationships. Gaslighting, again, is a type of manipulation that is frequently found in these relationships, but because it is so singular, it is often regarded as a separate type of abuse. The term represents the unique ability of the narcissist to exert control over those around him or her, leading them to doubt that they understand the distinction between reality and fantasy.

This is the crux of gaslighting

The ability of the narcissist to cause the target to question their sanity. The narcissist is able to do this because they are masters at constructing a false reality that others believe in. For example, the narcissist can carefully create and spread a damaging lie that other people accept. Even the person the lie is about may begin to accept the lie, which is the goal.

For example, a vindictive or seductive narcissist may tell others that a co-worker, roommate, or associate is having problems at work and is about to lose their job. The narcissist says that this person has been caught violating office policy. This seems benign enough, but it is a powerful lie that it is easy for the target to believe. The target may then begin looking for another job (which might be the goal of the narcissist), they may subconsciously begin performing poorly at work (thus fulfilling the words of the narcissist), or they experience psychological effects like anxiety and paranoia.

Gaslighting can be more vicious

A narcissist may steal things from your desk or move them around, which may cause you confusion and doubt. They may follow you or get others to follow you to make you paranoid. They can engage in a host of activities designed to loosen your grip on reality. This manipulation also serves to isolate you.

Isolation is a result of narcissistic abuse that can be considered another form of abuse

Most people learning about narcissism and its effects for the first time have difficulty understanding just how damaging isolation is. Individuals who are isolated not only experience psychological symptoms like depression and anxiety, they experience physical symptoms due to a release of cortisol and other hormones, and they are at much higher risk of suicide than the general population.

As we have seen, the narcissist isolates their partner because they have a codependent need to keep the partner in the relationship. You, as the partner of the narcissist, serve the important role of enabling and encouraging their distorted, archaic self. In order to maintain this self, they will belittle, bully, and engage in other abusive behaviors. These behaviors serve to isolate you by lowering your self-esteem and making you depressed, but the narcissist also actively attempts to isolate you by discouraging you from interacting with family and friends or planting the notion that these people dislike you and would not want to be around you.

As the reader may gleam, gaslighting is a type of abuse that pervades the other types because the narcissist requires the reality of the target to be distorted. In simplest terms, if you saw the narcissist for who they really were (and yourself for who you really are), you probably would not want to be in a relationship with the narcissist or around them at all. The false reality the narcissist constructs in there, and your life is in itself a form of gaslighting.

Some indications that you may be a victim of gaslighting include:

- Feeling excessive doubts that you cannot control or explain
- Feeling that the narcissist knows more than you do about everything (even about yourself)
- Feeling that your sense of normal has changed
- Feeling excessive paranoia without a clear cause
- Becoming silent and withdrawn
- Feeling hypersensitive and hyper-vigilant in your normal environment

Phases of Abuse

The abuse cycle is divided into six phases: idealize, devalue, discard, destroy, and hoover. The narcissist naturally engages in this cycle in every relationship that they are involved in. This is not limited to romantic relationships. As the reader may already know, the narcissist is willing to discard even the closest blood relative without a passing thought.

The phases of abuse are also related to the phases of the narcissistic relationship. The idealization phase occurs early on in the narcissistic relationship. This phase may also include so-called love-bombing, which is designed to give the target an idealized view of the narcissist and the relationship. This merely sets the stage for abuse by reeling the target in with a fictitious idea of who the narcissist is. The narcissist wants you to trust them and see them as superior. Idealization allows them to do this by establishing the sort of rapport that human beings usually establish with one another, but which the narcissist is doing manipulatively and deceptively.

Indeed, many people have difficulty leaving narcissists because of the idealized images that were established in the idealization phase. Those who are abused by the narcissist and do not leave eventually will be discarded when the narcissist tires of them or no longer needs them. Before the narcissist discards their partner, they devalue them. This is a type of abusive behavior that involves belittling, bullying, and other behaviors that are designed to establish the relationship dynamic the narcissist wants. In reality, the narcissist does not value you and thinks you are less than they are, so they will naturally say things that reflect how they feel. The point, of course, is that the narcissist sometimes abuses intentionally, but other times they do it merely as an extension of the sort of people they are.

Destruction is a vindictive behavior. To return to the phases of narcissistic abuse, recall that the first type of emotional abuse is a type of manipulation that occurs with idealization. This is followed by more overt emotional abuse in the form of the demeaning and belittling remarks and implications the narcissist makes. Even disregarding your wants and needs is a form of abuse. These serve to devalue you.

We mentioned isolation as a phase of abuse, but we did not talk about disconnection. Isolation can be both physical and emotional. You can isolate yourself by remaining at home or in another location where you are removed from others, but you can also be isolated mentally. The narcissist is skillful at causing you to be both physically and emotionally isolated. A result of this isolation is a disconnection. Human beings normally connect with others of their kind, but a disconnected person has difficulty forming bonds with others and suffers all the physical and mental problems that stem from this.

CHAPTER 4:

Narcissistic Tactics

You can be able to tell if the person you are in a relationship with is a narcissist based on the kind of behavior he/she exhibits throughout the duration of your relationship. Ideally, you want to be able to figure out if your boyfriend, girlfriend, or even an acquaintance has narcissistic tendencies as soon as possible so that you can sever ties with him/her before you are too invested in that relationship. Here are ten things that a narcissist will always do in a relationship.

He Will Try to Charm You

Narcissists can be quite charismatic and charming when they want something from you. If you are in a relationship with one, he will go out of his way to make you feel special in the beginning so that you trust him enough to let your guard down. As long as you are serving the purpose he wants you to serve; the narcissist will give you a lot of attention and make you feel like you are the center of his world. If someone puts you on a pedestal during the early stages of your relationship, you should pay more attention to the way they act, just to see if they are faking it.

He Will Make You Feel Worthless

After you have been hanging out with a narcissist for a while, you will notice that when you have any sort of disagreement or argument, his first instinct is to dismiss you in a way that makes you feel worthless. He will criticize you in the sort of contemptuous tone that will make you feel dehumanized. When you disagree with ordinary people, you always get the feeling that your opinion matters to them, but with a narcissist, that is not the case. All the things about you that the narcissist claimed to like when he was charming you will somehow turn into negative attributes, and the narcissist will portray himself as a "saint" for putting up with those attributes.

He Will Hog Your Conversations

Narcissists are in love with the way people perceive them, so they will take every chance to talk about themselves. Whenever you try to have a conversation, the topic is always going to change, and it will suddenly be about them. It's never a 2-way conversation with a narcissist unless he is trying to manipulate you into thinking he cares about you. You will get to a point where you really struggle to get him to hear your views or to get him to acknowledge your feelings. When you start telling a story about something that happened to you at work, you will never get to the end of it because he is going to start his own story before you are done with yours. If you make comments on certain topics of conversation, your comments will be ignored, dismissed, or even corrected unnecessarily.

He Will Violate Your Boundaries

From very early in the relationship, the narcissist will start showing disregard for your personal boundaries. You will notice that he violates your personal space, and he has no qualms about asking you to do him favors that he has by no means earned. He will borrow your personal items or even money and fail to return it, and when you ask, he is going to say that he didn't know it was such a big deal to you—the point is to make you seem petty for insisting on boundaries that most decent people would consider reasonable.

He Will Break the Rules

The narcissist will break the rules that you set for your relationship, and other social rules, without any compunction. The problem is that sometimes, we are initially attracted to rule-breakers because they seem to be "bad boys" or "rebels," but those traits are in fact tale-tell signs of narcissism. A person who breaks social norms is definitely going to break relationship rules because relationships are essentially social contracts. If someone is trying to charm you, but in your first few interactions, you observe that he cuts lines, tips poorly, disregards traffic rules, etc., you can be certain that you are dealing with a narcissist.

He Will Try to Change You

When you are in a relationship with someone, they are definitely going to change you in a few minor ways (often unintentionally). However, when you are dealing with a narcissist, he is going to make a deliberate and perceptible effort to change you, and more often than not, it won't be for the better. He will try to break you, and he will try to make you more subservient to him.

You will find yourself making concession after concession, until, in the end; any objective observer can tell you that you are under his thumb. He will cause you to lose your sense of identity so that you end up being a mere extension of him. When you get out of that relationship, you will find it difficult to figure out who you are as an individual because he would have spent the entire duration of the relationship defining and redefining you.

He Will Exhibit a Sense of Entitlement

The narcissist will demonstrate a sense of entitlement for the most part of your relationship. At first, he may seem generous and considerate just to draw you in, but after that, you will see his entitlement rear its ugly head. He will be expecting preferential treatment all the time, and he will expect you to make him a priority in your life (even ahead of your own career or your family). There will be a clear disconnect between what he offers and what he expects, and he is going to want to be the center of your universe.

He Will Try to Isolate You

Any narcissist who wants to control you and make you subservient to him understands that you have a support system of friends and family who won't stand by and let him harm you. So, one of the things he will do once he has faked affection and earned some of your trust is he is going to try and isolate you. He will insist that every time you hang out, you shouldn't bring anyone along. He will make up lies to drive a wedge between you and your friends. He will play into the conflicts that exist between you and your family members to make you lean on them a lot less. If you let him get rid of your support system, he will have free reign, and you won't stand a chance against his manipulation.

He Will Express A Lot of Negative Emotions

Narcissists trade on negative emotions because they want to be the center of attention. When you are in a relationship with one, he is going to be upset when you don't do what he wants, when you are slightly critical of him, or when you don't give him the attention he is looking for.

He is going to use anger, insincere sadness, and other negative emotions to make you insecure, to get your attention, or to gain a sense of control over you. If someone you are dating throws a tantrum over minor disagreements or when you aren't able to give him attention, it means that he has a fragile ego, which is a clear sign that he could be a narcissist.

He Will Play the Blame Game

This is perhaps the most common indicator that you are in a relationship with a narcissist. He will never admit to any wrongdoing, and he will always find a way of turning everything into your fault. When anything doesn't go according to plan, he will always point out your part in it, even if he too could have done something to change the outcome of the event. He will never take responsibility for anything, and when he takes action to solve a mutual problem that you have, he will always make it clear that you owe him.

CHAPTER 5:

How to Protect Yourself When Divorcing a Narcissist

Be Firm in Your Decision

Now we're moving on to the practical side. By reaching this stage it's likely that you've decided that you're right in your choice to divorce the narcissist in your life and you're ready to start the process.

That's good news, and you can be assured that it's a decision that will serve you well in years to come. For now, however, it's vital that you understand what is in front of you.

If you're not sure of your choice or if you're wavering, you're more likely to give in to the continued manipulation and demands of the narcissist. As we'll explore as we move through these steps, it's very unlikely that your partner is going to just accept the decision and make life easier. If anything, they're likely to do everything to make it harder, because they will take your choice to divorce them as a serious personal dig, something that they just can't handle. That means, your decision has to be a solid one, to avoid you changing your mind when a little pressure comes your way.

Assess the Situation Carefully

For sure, everyone is a little different and that means your situation might not fit the description we've given completely, but you will see similarities.

That is the whole point of this – to give you peace of mind that you're right, that you're not going crazy, that you don't have to deal with this and that if you want to divorce your partner because you're simply not happy, you're perfectly within your rights to do so.

However, that doesn't mean you should take the decision lightly.

Ending a marriage, any marriage is difficult and you need to be very sure that you're making the right choice for you. Starting divorce proceedings and then stopping them halfway through is not only distressing and upsetting for all involved, but it's also likely to cost you a fair amount of money in legal fees. In addition, starting divorce proceedings and then changing your mind is not sending the right message to your narcissistic partner.

They will take this as a win, that they've controlled you and changed your mind.

They might turn on the charm for a while, keeping you right where they want you and making sure that you don't get any ideas about leaving again, but after a while, everything will just go back to the way it was before, if not worse. They now have this episode to throw at you during moments of manipulation.

So, when you decide to start divorcing your partner, you have to be sure that it's what you want and it's the decision you're going to move forwards with, no matter what.

Be rock sure and steady in your choice. It's normal to have moments of worry, but that doesn't mean you should change your mind.

Adopt a Positive Mindset

Use every single part of your being to try and create a positive mindset. It can be hard in the circumstances but you have to try your best and focus on a brighter future. This will help you to overcome the difficulties that can arise when going through any type of divorce.

Divorcing your partner isn't just a case of – I don't want this anymore, it's a long and arduous process of unpicking the reasons why the relationship has failed, going through the necessary legal processes, splitting all belongings and coming to agreements. In the normal run of things, that can be very hard and very emotional, especially when there are still residual feelings in place. However, when you are divorcing a narcissist, it can be harder simply because trying to divide everything and come to agreements is borderline impossible without medical help.

Knowing this means that you're not going to have any nasty surprises. If you need to come up with a positive affirmation to use wherever things get tough, go do. Put into place mechanisms to help you feel positive and uplifted, whether that's heading out for a run whenever you feel like stress is starting to overwhelm you or simply focusing on your own self-care. It's likely to feel odd at first, focusing on yourself, because you've been so used to being denied this basic right for so long. However, go with it and understand that it's your need and you're right to look after yourself.

Move Forwards with Purpose

Once you're sure that you want to go down this route, you've tried your best to be as positive about it as possible, move forwards with purpose. Keep your eyes on the prize, i.e. that brighter future, and push through the hardships that will come your way. We're not attempting to make this sound harder than it is, but we want you to be prepared for the reality of divorce, not least divorcing a narcissist. Put a plan together and work through it slowly and methodically.

Points to Remember

This part has been the first one in your step by step guide to divorcing a narcissist. It is about being very sure about your decision because without that foundation your future happiness will remain very unsure. Canceling divorce proceedings halfway through is not a good idea, not least for your bank account. The main points to take from are:

- You need to be sure in your decision before you start divorce proceedings;

- Reading the informational chapters before will help you understand whether or not you really are affected by narcissism;

- Unfortunately, divorcing a narcissist is a long and arduous road and one which is likely to be difficult at some point. Being as positive as possible will allow you to see the process through;

- Once you're sure of your choice, you must move forwards with strength and purpose.

Know What Is In Front Of You

You've made your decision and you're sure divorce is what you want. Now, you need to do your research and know what is in front of you.

Your road throughout this divorce journey will be unique and will vary from person to person. Everyone has different situations and circumstances and that means your specifics will be unique. If you have children together, your divorce is likely to be a little more difficult, compared to someone who doesn't have children.

It's vital that you make a plan in terms of your finances and where you're going to live and be prepared for whatever else may be thrown at you.

We are going to talk about some of the situations that you need to focus on and some of the problems that might come your way. If you don't have children, the process of dividing up your belongings could be very difficult indeed, and if you own a house together, all of that needs to be dealt with.

You also need to know that your narcissist is not likely to behave well throughout this process. The fact you are divorcing them is a real kick in the teeth to them, and they're going to take it extremely personally, viewing it as a stain on their character. They will throw everything at you in order to punish you for this and also to turn everyone's attention back onto them, viewing them as the hero in the story.

Expect the Worst

We've all heard the old 'expect the worst, hope for the best' line and that's what you need to do during a divorce of this kind. You need to realize that your narcissist is not going to play fair or kind. They're going to throw everything at you, they're going to make you look like the bad one and you're going to have to convince everyone around you that you're not the one in the wrong. At least, that's the way it will feel. We are all far more experienced and knowledgeable about narcissism these days and divorce courts have seen countless situations of this kind. That means you can be sure that everything will be fair in the eyes of those who are dealing with it from a legal point of view. However, don't expect fair from your partner.

It's probably against the rule being positive to say this, but you need to think of the worst-case scenario here and try and prepare for it. By doing that, you're not going to be shocked or momentarily dumbfounded by what your narcissist says or does.

Remember, divorcing a narcissist is a serious kick in the teeth to them, so you cannot expect anything positive from them.

Planning Your Finances and Housing

If you share finances at this point, you need to make sure that you have the cash to be independent at the start. Your narcissist could quite possibly cut off access to joint accounts and whilst we don't know for sure that this will happen, it's something to be prepared for.

Ahead of time, start putting money aside for the period of time before the divorce is finalized and settled. If you're working and you have your own money, make sure your partner doesn't have access to it.

You should also look into possible benefits you can apply for if you're going to be struggling financially in the meantime. There are many places you can go to for help and advice and here you'll be able to find out if you're eligible for any financial help and how to apply for it. Find all of this information out before you leave, so you know what you're dealing with and you don't have any unnecessary shocks or surprises.

Of course, it's likely that as a married couple you're sharing a house. If you own the house between you, you have a mortgage then when the divorce is all finalized the house will make up part of the items and assets which are divided between you, however, for now that needs to be put to one side.

CHAPTER 6:

The Path to Recovery Freedom

One of the things that you have to realize is that a narcissist does not see the need to seek help from a therapist because after all, they think that there is nothing wrong with them. Recovery is for those who have been through abuse. If you have been or are in a relationship with a narcissist, it is high time that you left and sought help from a professional. It is this kind of support that you need to rebuild your self-confidence and bounce back to your self-esteem. Trust me; you are better than you have ever thought possible. The narcissist might have managed to puncture your self-confidence and even crush your self-esteem, but most importantly you are just a victim. You are not unworthy like they want you to believe. Finding a health professional that has a specialty in trauma recovery will help you journey through the healing process to recovery. If you are not able to leave the relationship, a therapist can also help you to learn the best ways in which you can communicate effectively with your abuser so that you can set boundaries that they will respect and hence, protect you so that they will no longer take advantage of you. Here are some of the steps that you will have to go through to help you journey through healing to recovery:

Step 1: Cut Contact

Once you have left the relationship, keep it at that! Stop maintaining contact with your abuser. The main reason why you left is that the situation was not working for you. Therefore, there is nothing that will happen that can make things better. The best way to recover from abuse is for you to block all forms of communication.

If you have joint custody of children, you may not be able to wipe this person entirely from your life. It is therefore advisable to create a strict custom contract, according to which you only communicate on matters regarding your children using third-party channels exclusively! Otherwise, ensure that you have set up court orders for all forms of agreements.

Think about the extreme trauma bonding, the gross abuse, and the addiction that you had with the narcissist. Sometimes the best way is for you to accept that the only way you can recover from such damage is to pull away and cut your losses once and for all. Think of abstaining as a way of protecting yourself from hurt. In other words, each time you initiate contact with your abuser, you are handing them the ammunition to blow you off.

Remember that you lived with them and so they know what your weak points are and how they can wound you even more profoundly. It is not until we heal that we will stop forcing ourselves on the narcissist for love or craving them or even justifying to ourselves giving them a second chance. When we completely stop contact, then we can begin to heal.

Step 2: Release That Trauma So That You Begin Functioning Again

If we are going to heal, we have to be willing to reclaim our power. We have to do the exact opposite of what we used to believe; 'I can fix him/her, I will feel better.' Your power belongs inside you. The moment you take your focus away from your abuser then you will be able to channel that power into rebuilding your self-love and paying closer attention to making yourself whole again.

At first, it might seem like understanding who a narcissist is and what they do is essential. But the real truth is that these things cannot heal your internal trauma. What you need to do is to decide to let go of that horrific experience so that you can be at peace. You will begin to rise, get relief, and balance again once you have decided to take your power where it belongs-inside you.

Step 3: Forgive Yourself for What You Have Been Through

When the insecure and wounded parts of us are still in pain, we often are pushed into behaving like children who are damaged. We are often looking for people's approval and especially from our abuser, we hand our abuser the power to treat us as they see fit. And that's the time you will realize that you have given them all your resources: money, time and health. The most unfortunate thing is that while doing that, you end up hurting the people that matter the most in your life... your children, siblings, parents, and friends.

Yes, it might be hard to forgive yourself for this, but you can do that if you want to rebuild your life and everything that you lost to your abuser. By working through your healing process, you will soon find resolution and acceptance. You can move away from lacking self-love and respect to living a life full of truth and responsibility and well-being.

You will realize that, when you forgive yourself, you acknowledge that this was all a learning curve and this is the experience you learned, and hence, you are going to use that to reclaim your life. It is when you release your regrets and self-judgments that you can start setting yourself free to realize greatness in your life irrespective of what stage you are at. This is the point when you will begin to feel hope again, hope that will steer you forward into fulfillment and a life full of purpose.

Step 4: Release Everything and Heal All Your Fears of the Abuser and What They Might Do Next

Do you know what bait to a narcissist is? Anxiety, pain, and distress. These are the things that can perpetuate another cycle of abuse no matter how we tell ourselves that we have separated from them. It is indeed true that abusers can be relentless. In most cases, they do not like being losers. But one thing that you have to understand is that they are not as powerful and impactful as you may have thought them to be.

They need you to fear and go through pain so that they can function. Once you have healed your emotional trauma, they fall apart. Therefore, it is crucial that you become grounded and stoic by not feeding into their drama; this way they will soon wither away along with their power and credibility.

Step 5: Release the Connection to Your Abuser

So many people have likened their freedom from a narcissist to that of exorcism. When we liberate ourselves from the darkness that filled our beings, we are allowing ourselves to detox and let light and life to come in. If that light has to take over the shade, the darkness has to leave so that there is space for something new to come in. In the same manner, it is essential that you release all the parts that were trapped by your abuser so that you can tap into a more supernatural power, the power of pure creativity.

When you disentangle yourself from the narcissist, it is not just about cutting the cord; it is also about releasing all the belief systems that you might have associated yourself with subconsciously. It is only then that you can break free to be a new person and not a target of a narcissist.

Even though it might be tempting to seek revenge on your abuser, this is something that you have to try hard to avoid. Rage has the power of pulling you back into deeper darkness and a game that your abuser is an expert at, in the first place. The best form of revenge is one in which you decide to take back your freedom and render your abuser irrelevant.

And it is likely going to crush their ego, and they will be powerless and at a loss that they cannot even affect you. Often they are in despair when it hits that you are a constant reminder of their extinction. It is at this point that this ends and your soul contracts to allow love and healing in so that you can be whole again.

Step 6: Realize Your Liberation, Truth, and Freedom

Traditionally, we learn that loving ourselves is a very selfish act. However, when it comes to finding liberation and freedom from the hands of our abusers, it is a very critical step that allows us to take in the truth and let it set us free from captivity. Yes, it is something incredibly difficult to do, but it is a necessary step toward achieving liberation.

Society has taught us that we are treated by others the same way we treat them. However, this is a false premise because we get treatment according to the way we treat ourselves. In other words, the measure of love that we get from others is equivalent to that we feel about ourselves.

Therefore, when we open up to healing and recovery, we are opening the doors for others to love us in reality and in more healthy ways than ever before. It is this act that serves as a template by which we teach our children so that they do not carry around subconscious patterns of abuse that were passed to them by our ancestors. This positive modeling only starts when we decide to take responsibility for our happiness and freedom. We slowly become the change that we would wish to see so that we can let go of being someone's victim and stop handing other people our power.

In other words, we take back our lives by doing everything necessary to aid our inner healing irrespective of what the narcissist does or does not do, something that's now irrelevant either way. It is at this point that we can thrive despite what we have been through and what has happened to us.

CHAPTER 7:

Tactics to Help you Deal with the Divorce

Isn't this a statement you tell yourself every day!? It plays in your mind like a mantra, the self- affirmation reminding you that going in the right direction will be worth it in the end. It should be so easy- why stay with someone who has no empathy, care, or kindness towards you, and who wants to see you suffer? Yet it is not as easy as it seems, hence why you need to repeat statements such as this.

This is one thing that many people don't tell you when taking the steps to divorce a narcissist. You need mantras or affirmation- like statements to keep you on course, remind you that this really is in your best interests and that it will be worth it in the end. The psychological, mental, and emotional abuse and trauma you have suffered are real, and regardless of how many times you have been gaslighted, or made to appear crazy, in the wrong or losing the plot, you know the truth in the core of your cells. Being with a narcissist is completely detrimental to your health.

A covert narcissist is exactly this – covert; still in the shadows of their own manipulations, delusions, and shady- hurtful character. They are not (yet) in the open or publicly acknowledged, and is this because you have not yet made the decision to allow them to be seen in their true light? Taking a stand and choosing, with your own free will, inner strength and sheer conviction, that you will no longer allow yourself to be abused, victimized or manipulated allow your partner to be seen, and for you to subsequently finally take the steps necessary to be free from their abuse.

Of course, all of this is something you know – so see these words as a reflection of your own psyche and conscious mind telling you exactly how it is. The fact that you are reading this and have chosen, consciously, to align with your true self and leave your narcissistic partner for good implies that you are already well on course. This is confirmation, and you are heading in the right direction! You are strong beyond measure.

Divorcing a Narcissist: Stop Reacting!

Reaction. The reaction is not the same as a response. When you respond to someone or something, you provide space, wisdom, and awareness to connect on a mature and responsible level. Responding allows for authenticity, the calmness of thought, and clarity in communication. Yet, reacting is something completely different.

The key to your narcissistic partner's success is in your reaction. They need people to become emotionally entwined and engaged with their stories. If there is no reaction then there is no exchange- no one is appeasing or empowering them. Power is a great word to be aware of here. The reaction provides a narcissist's empowerment or a more accurately faulty sense of empowerment. Causing pain, hurt, and manipulation to others is not empowerment. Regardless, reacting provides the sustenance that a narcissist needs, so the best way to heal and begin your own journey of empowerment is to stop reacting and start responding.

Things to Be Mindful Of: How You May Be Reacting!

Your partner attempts to provoke a reaction and you allow it. Instead of taking a moment to slow down, be calm inside, and recognize the intentions of causing destruction, chaos, and harm; you play to their manipulations. Thus, a vicious and highly repetitive cycle can begin and continue for hours or even days on end. The key is to detach and not get caught up in their games. It can be easier said than done, however, the tips and techniques for effective response below can really help with this.

'Snide remarks.' Expanding from example 1, at this stage, your partner should know you very well and therefore know your triggers. Snide remarks or specific comments are a very effective way to get a reaction from you and subsequently enable them to continue in their ways.

'Awareness goes where energy flows!' If you don't give your attention, time, or energy to something, how can it perpetuate? The answer is that it can't. The intentions and motivations of your partner require energy and attention, otherwise, they are formless.

Watch out for the signs. Assuming you have been with your partner for a while you will know the signs to when they are going to begin their games. If they are bored or displaying signs of frustration, stimulation, or boredom this is a sure warning that you will soon become their target for their stimulation. A narcissist needs that 'spark' to feed their egocentricity, self-centeredness, and feelings of self-worth. Without it, their illusions start to crumble down and they have no choice but to look within, seek help, and ways to change; which are of course very rare for a narcissist.

If you feel yourself becoming stressed, anxious, nervous, or heated inside, these are sure signs that you are on the verge of a reaction. Unlike in partnerships where narcissism is not present or a key theme, and where most people are allowed a few moments of blowing off steam or showing weakness; in this relationship, you are not provided the patience, compassion or support necessary. This means that even when or if your partner does happen to be in a serene, kind, or non-narcissistic space you may unfortunately spark them with your own reactive behaviors. It is extremely rare for a true narcissist to see you becoming upset or worked up on your own accord and not use it as a chance for drama, or further manipulation.

A Deeper Look into Divorce and Reaction

Divorce is a serious thing. The process inevitably means that you have decided to part ways, restart your life, and take back your individual resources, belongings, and physical necessities. This in itself is a major red flag in a codependent- narcissist relationship! Your partner's entire identity is merged in the reality that he or she can feed off you, use you as their hidden and subtle yet powerful support system, and bounce off your kindness, empathy, and positive attributes. So, once you starting responding this destroys their world. This can only happen when you begin to respond.

How to Manage Conflict

Managing conflict is the same if not similar to learning how to respond. When dealing with someone with deeply buried narcissism, you need to know how to respond appropriately and in a way that doesn't cause further harm to yourself. Once again, you are not responsible for the narcissist's energy. You may have spent years being the most patient, loyal, loving, and understanding or empathetic partner, yet these qualities are all lost on them. Managing conflict during or after the divorce proceedings should not be viewed as any different. Please do not make the mistake of thinking that now you are finally free, or soon to be free, that your partner will suddenly 'see sense' or have a heartfelt awakening. They will not. A narcissist will always view you as their scapegoat and wall or mirror to project their stuff onto, so now you are taking the correct steps and working towards your own wellbeing and happiness; they do not want to let go or give you up so easily. The following steps may seem simple or effortlessly implemented, yet they are not! Narcissists will do everything in their power to maintain their illusion of power, and try to keep you entrapped in their games until it really is all over. So, in order to combat this and manage conflict successfully, do stay committed and completely aligned to the following. They are all necessary for your happiness, peace of mind, and success.

I. Patience

The key to your success when going through a divorce or separation is to focus on your own self and personal qualities. The narcissist has spent months, years, or even decades (hopefully not!) unwilling to change, so they are not going to start now. This signifies that the only way to get through this and see your own intentions and goals materialized is to stay centered and focused on yourself. Having patience is the first step.

II. Staying Centered: Personal Boundaries!

Nothing and no one can take away your power, and this is something to keep in mind when separating from a narcissist. Actually, don't just keep it in mind; know it within. You hold great personal power and with strong boundaries, your mental projections can act as a shield to all of your partner's bs.

III. Kindness, Tolerance and Self- Respect

Above anything else, you need to have self- respect. This links with kindness and tolerance, which are both necessary to manage and deal with conflict harmoniously. The self- respect part is the trinity due to the fact that you won't receive much kindness or respect from your partner, unfortunately. However, you should seek to remain kind and tolerant during the process. There is great truth in the validity of the power of the law of attraction. We attract, magnetize, and harmonize to us what we give out, so any energy or intentions we project we will receive. If you are sending out harmful, hurtful, or separation based vibrations- you shall receive more from your partner. In other words, you cannot fight chaos and narcissism with more destruction or ill wishes! Showing kindness and respect, even if in neutral and indifferent civil ways, will allow you to remain sane, clear-headed, and calm; also enabling you to stay as clear as possible from your partner's detrimental motivations.

IV. Being Your Own Best Friend, Lover and Soul mate

To succeed, you need to be your own best friend, lover, and soul mate. You need to practice self- love and show up for yourself (because your narcissistic partner isn't going to). Being your best self for you allows you to be your best self for others.

Even if your partner is incapable of rationality or niceness, this commitment to being the best version of you still has a positive effect. Subtle energy and intentions are real and showing up for yourself in a way which states that you are self- loving, self- respecting and not going to tolerate anything less than harmonious and ethical cooperation, means that the situation will flow better than if you didn't commit to these things. Your vibe projects outwards also influencing physical reality and the experiences you attract. How divorce or separation proceedings go can all be changed and shaped by your mindset.

V. Gaining Support

The importance of peer, family, and friendship support cannot be disregarded when divorcing a narcissist. Your ability to manage conflict is largely tied in with the amount of support you receive. It can be both a coping mechanism and an essential aspect of your recovery and conflict resolution. Narcissists thrive off the social support and cooperation of others.

CHAPTER 8:

Divorce and Your Children

Divorce affects kids, period. There is plenty of disagreement on just what those effects are, but few would argue that experiencing the divorce of their parents has no impact on children. Some would argue that children of divorce are doomed to a life of depression, failed relationships, and eventually divorce. Others would argue that even though there may be short-term pain, the divorce of their parents has no significant impact on a child. I don't agree with either extreme.

First of all, we are all responsible for our own actions. While experiencing the divorce of their parents may make it statistically more likely that a person will get divorced themselves, ultimately each one of us has the ability to choose how much we let things from our past affect us. To blame failed relationships on the divorce of your parents is a cop-out.

On the opposite extreme, there are definitely cases where the parents' divorce is in the best interest of the child. This is usually to extract the child from a bad situation such as abuse, addiction, alcoholism, open infidelity, etc. In these cases, the factors contributing to the divorce will likely have a negative impact on the child even though the divorce is necessary for their emotional or physical protection.

A study was conducted recently by Bowling Green State University and Iowa University that underscores the fact that divorce does impact children. In this study, researchers looked at children with half-siblings, specifically situations where adolescents had half-siblings with the same mother but different fathers. The results were enlightening, indicating that "by age 15 teens who have a half-sibling by a different father are roughly 65 percent more likely to have used drugs. This held true even after the results were adjusted for family background, family instability, and socio-economic factors. The results were more pronounced in firstborn children than siblings later in the birth order.

So what does all this mean?

This study offers proof that divorce hurts kids. It also shows that for younger kids, seeing their mother start a new family with someone other than their father hurts even more. Adolescents in this situation are hurting to the point of turning to drugs and sex to ease their pain.

My goal here is not to put a guilt trip on anyone who has remarried and is starting a new family. I would, however, urge you to take special notice of how your adolescent or pre-adolescent children are adjusting to the new blended family.

If you are reading this, you are seeking some help in dealing with your divorce and that puts you way ahead of most people. But, be aware that your kids may need some help too. Get them the help they need to adjust to the new family situation from a pastor, counselor, or other trusted adviser. Doing so will likely prevent them from turning to drugs or sex to deal with the pain if they are struggling to adjust.

If you haven't started a new relationship yet, please consider the impact it will have on your kids before you do. I have heard some family specialists recommend waiting until your kids are out of the house before you even begin dating.

My hope for you is that you will wait until you are healed to begin dating. Then, when you do venture into new relationships, consider your children's feelings as you proceed. Kids are resilient and they can handle a lot. Everything you do to ease their transition from divorce to Mom or Dad dating, to Mom or Dad getting re-married, will only help them. If you see that they are struggling with the adjustment, get them some professional guidance. Help them deal with their emotions before they turn to drugs, alcohol, or sex.

How and What to Tell Kids

- **Tell the Truth**

The best thing you can do is to just tell your kids the truth, but not necessarily the whole truth. For example, if your spouse is having an affair, your children don't need to know all the sordid details, they only need to know that sometimes things happen that you don't want to happen. You also need to adjust what you tell your children based on their age. A child of three has a different level of understanding than a child of seven, and a child of seven has a different level of understanding than a teenager.

Avoid speaking negatively about your ex, especially to the children. He is, and always will be, your child's parent and your child loves him. You need to do everything you can to help your child maintain a healthy relationship with his or her other parent. Some of the best advice I received from the Divorce Care material was that the truth will come out. You don't have to be the one to tell your children what really happened—they will eventually find out on their own.

- **Tell Them It's Not Their Fault!**

Many children will blame themselves for their parents' divorce. This is normal, but it is something that can be minimized if both parents reassure the child that this is something between Mom and Dad and has nothing to do with them. If the child has experienced feelings of abandonment before, as is alluded to in this question, then it can be especially important that she understands it's not her fault. She may be inclined to think there is something wrong with her, and you need to convince her that this is not true.

Answer your child's questions as truthfully as you can without giving in to negativity. This can be difficult, especially with older children. They can sense when there is more to the story and will often probe to find out what you are leaving out. If you are faced with an overly inquisitive child, just reiterate that the divorce was an issue between their parents and some details are private.

One of the greatest sources of fear for children during a divorce is the uncertainty of how life is going to change. Try to give your child as much information as possible about how life will be different after the divorce. As soon as the details are decided, let them know what the living arrangements will be, if they will be changing schools, how often you will see them, etc. The more time they have to adjust to the changes before they actually happen, the better your children will be prepared to handle them.

CHAPTER 9:

The Aftermath

The aftermath of dealing with a narcissist can be truly felt only once you go no contact and have them no longer in your life. The effects of narcissistic abuse are long-lasting and go way beyond the direct contact with the narcissist and even once they are no longer present in your life, the toxic cloud above your head still remains. Gaslighting, drama, lying, isolation, and a series of other manipulation techniques we talked about leave you mentally numb to the point that even dealing with everyday tasks feels like a burden. The consequences of having such individuals in your life are many, as you are affected on all levels of your conscious and unconscious being. In other words, you feel broken and damaged in the mental, physical, emotional, and spiritual planes. In addition, in cases of many survivors, the narcissist also affected their material reality, which resulted in a loss of status, friends, money, or property.

Survivors of narcissistic suffer a wide range of mental health issues as a result of long-term manipulation and devaluing, all of which have roots at the beginning stages of a relationship with a narcissist. Anxiety and paranoia are some of the most common reactions to being mentally and emotionally abused and are all part of a PTSD, post-traumatic stress disorder. Because of the constant distress and chaos survivors have been part of, they experience flashbacks, intense headaches, have trouble sleeping or intense nightmares. The life with a narcissist leaves our brain in a state of shock and extreme confusion, and traumatizes the mind, causing troubles with concentration and agitation. Survivors have trouble communicating and may experience social anxiety and agoraphobia, the fear of open space, and crowded places. The feeling of isolation stemming from the days of a relationship persists and people who dealt with a narcissist feel too vulnerable to expose themselves to the outer world, which is often followed by a state of paranoia and beliefs that people are evil and want to cause us harm. It is like a constant state of fight or flight.

Since gaslighting is one of the most dangerous, if not the most dangerous form of playing with one's mind, many experiences mild to severe realization, where one feels like they and the outer world are somehow separated. Because of the state of shock, the mind activates these two coping mechanisms, which are a normal response to prolonged stress but can be troublesome if not treated.

If you feel like you are an actor in your own life, a ghost of your former self who is not able to feel or be present in reality, it is likely that your mind is just trying to protect you until you heal by shutting the reality off. It is possible that to feel this way even during the relationship, starting as early as the devaluation phase, in which case the depersonalization and realization just deepen once they are gone, until you start to heal.

Another very common side-effect of being involved with a narcissist is depression. Survivors feel blue, have no motivation to take care of themselves and life gets to the point where even taking a shower seems like a huge task. Depression can be mild, but unfortunately, can also be fatal, causing thoughts of ending one's life or even suicide. The life and has been drained and the survivor is left in a fog, with no self-esteem, no drive, and no hope for a better future. All energy was given to the narcissist and the relationship that they just can't find the strength to continue with their life, especially if love for the narcissist is still there. You are made to believe there is nothing about you to love. Your dreams and ambitions have been extinguished and you believe you are not lovable unless you are perfect or can fulfill someone's demands. You don't feel good enough, let alone capable of moving on, so who wouldn't feel depressed? Narcissists are like predators who feed off of other people's energy—they take your light and give you their darkness. And they will show absolutely no remorse for what you are going through, but that is okay because you will heal and they will always be stuck their pathological ways.

The effects of narcissistic abuse are such that avoidance feels like an escape. The constant feeling of not knowing what to expect from the narcissist is combined with low self-esteem and a feeling of utter worthlessness. Because of that, survivors feel incompetent and view themselves how a narcissist described them. They see themselves through narcissist's glasses and believe they will be rejected, denied, and discarded everywhere they go, and all of this together causes them a lot of anxiety.

Since the abuse has damaged the core of self, survivors feel like they don't have an identity, as a relationship with a narcissist is a codependent one, and thanks to constant projection, there is no clear line between who is who. When it all ends, many don't know who they are, feel like nothing has meaning anymore, and feel powerless. Anyone who has dealt with a covert knows very well how it feels like not to be allowed to be authentic, to thrive, how it is to feel alone while being in a relationship, to feel guilty for standing up for yourself and putting healthy boundaries. Such a person knows what it is like to be trapped in guilt for things that are not your fault all the time, to be afraid to express oneself, and doubt every decision you make.

Don't feel ashamed if you feel this way. You are not weak, you are completely opposite. Know that you are not alone, even if it feels like it. There are others who, just like you, suffer from the effects of loving a narcissist and they too feel alone. Some survivors find escape in substance abuse, some battle with sexual dysfunction and some develop a physical illness or eating disorder due to constant stress and feeling not good enough or beautiful enough. If any of this resonates, just don't feel down about yourself.

Don't blame yourself as it is not your fault. These are all very human and very normal reactions to being exposed to months and years of narcissistic abuse. And most importantly, don't compare yourself to others who are able to live their life to the fullest shortly after a breakup, as a relationship you had was far from normal or healthy.

All of this happens because you suddenly start to realize with whom you have dealt with, and as time goes by, things start making more sense. You start noticing your part in the game, but most importantly, you start seeing the narcissist for who they truly are. However, in the beginning, truth is hard to comprehend and your mind might as well try to protect you from a flood of emotions until you're ready to face it. Unlike the narcissist, you are a healthy individual who was infected with someone else's virus and you can get back on track and you can restore your life. Even if breathing feels like a burden now, one day you will look at your relationship with them and be proud of yourself, because you will win this and you will endure, no matter how impossible it feels at the moment.

CHAPTER 10:

The Path to Recovery Freedom

Many people will breathe a sigh of relief after the divorce is finalized just to realize that things are not as done as they would like them to be. We are going to take a look at the different things the narcissist may attempt to bring you back into their war zone and the reactions you should have to ensure you shut them down each and every time.

You must also realize that the time it takes to heal from the abuse you suffer when a narcissist can take quite a bit of time. Depending on the severity of the abuse, you may be looking at some serious long-term damage. Understanding that you have been through a traumatic event is the first step toward healing. We will look at a variety of different things you may be facing when it comes to healing and the steps you can take to regain control, self-confidence, and happiness.

Post-Divorce Combat with a Narcissist

Those that divorce narcissists quickly find that life is still difficult even when the court hearings are over. You must never forget that the narcissist has an inane need for attention. They need the focus of the world to be on them. This is completely exhausting and probably at least part of the reason you divorced them. When you were married to the narcissist, you were never enough, and that is not going to change now that you have divorced them.

Once you divorce a narcissist, you must understand that things are not going to simply become peaches and cream. Realistically, there may not be a ton of differences at all, to begin with. You have to remember that while you will be growing, healing, and changing, the narcissist will not. They will not be able to see that they have made mistakes, and they will continue to try and gain your attention at pretty much any cost. They will not be concerned about the consequences.

Finding the strength, power, and drive to reclaim your life is no easy feat. It is something that will have to be worked toward. There are many aftereffects that can play a role, and it can feel like a war zone when it comes to dealing with the narcissist that you just divorced. You will be facing a variety of different challenges. Let's take a look at some of the things that you may experience after finalizing your divorce with the narcissist in your life.

You may find that you are still in a frequent state of confusion. Narcissists will use things like gaslighting, criticism, lies, and double standards to make you feel crazy and confused. You must remember they love to play these kinds of games so that they have full power and control. Once you are outside of the relationship, the damage that this kind of thing can have on a person is lasting.

You will need to work on rebuilding your self-esteem and your ability to trust your own thoughts, memories, and feelings.

Be aware that the narcissist that you just divorced will still try and continue to play these games with you. They are so used to winning when you are around that they will seek it out. It can be difficult to avoid interaction with your ex. This is especially true when there are children involved.

Having a strategy to deal with many situations where you need to be in contact with your ex is a great start. Don't be afraid to reach out to a friend or family member to join you for face to face conversations with the narcissist. They can help cement what actually happened, which can, in turn, help you learn to trust yourself more. The manipulation game may have worked on you for a long period of time, but you don't have to let it go on forever.

You should also understand that changing your phone number and possibly the locks on your house can also be a great course of action. Some even find that they need to change the email address and things of that nature. They do this because a narcissist is a person of tenacity. They will likely want to continue to have your attention and will go to great lengths to do it.

Some people that have divorced narcissists end up having issues with the ex, bombarding them with nasty text messages, emails, and other forms of communication.

If you have a volatile narcissistic ex-spouse, you may also want to inform your friends, family, and place of business. You never know what type of slanderous things the narcissist may try to soil your name and reputation. By making the people in your life aware of what is going on, you are taking a proactive approach to keeping the narcissist out of your life forever. Completely cutting ties when you can is the best option.

For those of you who have suffered the abuse of a narcissist for a long amount of time, don't be afraid to ask for help. It can be hard to trust yourself in the early time after leaving a narcissist.

They have spent all of their time wearing you down so that you would have no confidence or conviction in life. It takes time to work through these issues and asking for help to get through daily life can be very helpful in building your confidence and showing yourself that you can, indeed, do it without the narcissist.

More than likely, the narcissist in your life is not going to simply disappear. You can pretty much guarantee it if there are children involved.

While you may not be able to cut ties completely, you will need to set very clear boundaries. The narcissist may ignore them. If they do make sure to jot down what is going on so that if you end up back in court, you have the evidence you need to show the true colors of your ex-spouse.

When you divorce a narcissist, you take away a decent amount of their power, and they hate it. They will use a variety of different tactics to draw you back in so they can continue to use you for their own purposes. By creating chaos, they believe that they will also gain control. This can be some control over you and/or the children that the two of you have. You may find that they ignore orders from the court, or they start making false claims against you. These things are both done to rope you in and ensure that you continue to play the narcissists game. You can't stop them from doing these types of things, but you can know that they are coming, which can give you time to figure out the best way to handle it when it does.

If there are kids involved, you should also be prepared for your ex to try and use them against you or, even worse, turn them against you. The narcissist can be very charming, and when they want to, they can appear to be a great parent and person. Depending on the age of your children and the experience they have had with the narcissist, the thought of this can be emotionally devastating.

You must know that you cannot control what happens when your kids are with their narcissistic parent; you can only control your own personal reactions and actions.

It may seem like a great idea to fill your children in on who their other parent actually is, but this can actually do more harm than good. Kids are actually pretty smart when it comes to the intent that people hold. They will quickly realize which parent is truly there for them and supporting them in a healthy way and which parent is not. You should not speak poorly of your ex or use your children to spy on what is happening at your ex's house.

Don't stoop to the level of the narcissist and use your children as pawns in a never-ending game of non-sense. Instead, protect them and show them what a healthy relationship between a parent and a child should look like. If they have questions or concerns, be open and honest with them. Answer their questions with kindness and compassion toward the other parent. They will see that you are trying, and all it will do is tighten the bonds between you.

Taking the high road is not always easy; however, it is always going to be the best answer to the question of how to handle the children during and after a divorce.

Realize that they have nothing to do with it and do your very best to keep them out of it. This can be so hard when you are dealing with a narcissist. They do not care enough about anyone to not include them in their nefarious games. Shielding your children, the best you can by providing them with genuine love and support is the best thing you can do when they have to deal with a narcissistic parent. Remember not to take the things your ex says to heart and encourage your kids to think for themselves.

Obviously, every situation is different, and each person's experience with a narcissist can vary. Some of you may be lucky, and the narcissist will move on quickly, leaving you alone to pick up the pieces and take back the control in your life. For those of you that are not so lucky don't give up. Stay strong and focused on healing and starting your life over once the divorce is finalized.

Eventually, they will prey on someone else, and in the meantime, you will continue to build the skills you need to handle them in a way that will not bring harm to yourself or to your children.

Healing From a Narcissistic Marriage

Healing from divorce is not an easy thing. Healing after divorcing a narcissist is even harder. They will go to great lengths to continue to keep control over you. What you once believed about human decency will be unraveled once you have experienced the pain of divorcing a narcissist. Their behavior is completely deplorable and devastating.

One of the reasons that it is more difficult to heal from a divorce with a narcissist as compared to a regular divorce is that being with a narcissist is more like war than it will ever be like love. Most relationships have good memories, and it allows us to get over the loss of the relationship. The memories of a relationship with a narcissist will be memories of feeling helpless, belittled, and crazy. Let's take a look at a few other reasons that healing from a narcissistic relationship is more difficult than recovering from a normal break-up.

One of the biggest hurdles to overcome is accepting the fact that your entire relationship with your ex was one-sided. It was only ever about the narcissist and what they wanted or needed. This is a truth that can be hard to swallow. When you are devoted to someone, you hope and oftentimes expect that they are also devoted to you.

CHAPTER 11:

Redefining Yourself After Abuse

Despite the fact that narcissistic abuse can leave behind marks or injuries so deep that you may feel that you will never be able to truly cleanse yourself of them, you can recover from it. Of course, you can never turn back time, and therefore erasing the effect of narcissistic abuse altogether is impossible but you can get yourself back to your healthy self. You can care for yourself and help yourself heal. Even though, in the throes of abuse, you may not be able to recognize the person you see when you look in the mirror, you can get that sense of identity back. You can reclaim it and if you are willing to put in the effort, you will get it back.

It does not matter how long the relationship you were in lasted, nor does it matter how much abuse you endured, you can always hope to heal. While the healing process is not easy by any means, it is possible, and you will be able to do it. This will guide you, step by step, through the process of healing, pointing you in the right direction so you can begin to work on yourself. As you work, you will get to the point where you recognize your smile in the mirror. You will feel peace of mind for the first time in ages. You will feel happier, and maybe even love, again. No matter what the narcissist has told you, you are capable of change and healing, and you absolutely deserve a life filled with happiness and peace. You are worthy of love. You are worthy of respect. You are worthy of loving the person you see looking back at you in the mirror.

Acknowledge Your Abuse

Healing begins with acknowledgment. If you cannot acknowledge that what the narcissist has put you through is abuse, you may not be ready for this process. By recognizing what happened as the abuse it was, you will be able to take the steps necessary to correct for it and heal. You will erase any of the denials you have hidden the abuse behind as long as it occurred by naming it. Naming it abuse releases your blame in the abuse. No one asks for their loved ones to hurt them the way the narcissist may have hurt you, nor does anyone deserve it. When you say that the narcissist abused you, you say that the narcissist made a conscious decision to inflict unwanted harm upon you, and that pushes the blame you may have internalized from yourself onto the narcissist. With that blame lifted, you will be able to begin working on yourself.

As you go through this process, do not forget that you only control yourself. You must be responsible for yourself but you do not control how those around you react. Even if you did something as cruel as punching someone on the street, you are not in control of the other person's reaction. You did not deserve what the narcissist did to you, regardless of how minor or extreme the narcissist's manipulation may seem to you. You were an unfortunate victim, chosen because your own traits made you desirable. Instead of lamenting that some of your traits made you a victim, you should celebrate the ones that attract a narcissist—empathy and compassion are fantastic for people to have. Being patient and seeking peace is an admirable way to live. These are not bad traits to have and they do not make you a lesser person. These are traits of a good person. In this situation, the narcissist took advantage of the good person you are and used your best traits against you. Treat yourself kindly as you consider this and remember that you did not ask for it to happen.

Forgiveness and Compassion for Yourself

With the acknowledgment of the abuse, you can then move on to forgive yourself. As you established, your traits and strengths should be celebrated, not punished.

Forgive yourself for blaming yourself for the abuse so you can begin to celebrate those parts of yourself. You will be able to forgive yourself for not seeing the red flags when they happened, reminding yourself that your good nature may have been to see the good in everyone but ultimately the narcissist choosing to take advantage of that is not your fault.

You can forgive yourself for not leaving the relationship sooner, reminding yourself that you tried desperately to care for the narcissist, truly loving who he was, and that love was taken advantage of. Your good heart, your compassion, and kindness when you see someone suffering, were taken advantage of. When you recognize that, you can forgive yourself.

Remember, forgiveness does not necessarily come easy but you deserve to forgive yourself. You did not intend for the situation to get as bad as it did and you are making an effort to heal the best that you can. You did your best in the situation with what you had, and that is enough. Yes, you were in a bad situation for a period of time but you survived. You were strong enough to cope as it happened and you were strong enough to say you are ready to get help and begin healing just by virtue of having opened this and reading as far as you have. That deserves celebrating as you work through healing.

Remind yourself to give yourself the compassion you would show other people. If your friend came to you in this situation, telling you the story you yourself have, how would you react? Would you be supportive? Would you be kind and understanding? Or would you look at her with a cold, hard look, and tell her that she should have tried harder to leave in the beginning? Would you have told her that the abuse was her own fault and that she had been asking for it? The answer is most likely no, you would not. Treat yourself with that same compassion as well. You must forgive yourself and treat yourself kindly if you hope to move on toward healing the rest of you.

Grieve Properly

Despite the fact that your relationship with the narcissist took a turn toward abusive, you still likely developed real, strong feelings for her. You loved her, or rather, the idea of her that she originally presented to you when attempting the love bombing stage, when she mirrored your heart's desires. You fell in love with an idea, which quickly was obliterated by the narcissist that was left behind, staring back at you with the face of the one you loved as if your loved one had suddenly become possessed. You deserve the chance to grieve that relationship. Though the person that you loved was never a real person, she was real to you, and because of that, you should allow yourself to grieve. If not for the person you lost, then grieve for not getting the relationship you deserved when you fell in love with the narcissist.

Grief involves five stages that occur, though they may not happen linearly. Grief also comes and goes and while you may feel better one day, you might suddenly be shocked by feelings of sorrow when you realize that you are once again missing the narcissist. This is normal, and grief is one of those things that never fully goes away; you just learn to live with it.

The first stage of grief is denial. You tell yourself that the relationship does not need to end. You may try to convince yourself that what has happened in your relationship does not warrant breaking up. This is to protect yourself from the pain you will feel when it is officially over. Next, you go through anger. At this stage, you acknowledge the truth in front of you: The narcissist was abusive. At this point, you recognize the narcissist for who she is, and that enrages you. The thought of your abuse, or the abuser that inflicted it, is enough to send you into a fury. Third, you reach bargaining. At this stage, the anger has subsided somewhat, and you tell yourself that there are ways or reasons that the relationship could continue to work. You tell yourself that if you try a little harder, or do a little more, then the abuse would no longer happen. This would be enough to save the relationship, you tell yourself, and you try to grapple with that, even if your bargaining chip ends up being your own wellbeing, such as deciding that you are willing to martyr yourself for the narcissist because you love her. Next, you hit the stage of depression. Here, you acknowledge that the relationship is over. You see that things can never be acceptable, and that dissipates the hope you felt. Lastly, you reach acceptance. At this point, though you may not agree with what happened or that your relationship had to end, you accept the end result and no longer try to fight it.

Release Negative Feelings

As a primary target for a narcissist, you are likely empathetic to some degree. As an empath, you likely have a propensity to absorb the emotions of those around you. You may have internalized some of the narcissist's own negativity because of the exposure to them. You may see some of the narcissist's negative traits in you, such as realizing that you are snapping at people the same way he snapped at you or that you have been thinking about yourself in the way that the narcissist thought of himself. You might feel uncharacteristically angry at the world. No matter the negative feelings, you need to develop an outlet for them.

If left alone, you may feel as though you're very self is festering within you, as though the toxicity from the narcissist still threatens to overwhelm you and turn you into someone you know you are not. The solution to this is to find a good outlet for yourself. Some people pour themselves into a creative hobby, such as drawing, writing, painting, music, dance, or any other form of creating something else. They literally channel their feelings into their art, allowing the negativity to flow through them and out into the world so it can no longer consume them. Others choose physical exercise as an outlet, choosing to sweat out the negativity with each rep of the weight set, or with each mile run. Others still may decide to nurture something else, such as growing and tending to a garden, bringing back those tender feelings that were once familiar to them. No matter what you choose as your healthy outlet, what is important is that you feel better after engaging in it and that you see that your general outlook and mood is improving the more you do it. Anything is acceptable here so long as it allows you to channel your negativity in a way that works for you and that you enjoy.

Find Support Networks

Support networks may be one of the most intimidating parts of healing. Support networks imply that you will be opening up to others about the abuse you endured in person, face to face with others. Some people are not comfortable with this idea but luckily, the internet has made finding groups of people like you easier than ever before.

CHAPTER 12:

Discover Your True Worth

Your self-esteem and self-worth are the value that you placed upon yourself. They are a reflection of whether or not you like yourself. They reflect whether and not you feel that you deserve to be happy and whether or not you show yourself kindness and compassion. They reflect whether or not you are comfortable with your strengths and are aware of the positive things that make you. Your self-worth and self-esteem tell everyone whether or not you believe that you as an individual matter.

Your narcissistic former partner did a number on you so it is understandable if your self-esteem and self-worth are not up to par with what they should be. The first step in rectifying that is becoming more self-aware. You need to have a baseline for what you generally feel about yourself so that you can then use that as a guideline to move forward and increase your self-esteem and self-worth accordingly. Education is your best friend.

Self-esteem and self-worth are not the same things although they might be described as flip sides of the same coin. While your self-esteem is a general gauge for what you think, believe and feel about yourself, your self-worth is recognizing that you can be even greater than these things. High self-worth comes from recognizing that you are lovable, that you are a necessary component to this life, and that your value is beyond measure. In simple terms, self-esteem speaks to you thinking that you are lovable, necessary, and valuable but not necessarily believing this while self-worth is having that absolute conviction of the fact. As a result, having high self-esteem does not equate to having a high sense of self-worth.

Luckily, if you are currently suffering from low self-worth and self-esteem, you are not stuck in this condition forever. There are things that you can do to build your sense of self-worth. Below you will find 5 such measures.

Talk to Yourself Kindly

You may not have realized it but the voice of the narcissist that you lived with for so long may have become your internal voice. Of course, this voice is constantly criticizing you and dismissing your needs as fickle things.

The internal dialogue that goes on in your head is known as self-talk. You may not realize it yet but you have the power to influence what is said because this talk is influenced by your thoughts, ideas, beliefs, and things that you are unsure about. These thoughts, ideas, and others center on your perception of the world around you, other people, and yourself.

This is why self-talk has the power to be both negative and positive. As a result, if you have a negative outlook on life and yourself, your self-talk will predominantly be negative. On the other hand, if you have a more optimistic outlook and personality then this self-talk will be more positive and hopeful.

Self-talk can be influenced by your current level of self-esteem and self-worth. On the other hand, you can increase your sense of self-esteem and self-worth by practicing more positive self-talk.

Even though practicing positive self-talk has so many great benefits, our instinctive human reaction is to practice negative self-talk. This is an evolutionary trait that was used in the time of our ancestors to up the rate of survival. Having a pessimistic view allowed cavemen to better predict the worst-case scenario so that they could be prepared. Even though this practice is not necessary for survival in most cases in modern society, it is still something that persists in the human psyche.

Therefore, to beat this natural human inclination and circumstances that promote it, you must first be aware of what it is and how it happens. Negative self-talk falls into one of four categories. They are:

- Catastrophizing. These types of negative thoughts make the person expect the worst at all times even going so far as to defy logic in the expectation.

- Personalizing. These types of negative thoughts make a person blame themselves for everything that happens even if the circumstances are far out of their reach to control.

- Magnifying. These types of negative thoughts make a person focus on the negative aspects of a situation while blatantly ignoring any and all positives that came out of that situation.

- Polarizing. These types of thoughts take on an either-or approach. Things are only good or bad, or black or white. There is no middle ground and as such, thoughts tend to favor the black or bad.

Now that you are aware of the type of negative thoughts that can persist in your mind, you can then learn to switch them around so that they are more positive. This is a practice that takes a conscious effort on your part to monitor what type of talk goes on in your head.

Let us practice with a few examples.

Your negative thought can be, I have failed and so, will be a failure forever. You can switch that negative self-talk and practice a more positive outlook by instead thinking something like, I am proud of my effort because it took much courage to go outside of my comfort zone.

Another negative thought may take a form like, I am out of shape and should not bother trying to achieve my ideal weight. A positive thought to counter that should be, I am capable and persistent and will do what is necessary to ensure that I become as healthy as can be.

Practicing positive self-talk is another process that does not happen overnight. You have to be persistent and consistent with it to see results. This will allow you to develop a new habit whereby your natural inclination is to take on a positive outlook on the world and yourself. That positive outlook will help boost your sense of self-esteem and self-worth. Tips you can employ to do this include:

- Identifying things that trigger negative self-talk. For example, your work life may be a circumstance where you experience a lot of negative self-talk. Identify what about that situation triggers those thoughts so that you can mentally prepare yourself to counter these thoughts with positive self-talk.

- Stop and evaluate how you feel often. Do this especially when you feel down as this is a time where negative thoughts are likely to manifest.

- Surround yourself with positive people. It is unfortunate to say but you are the company that you keep. Therefore, if you find yourself hanging around people that are perpetually negative then your internal dialogue will take on that energy. Actively choose the type of energy that you absorb and hang out with people who promote positive vibes and interactions.

- Learn to use humor to counter negative self-talk. Humor allows a person to feel lighter and less stressed and therefore, less likely to give in to negative self-talk.

- Use positive affirmations. These statements boost the likelihood that you will take on a more positive outlook and therefore, use positive self-talk to communicate with yourself.

You are now the one in control of your thoughts. Taken even that power away from the narcissist and replace his voice with one the uplifts and empowers you.

Work on Your Self-Image

Your self-image is what you believe about your personality, appearance, and abilities. The narcissist would have taken punches at your self-image as well to suit his purpose of manipulating and controlling you. He would have made you see your physical appearance, your capabilities, and your personality through a lens of his making. This is your wake-up call to look at yourself through a new lens. The best way to cultivate that new lens is to first work on acknowledging the things that you are good at.

Next, if there are things about your personality that you do not like, acknowledge what they are and work on changing them. Personality is a fluid thing. You can change it anytime. You have seen how being in the presence of the narcissist can change your personality for the worst. Now you can work on changing it for the best. One of the surest ways to do this is by changes bad habits that you may have such as being abrasive. Taking on more positive personality traits like being more kind and honest goes a long way in boosting self-image.

One of the hardest-hitting contributing factors for poor self-image is body image. Weight, how we dress, our facial features… All of it and more play a part in how we feel about ourselves. Again, this is something that you can take control of. You need to learn to feel comfortable in your own skin and to see the beauty in you. Beauty is not just skin deep. It is about how you carry yourself, how accepting you are of yourself, and how open you are to the fact that you are a beautiful person. Beauty is not a state of the body. It is a state of mind.

Things you can do to promote a more positive body image include:

- Celebrating and appreciating all the things that your body can do. You can run. You can dance. You can breathe. You exist… All of these things make you special and beautiful no matter how simple or common they are.

- When you need reminding, make a list of the top 10 things that you like about yourself. Read this list often and place it in an area where it is easily visible and accessible to you. This frequent reminder of your likable traits solidifies the facts in your mind and therefore, boosts your sense of self-worth.

- Turn negative self-talk about your body image into positive self-talk.

- Wear clothes that make you feel comfortable and good about your body. Do not try to fit into the social norm. Work with your own body shape, size, and your own needs, not against them to fit in with the current trend.

- Do not allow yourself to be fooled by mass media and social media messages about you what you should be or look like. What you are is beautiful and there is no need to change to fit into a mold.

Be Proud of the Fact That You Are a Survivor of Narcissist Abuse

This narcissist tried to break you but just from reading this I know that you are not broken, merely cracked. A crack can be mended and be transformed into something truly beautiful and inspiring as exampled by you.

Not many people can go through the things that you have gone through and still make it out on top. You are strong and resilient and both of these traits deserve to be celebrated and appreciated, especially by you. Not only have you survived this abuse and taken steps to get out of the vicious cycle, but you have also taken steps to make a bigger, better, brighter future for yourself.

Focus on the change that you would like to make in your life and how you would like to go. As you manifest that change, you will notice the increased positivity in your mental, emotional, and spiritual environment.

CHAPTER 13:

When the Healing Gets Tough

Healing properly takes time, discipline, and determination. Imagine you broke your arm in several places, so you go to the hospital to get it repaired and instructions on what to do for the pain and to have a fully functioning arm once it heals. In order for this to happen, they have to break your arm again because it has started healing on its own, but improperly. If they do nothing, your arm will mend in a deformed manner, the bones will not be properly aligned. You agree to allow them to break and reset the broken bones so that it can heal properly and be fully functioning once it has completely healed. After the bones have been broken and realigned, you experience a lot of pain, and a cast is placed on your arm to keep it stabilized for several weeks to ensure proper healing.

If the cast is removed prematurely, you run the risk of the bones moving and becoming misaligned and causing it to look abnormal, compromising full mobility of the arm. You agree to the process and keep the cast on, and you keep your arm in a sling throughout the day to ensure proper healing. To function through the pain while the arm is healing, you are given instructions to take pain medication several times a day and instructed to restrict your activities until the cast is removed. After a few months of complying with the doctor's orders, the cast is removed and your arm looks a little thin, but you are able to move it and the pain has subsided.

Just as the physical body has to be nursed and assisted to heal when bones are broken, your eternal body, and your soul—mind, and emotions—has to be nurtured and assisted when you have been wounded or broken emotionally from a failed marriage.

You must be guided through the healing process to ensure that you heal properly and are nurtured. Prescribed exercises and instructions are the medication that will help you heal properly. When you are feeling the pain from the wounds and the flood of different emotions associated with your grief, you may become overwhelmed.

The assistance I've provided will help you stay on track and continue to heal in a healthy manner. Not working through your emotions properly can delay your healing and cause you to stuff the emotions inside to avoid them. Avoiding the pain and not processing the varying emotions can lead to bitterness, resentment, anger, and depression and can adversely impact your ability to build healthy relationships in the future, as well as impact your ability to return to complete healthy functioning and interaction with others.

You may start lashing out at the children or having anger outbursts with the people close to you. If you become depressed and are unable to pull out of it, your daily activities and routines can be adversely impacted.

To stay on track with your journey to wholeness, here are a few things to look for, identify, and push through so that you can stay on course and continue the work necessary for healthy healing.

Obstacles

You may want to resist reaching out and asking for help. Avoid ignoring the recommendation to have a few people or family members you can call upon to talk with and assist you with caring for you and with the children, if applicable. This support in your life is a vital part of your healing. You must be able to share how you are feeling. You will need someone to be real and transparent so that you don't keep the emotions and pain bottled up inside. You don't want the pressure to get so high that you explode in ways that could be harmful and inappropriate.

Remember, a support group for individuals working through a divorce or a professional therapist are also options if you don't have friends or family you can call upon who can identify with what you are going through or be the nurturing support you need.

When you are feeling different emotions, you may be tempted to try to avoid them by ignoring what you feel. If you keep them locked inside, you can't process them and if you don't work through them you won't heal properly. Resist the urge to not do the work, push your way through the different emotions. It may be painful and exhausting, but it will be so worth the work in the end. Remember to do the journaling as you face your pain and differing emotions. Describe what you are feeling, try to identify why you feel a certain way, and write it down. If you have a solution for something you've been dealing with writing it down. Write, write, and write, whatever the thoughts or feelings, just write. When you are at a settling point, write how you want to feel, some positive emotion that you want like joy, serenity, or love. Then, write down some positive affirmations.

Forgiving someone is a difficult challenge. It can be even more challenging if you believe the person does not deserve your forgiveness. And forgiving yourself can be difficult. Think about the heavy load of ill feelings inside—anger, bitterness, hate, and resentment—these emotions you are carrying around with you every day, they are you hurting you.

The tendency to ignore this portion (forgiving) of the healing can be tempting because you may feel they or you don't deserve to be forgiven. Ask yourself why, and let's add these feelings to the journal. If you are feeling stuck here, consider reaching out for some spiritual support or a professional therapist. Remember, forgiveness does not mean you have to be friends with someone. You don't even have to see or speak with the person again. Restoring interaction is not the point and neither is it the goal. Freedom from your past is the focus. The act of forgiving is a personal choice, and you have to first want to forgive to move forward. When dealing with abuse, you should reach out for professional support so that you can move cautiously through this.

You may get tired of the routine and not want to do this every day, but the repetition is what makes this work. Avoid the temptation to excuse yourself from the exercises in the, they're important to building up your self-image and confidence.

Our children are our most valuable treasures. Don't slip up and bring them into all the drama. Even if you are feeling lonely, avoid leaning on your children and venting to them about your ex and all the hurt you are feeling. The temptation may be strong to vent about all the bad things their dad has done or how he is hurting you or neglecting them. Don't do it. Don't paint a negative picture of their dad to them. Let them form their own opinions. You want them to be protected as much as possible from all the ugliness that can come with a divorce, and you want to give them a fair chance at believing in marriage when they're older and considering having a family.

Being too close to someone too soon can be a stumbling block to your healing. Move cautiously when thinking about dating. Getting involved too soon can pause your healing because you may want a mate to avoid grieving your ex, and you may end up in a rebound and wake up one day and say, "I don't like him." It's common for people to run to a new relationship to make themselves feel better. Be strong. Move slowly.

You may think carving out personal space to replenish yourself spiritually is not necessary. Even if you are not a Christian, taking time to de-stress and relax in solitude can be replenishing and is healthy emotionally and physically. With so much activity in our busy lives, you may find it hard to get away from the noise and focus on your spiritual growth and well-being. Spending time in prayer and reflecting on biblical teaching will strengthen you. Avoid the temptation to put nourishing your soul and spirit on the back burner. Make it a priority. It is so worth it.

When you are always helping others, it is easy to avoid doing what is good for you. Don't ignore yourself. Put you first. You deserve to feel good about yourself and to feel happy. Take the time necessary to do what is best for you. Don't let anything hold you back, girl. As my daughter would say, "Chop, chop, and get to it."

CHAPTER 14:

How to Learn to Live and Love After Being with a Narcissist

Mistakes to Avoid

Don't Believe That Knowledge Alone Will Keep You Safe. You bought this, you acquainted yourself thoroughly with the tactics and red flags that have let you know your partner, friend, or family member is indeed, a narcissist. That is only the first step, however. You had to implement new, unfamiliar, even unnatural behaviors just to regain some semblance of rationality so you could escape that narcissist, and therein lies the key to a successful recovery.

Now one of the most important things you have to do is continue the momentum you started by leaving (or deciding to leave, if you have not yet left). Persistence in action is what will deliver you from the heart of darkness, now and in the future. You have to keep going, keep pushing, keep trying, and never let your guard down. This is a lot to take, and a lot to handle. But it beats remaining in an environment designed to eventually kill you. No one can survive in a toxic environment forever.

Now that you know you must keep being active in your recovery, one of the most important things you'll need to understand is that your conscious mind does not have the tools it requires to heal your emotional, psychological damage that was caused by the narcissist. As a survivor, you have inner trauma that's going to have to be dealt with. Knowledge about narcissism, and even acknowledging what has happened won't repair the wounds deep within your heart. You're going to have to seek help for this, such as seeing a therapist well-versed in recovery from narcissistic abuse or join a support group. Any place where you can gain the wisdom of others who have gone before you will help you on the road to healing.

It would be relatively easy to look at the narcissist and see only the sadist, the manipulator, the cruel person who hurts others for fun. This point of view is not entirely accurate. The narcissist's problems run much deeper, and she is not hurting for fun, she's hurting other people because compared to non-narcissists, her reactions, observations, and perceptions of other people and herself are woefully fractured.

Never Leaving Your Place of Shame. Many of us will struggle to get past this step, especially those of us who once prided ourselves on being strong, tough, and self-reliant. Many men struggle deeply with being victims of narcissism; this is not something that's supposed to happen to them, right? Wrong. Narcissists target anyone who catches their interest, and they like to aim high. You were once capable of success, achievements, and love—and you will be, again, as soon as you get over blaming yourself for the abuse. You are not at fault—only the narcissist is.

Distraction, Instead of a Focal Shift. Further on we're going to talk about the need for a shift in focus while you recover. This is not the same as a constant distraction. Keeping yourself from thinking about what happened is only prolonging both the pain as well as the healing. You need to set aside some time on a regular basis to do some deep self-searching and work on tackling recovery, one step at a time.

Love on the Rebound. One of the most dangerous mistakes, replacing the missing "love," if it can be called that, with new love opens us to a particularly devious occurrence: meeting and becoming victim to yet another narcissist. At this stage in the game, you are not recovered, rebuilt, or reclaimed enough to be steady on your feet. You wouldn't be able to see the next abuser coming, even armed with the knowledge of what it takes to be a narcissist. You might accidentally (or on purpose) let slip about the abuse you suffered at the hands of your ex, and this could provide the new predator tons of ammunition in winning you over, sweeping you off your feet, then controlling your every move as both your savior and your new commander.

Additionally, you might have a lot of dark feelings after your traumatic experience—even if the new love is a genuine, well-meaning person, do you want to expose them to all the anger, resentment, and pain you've had to hide for so long? It's in there, even if you believe you've let it go. Only time and self-work can get it out, and so early on in your healing process is not the time to begin a new romance.

Don't Stalk the Narcissist. Of course, we don't do this because we want them back (usually), but because we're afraid. We want to keep up a perimeter of defenses and being pre-emptive and going on the offensive to see what the narcissist is up to seems perfectly natural, and it is. However, it also opens you up to contact. You must steadfastly adhere to the No Contact rule if you want to survive recovery and get your life back.

In addition, you might catch a glimpse of the person we call "The Replacement." The narcissist loathes being alone; she must have someone to feed her need for narcissistic supply or she will quickly self-destruct, so in your absence, she will find another victim. If you were to watch this play out on social media, you would be devastated and horrified to see that the exact process of "love-bombing," down to the places the narcissist goes with their new beau, to important proclamations of love and events they post about, almost exactly match yours when your relationship was in its inception. This can cause feelings of jealousy and hurt, even if we believe that we absolutely despise our former abuser. We might be tempted to reach out—perhaps tricking ourselves into believing that we are burying the hatchet. Even a simple message of "Congratulations, I'm so happy for you" can lead to terrible consequences.

Rebuilding Your Self

This may seem like an impossible task, or at least, a daunting one. How does one go about the business of rebuilding self? To start, you need to quickly and firmly establish boundaries.

Because you are reacquainting yourself with what it means to have boundaries, it's important to take things slowly with new friendships, and leave dating until you've healed much more. Practice moments of boundary-enforcement during moments you're comfortable. If a social setting is too much for you right now, give yourself permission to opt out.

Reclaiming Your Reality

Forgive yourself and seek reminders of who you are. This is another time-consuming process, and should never be rushed. Don't allow so-called friends and family members guilt you into "getting over it"; this is especially true for men recovering from abuse. Take as much time as you need and tell those who would push too hard to take a hike. This is an important first step in recovering yourself. You were a strong, capable person once, and you will be again. The first thing you need to do is treat yourself with respect, and demand that others in your close circles do, too.

Seek out friends and family who were close to you during the good times before you met the narcissist. Ask them to help you; perhaps plan a trip to a place you had some good times or re-read articles or stories you wrote that garnered praise. Pull out old sports trophies and look through yearbooks and albums. You are on a mission to find you. You're out there somewhere, waiting to once again live happily. The narcissist never new you—they never even saw you. Don't be afraid to like yourself again; it's necessary to achieve success and joy in life.

Redefining Your Belief System

Understand that a part of you knew that abuse was happening, and don't think less of yourself because of it. It's time to acknowledge the truth of what happened to you:

- You were tricked (because the other person is a narcissist).

- You were lied to (because the other person is a narcissist).

- You were manipulated (because the other person is a narcissist).

- You were hurt (because the other person is a narcissist).

- You were abused (because the other person is a narcissist).

The reason for the repetition is to help you get it into your head that there is only one reason these things happened, and that reason is listed above. You did not deserve to be hurt. You did nothing that warranted the abuse. You are simply not to blame.

Most people do not abuse others. There are so many people out there who would never dream of hurting you, who at the very least would show you a minimum of respect, and at the most would love you for the person you are, not the shadow they wish to torment. What you're doing now is strengthening yourself, so that you can once again believe that there's good in the world. Always remember, take this process one step at a time, and don't feel as if you're not making the process fast enough.

Rebuilding Your Trust

This part of the process may take the longest. This is a difficult part.

When dealing with people in your various friendships and acquaintances, give people the opportunity to show their intention. Call them on it. Ask them about their intentions. You can do this neutrally, even in a friendly tone—this is not a call to arms and you never need to sound combative. Being assertive and seeing with both eyes open is a healthy way of dealing with other people. Don't be afraid to take the initiative.

You're going to reach a point where you realize that part of you knew what was going on while you were with your abuser, and that's going to hurt. That will feel like a metric ton of shame, but you have to process it. All of us want to be happy; we want love, we want joy. You were holding out for that, but it never came. This is not your fault.

You're going to have to examine why you made the choices you did that brought you together with the narcissist—again, this is not blame. It's understanding yourself. Self-inquiry is one of the hardest but most important steps of the healing process. By learning about your vulnerabilities, you can learn how to better protect yourself in the future and learn how to forgive yourself because of the past.

Taking Steps towards Loving Again

Heal your inner child. Reclaim your joy. Look at relationships in a balanced, healthy way. What can I bring to the table? What am I asking of a new partner?

To start, you will need to shift your focus away from the concept of love for a while. This might seem counterintuitive, but you have a lot of rebuilding to do.

Finally, you are going to need a lot of patience. You will not be rebuilt in a day, just like that famous Italian city. You're healing and recovery will take time, as much time as it needs, and you are worth every minute it takes. You deserve to be happy and to be loved in a healthy, uplifting way.

CHAPTER 15:

Transforming Your Future Interactions

Moving Forward

Handling an unhealthy/extreme narcissist is not an easy task, whether you choose to walk away or remain engaged in their lives to some degree. If you decide to walk away and cut contact, how you handle this move is an important consideration. For non-abusive narcissists, being empathetic and considerate ensures that you can walk away feeling positive about your actions. Remember, the narcissist is unable to empathize at times, and this is often due to increased emotional sensitivity. Letting them down gently without confrontation or exposing them may be the kindest route to prevent them from suffering a major blow to their self-esteem. However, in relationships where abuse is present, it may be advisable to cut the relationship swiftly, or in whatever way is safe and expedient for you.

When the Narcissist Returns—like any person involved in a relationship, it is likely that the narcissist will at some point think of you and contact you. Depending on your relationship and the individual, they may be very hurt, angry, or suspicious about why you are no longer involved with them. This may be understandably so. For example, if you decided to stop speaking to a parent because their actions were detrimental to your well-being- their parental love for you (whether hidden or clearly displayed) will not simply disappear. It is claimed by many that narcissists do not love, but this is rarely the case, and only applicable at the very upper limits of the scale. It is more likely that they are unable to express or show their love in the presence of other people. Many narcissists find that their loving feelings become apparent when they emerge temporarily from the grips of their addiction to narcissistic supply.

They may contact you in a caring, human manner, to gloat, or in a manipulative attempt to reel you back in and gain something they want from you. Each situation, like each individual, is different. When possible, in response to these contact attempts, empathy is advisable, but delivered in a way that does not invite hope, questions, or doubts. Be firm and stand by what you know is best, rather than being open to what they may offer you.

For example, if you have left a relationship with an emotionally abusive narcissist you may find that they contact you again in the future. Refusing contact is advisable, rather than discussing or reasoning with them, as no good can come from the interaction, only further harm. If they increase their attempts to contact you, become angry, emotional, or abusive, a strict attitude of no reaction can eventually force them to gain control of themselves, and move on. However, if you have been keeping your distance from a non-abusive family member—with unhealthy but not overwhelming narcissistic tendencies—you might welcome the opportunity to have a positive and well-meaning conversation. This does not mean that you are opening yourself up for dangerous or pre-emptive closeness but simply means that you are experimenting with being present in their lives, so long as they are able to behave in a reasonable manner. If they are still unable to behave well, then you may decide whether you want to continue the relationship or increase the distance further.

How to Change a Narcissist – Essentially, if someone is being unhealthily narcissistic, it is up to them to notice and correct their behavior, rather than anyone else to point it out to them and risk the backlash from a narcissistic injury. Healthy narcissism may work well, but it is important that it does not develop into dependence on approval and attention to an extreme degree in the long run. Highly narcissistic people are usually unaware that they are so, as they live very often in a state of denial and are unlikely to attempt to improve or work on themselves. In some cases, suspecting or being diagnosed with having NPD can provide significant motivation for people to change, as was found by Dr. Craig Malkin of Harvard medical school. During online discussions on identifying narcissism, he found the most distressed and heartfelt pleas for help and advice on how to improve came not from people in the lives of narcissists, but from those that had been diagnosed with or suspected they had NPD.

Happily, he believes that narcissists are able to change the ways in which they see the world, but that this rarely happens. This is because, in the case of narcissists, many will live, perpetually unaware or in denial of their skewed lens, and will never attempt to improve it. Although we cannot condemn those that want to change with a sentence of "irrevocably permanent narcissism"—for change to happen a person has to want to change and be capable of facing the work necessary to make improvements. It is no one else's responsibility to make this happen but the person who is overly narcissistic themselves.

This means that if you are caught up in the life of a narcissist, whether you decide to make them aware of your suspicions or not, nothing can make them improve unless they decide that they are ready to do so. This decision may come at a point of desperation, and real progress- if it comes at all- may take many years to solidify.

To overcome narcissism, the first step is to recognize the role of addiction to narcissistic supply and stop attempting to secure it. Accepting that being ordinary is okay is essential, and that no matter what successes or failures life brings—a person can never become more than just a person- equal to everyone else. The urge to stand out from to overcome narcissism, the first step is to recognize the role of addiction to narcissistic supply and stop attempting to secure it. Accepting that being ordinary is okay is essential, and that no matter what successes or failures life brings- a person can never become more than just a person- equal to everyone else. The urge to stand out from the crowd needs to be quashed.

If it's impossible to stop supplying the ego—then aligning this need with a positive cause can at least make a difference in the world. Like any addiction, fighting it can be extremely difficult, and overcoming it whilst still being intoxicated is highly unlikely to happen. Rather than fighting to remain in control of narcissism, the narcissist must take responsibility for starving it and going "cold turkey," as with any alcoholic or drug addict.

Assessing the Situation Objectively – you may be fully aware that you are a source of narcissistic supply, a target for manipulation, or abusive behavior. Perhaps it is clear that you must either break off or continue the relationship. But for those who are still in the questioning phase, unsure about what is happening and the extent to which they need to act, there are several exercises you can do to help you see more clearly. Extreme narcissistic people may be abusive if they are unhealthy enough, as they may be unable to be empathetic to others. If you're unsure as to whether you're involved in an abusive interaction, take a look at the following checklist. Many victims of abuse live in a state of denial regarding the true nature of the situation, making justifications for their loved ones and excusing their abusive behavior. Abuse can be an insidious process that can leave the victim feeling confused and upset for an extended period after it has finished. It can have crippling effects on the victim's sense of self-worth and confidence and should not be ignored or allowed to continue after it has been identified.

There are various types of abuse – emotional/psychological, sexual, physical, and financial/material. As a summary, you have the right to emotional support in your relationships, be heard by your partner, and be responded to with courtesy. You also have the right to have your feelings and experiences acknowledged as real and valid, clear, and informative answers to questions that concern you, to live free from criticism and judgment, live free from accusation and blame. You should receive encouragement, live free from emotional and physical threats and be respectfully asked to do things rather than "ordered." You should receive goodwill from your partner and live free from angry outbursts and rage. Each type of abuse has various indicators split out in the lists below. If you're unsure about whether you are experiencing abuse, identify which indicators apply to your relationship with the person in question. Multiple indicators mean that it is more likely that what you are experiencing classifies as abuse.

Conclusion

I commend you for reading through this. You invested in yourself. You made a commitment and kept it. I hope your heart has been stirred and your soul inspired. You have been given the gift of tools you can apply to rebuild your life. You have received encouragement and you've read stories of other women just like yourself. I'd like to reach out to you across space and time to give you a hug and to look into your eyes. I'd like to say to you, "You are amazing. You have a good heart and you are worthy of following your dreams. You have so much to give, and there is no one on this Earth who has the life experience, knowledge, and unique gifts that you possess. You matter, and you can rebuild your life to one of joy and purpose, and you can truly make a difference for others. This is your time to re-create yourself into the fullness of your being that has been suppressed for so long."

I wrote much of this either sitting in my sunny bay window in my kitchen, or in my motorhome parked by the water. Each time I sat down to write and pour out my soul to you, I breathed deeply, dropped into my heart, and infused my message with love. This is my love letter to the women who have been hurt, let down, betrayed, disappointed, humiliated, and led to believe they are somehow unlovable and unworthy. You are beautiful! You have so much to give.

When you release your fear, you will be filled with joy and hope. Fear is the opposite of love. Make the choice to live your life in love. Lead with your heart. Discover your message, and then share it, to inspire others to live their lives being all they're meant to be.

Now is the time for your new beginning. Anything you've ever longed for wished you could do, fantasized that perhaps "one day" you could achieve, can now be yours. I know that is a bold statement. I'll venture a guess that you read that and thought something like, "Me? I don't have the money, or the talent, or the skills. I'm too old. I'm past my prime. It's just too late for me." I assure you, it is never too late! Your life will not become grand overnight, but if you work through this, seek support, learn to love yourself, feed your soul, face your fears, and refuse to give up, you will rebuild your life and you will be happy. You will live a life of meaning and purpose.

Will you resign yourself to the alternative? Will you stay stuck, miserable, and unfulfilled? It is up to you, but you certainly do not have to settle for a directionless and small life. I pour my heart into my work with women because I truly believe women are powerful and amazing beyond words, and they deserve to live spectacular lives. We have been given false messages about our weaknesses, inadequacies, and imperfections. It's time to stand together in strength and celebration! We deserve happiness and fulfillment!

Move forward, in the direction of your dreams every day, even if it's in small increments. Surround yourself with people who support and inspire you. Keep the momentum going? Utilize the tools you've been given. Nurture yourself, on a daily basis. When you have decisions to make, breathe deeply, drop into your heart, and ask for guidance. Then follow your instincts and go forward. You are on a healing journey. You have life lessons to learn. You have great wisdom to draw from. You are in this life to contribute to the unique gifts and talents you've developed. What will your legacy be? What great things will you accomplish?

How do you feel now?

Do you feel well informed and confident that you're clear on the road ahead? Do you feel like you might be ready to take the first step towards initiating divorce proceedings? Have the contents of the book helped you to understand that none of this is your fault and that you're free to walk away?

We hope that you feel more positive at this stage. Whilst it's normal to feel sad at the same time because you're about to end a marriage that you hoped would last you a lifetime, it's important to realize that you do not deserve to live your life in the grips of a narcissist and their constant manipulation and control.

You can set yourself free, and whilst the road ahead may not be smooth, it will come to an end and leave you with a brighter future ahead.

Divorce of any kind is messy and difficult. Choosing your divorce attorney carefully is vital. As we've mentioned several times throughout the book, choosing an attorney who has specific experience and deep knowledge of narcissism is important. In this case, they can help you to navigate everything that the narcissist may throw your way and help you to end the divorce with a fair result.

If you have children, remember that they must always come first. We obviously don't have to tell you this, but it's a point that's worth making. When a divorce takes hold, things can become overwhelming and when you add narcissism to the mix, it's even easier for the whole situation to turn very sour indeed.

Stay as positive as you can be, focus on the future, understand that whilst the road ahead may not be easy, it will be worthwhile in the end. Choose your attorney carefully, be sure of what you want, plan everything out, and seek support from those close to you. If you have to mend some broken bridges in order to build up your support network, don't be afraid to do so.

Life does not have to be controlled by a narcissist. You do not have to be manipulated and you do not have to live your life trying to please someone who will never be pleased.

Look to the future with hope and happiness will come your way.

Believe in yourself. I believe in you. You've got this!

HEALING RACIAL TRAUMA

A PRACTICAL GUIDE TO HEALING THE SHAME, ANXIETY, FEAR, AND TACTICS IN ORDER TO DEVELOP FREEDOM

BETHANY KEY

Introduction

We will meet a few people of color along the way and read their stories of oppression, healing, and resilience. How many of you presently live with the poisonous plagues or perilous pitfalls of complex racial trauma? Are you still shrinking in the shadows of shame and sin from childhood or adolescent racial traumas? Have you experienced physical, psychological, emotional, and/or sexual abuse and terror over the course of your lifetime or within the past several years (or even decades)? Has the loss of a loved one catapulted you into the complex claws of racial trauma, a precarious path without a mindful map, or any concrete escape plan as it involves numerous intersections, roadblocks, and potholes on our minds, bodies, and spirits daily?

1. How brainwashing has been used to control the mind

Brainwashing is a type of psyche control that objectives an individual's capacity to settle on decisions without being forced or pressured.

2. Inferiority complex and racial trauma

In America, bigotry is normal and comes in different structures and shapes including police ruthlessness and racial profiling among others. This has brought about low confidence among the minority particularly blacks. As a matter of fact, low confidence is the main purpose behind inclusion in lawful offenses. Why? Since bigotry is about genuine force and when one individual is denied their capacity, they will respond to show their disappointment.

3. Superiority complex psychology

It is both absurd and ludicrous to realize that the prevalence complex is a type of guard system which individuals utilize to reward for the substandard complex. Such individuals accept that their worth is relied upon demeaning and harming others.

4. Assassinating a person's character with racial trauma

The brain science of prejudice includes character death

Character death can be portrayed as a planned and steady procedure that expects to insult or chaos up with the validity of an individual or gathering of individuals.

Individuals who kill others' characters utilize different strategies including misdirecting data, demeaning, slander, and control.

This may prompt dismissal by other people who may not have the foggiest idea about the genuine truth—does this ring a bell? Prejudice is incredible and will frequently retaliate through character death.

Nothing is outlandish

On the off chance that today we are living in very much assembled houses and not caverns, if today we are utilizing current ovens and not kindling, if today we are strolling completely dressed and not exposed, nothing is unimaginable. At some point—bigotry will be history.

Unlike treating a broken bone with a cast, the path to healing from racial trauma is one that can take dangerous detours and boisterous bumps on the road to recovery and resilience (literally!). Tan's quote about wounds is so valid and applicable to the visible and invisible ones that impacted my body, mind, and soul. Are you even conscious of your wounds from complex racial trauma? Did you endure or witness atrocious acts of domestic violence or intense scenes of intimate partner violence (IPV) when dating, married, or while growing up in a dysfunctional household or volatile situation? Are you currently still harboring woes and wounds beyond words from service in the military, exposure to war and violence as a former refugee or immigrant, or endured atrocious acts of rape, molestation, incest, or sexual assault? This will offer you some light amid the darkness that you have had to deal with for far too long.

CHAPTER 1:

Feelings of Shame, Guilt, and Anxiety

As a result of exploring life, love, and learning beyond labels in as far as what complex racial trauma is and its typical sources, we will present you with some relevant research, practical examples, and beneficial exercises to the understanding complex racial trauma's overlapping, revolving, and devastating physical, psychological, spiritual, socioemotional, sexual, behavioral, financial, and vocational ramifications. Our ability to rise above this diagnosis depends on our capacity to navigate all these complicated effects and manifestations, so channel the lyrics to "Eye of the Tiger," "Rise Up," or "Roar" "We Are The Champions," or whatever pumps you up to defy complex racial trauma.

Reverting back to the title of and the revolving doors' metaphor, how many of you feel automatic panic, fear, or just plain annoyance when entering revolving doors in any office building, tourist attraction, or hotel? I personally dislike the feeling of entering them as other people are also pushing simultaneously and following me so closely. It probably reflects the feelings and realizations that I do not have control, something that my racial trauma has caused me to struggle with most for most of my adult life.

How do people with complex racial trauma struggle with control issues? In my own case, whether I was trying to regulate my weight, grades, perceptions from others, achievements at work, I always felt like I had to be the best, so I was super competitive at work, in school, and with my peers. I also was highly distrusting and suspicious of everyone and everything. I never felt safe. Are you competitive, aloof, depressed, or anxious? I suffered from high anxiety as well as hyper-competitiveness. My inflated sense of ego also greatly hindered my relationship dynamics that caused me to be overly bossy, super controlling, and extremely suspicious of everyone and everything. Do any of these tendencies presently reflect your own struggles with complex racial trauma as far as managing the physical, psychological, spiritual, socioemotional, sexual, behavioral, financial, and vocational ramifications?

Put down the mops, toss aside the dustpans, and sideline the sweeper for this one. As you complete this essential exercise, think of your own life in terms of a house, dorm, or apartment metaphor. In order to be sane, happy, and healthy, we must clean each room equitably and live in each area for balance, right? Well, this mindful technique urges us to take an inventory of how complex racial trauma manifests in our own lives or "houses" before we do a clean "sweep" to purge the dust from the past. Answer honestly about any areas that warrant you to spring clean the racial trauma dust and cobwebs from the critical facets of your life and wellbeing holistically:

- Physical dirt.

- Psychological grime.
- Spiritual dust bunnies.

Additionally, it is important to clarify that DNA is not different between blacks and whites, in fact, it is almost exactly the same by far, what cannot be denied is that there are genetic variations but only within the African continent there is more genetic variety than in the whole rest of the world, a fact that has demonstrated that life started there and from there it spread to the whole planet. As a last important fact, there is no visual characteristic that allows us to differentiate the genetic similarities or differences in us, so classifying someone as white, brown, or black is an absurdity that expresses nothing more than the simple color of the skin.

Aware of the equality between all classes and colors, great movements have been created in order to assert the universal rights of human beings in the face of all kinds of contempt, movements led by men who are willing to give their own lives for that cause. There have been very important and renowned figures whose efforts came to make a considerable difference, although these worthy representatives have been key players in each victory obtained are not responsible for one hundred percent of them, there is a larger group of anonymous heroes who in silence and discipline have managed to create liberating enterprises, deserving greater credit although they are only satisfied with receiving the benefit of rights respected for them and theirs, but it is inevitable and regrettable reality, there is still much to be done.

Activism is necessary to gain new grounds and not lose those already won, let us remember that thanks to the constant and firm fight against discrimination and racial violence, it was possible to eradicate the separation and privileges in the use of public transport, alliances were created between multiple races in all sectors affected by poverty and hit by supremacist elitism, with this the well-known campaign of the poor obtained the law that allows the right to vote. A highly accentuated criticism in the middle of marches for the resources destined to senseless wars in Vietnam, same that would have a greater benefit if they were used in programs of aid to the poor, that mobilization was the one that originated the law of service of immigration and nationality. The agitation in the streets in defense of the universal guarantees of each individual, as long as it is persistent and under the slogan of non-violence, will generate firm and sustained results as it has happened in the past, we must raise our voices unanimously without lowering our arms but without generating regrettable disturbances that threaten the integrity of public goods. The tactic of the state security forces will always be to use violence and aggression to disperse the concentrations, let them be the violent ones without falling into their provocations because that is the bait they will use to destroy us, but when we raise our voices telling the truth but calmly our pleas will be heard in the right instances and sooner or later justice will come knocking at our door.

Men and women with extraordinary potential have been victims of a millennial sabotage that keeps them away from uncertainty but imprisons them and makes them smaller, destroys their character and decimates their will, preventing the large-scale development of self-realization and freedom of thought, action and time. Those responsible for this sabotage are already clearly identified and are known as the morality of conformity, the acceptance of facts as irrefutable divine predestination, and self-commiseration.

All human beings should constantly ask and question themselves because certain issues are considered attractively desirable and others extremely repulsive, who does not become a sheep unaware of the morality implanted by the media as right and wrong, this sheep accepts as absolute reality any fact, rumor, news or dubious affirmation because of the simple lack of own criteria because we have been educated from the first infantile schools to the most important university institutes that to question the teachers and the established precepts is something amoral and disrespectful, nevertheless, in that way we are suggested to accept everything without any type of claim that turns us to the convenience of a few in simple automatons within a system devised against us.

The most atrocious truths are hidden from the incredulous and passive gaze of public opinion, between information and disinformation a battle is led that seeks to subject each individual with strong pressure until he becomes so tiny and ridiculous that he only aspires to cover his most basic needs without any intention of standing out, that is to lose self-respect.

Who is at the top of the social food chain considers himself as the man who dictates the steps that society should take, the image of himself is that of a god incarnate with a supposed moral superiority to the rest and the others for him are just a flock that must obey his whims without any excuse. Paradoxically the majority behaves like that flock, only a few behave like free-thinking individuals capable of undertaking their own path, an idealism free of unfounded thoughts and a human character capable of benefiting many in their steps.

I raise my voice in these words when I ask myself about the whereabouts of the leaders who want to be part of a new generation of free from the oppressive chains of any supremacist system and build a society in which the color of your skin does not matter and your origins are not an impediment but neither are they a guarantee before the cultural environment, a community in which you can and must earn by your own merit access to better opportunities. What I propose is that no one should be despised but neither should things be put on a silver platter so easily that no one can appreciate the satisfaction of effort and sacrifice.

CHAPTER 2:

Forms of Racial Trauma

Racial trauma is real

There are various ways that people of color experience racial trauma: as stated below. This is the reality of people of color from generation to generation. We are a trauma bond and we carry this from our ancestors into the modern world. This has left us inadequate and inconstant pursue of self believe. We project our insecurities to others in society, all this because of a system that has left us at a disadvantage. We have been lead to believe we are less superior and we need guidance from the white man.

Transgenerational Racial trauma

The trauma across the family is called transgenerational racial trauma. We may be prone to certain individual attitudes or actions are modeled in our families or community.

We ask ourselves questions such as: Who am I?

Personal Racial Trauma

My family experienced personal racial trauma as we get to call each other names from the slave trade era. Names such as "nigga" that is a form of us personalizing such names as a form of copping. This is seen in hip-hop culture, yes it is a way of identity but also as a coping mechanism, we find power in empowering such words and not allowing the white people to call us back. We may thing this us empowering ourselves but it is a way of trauma coping passed down generation to generation.

Physical Trauma

This happens when one is physically beaten due to your beliefs. Such treatment has been ongoing and has led to the creation of hate groups that still exist in the modern-day, this has created fear in people of color as we feel oppressed and cannot speak out in case of injustice. In the modern era, politicians have taken advantage and use such groups to inflict pain on people of color knowing the public will blame us.

Vicarious Trauma

Vicarious trauma occurs when we hear of detailed trauma stories or watch of survivors of racial abuse i.e. on T.V, newspaper such stories cause us to relate and bring past fears to reality. TV has managed to make such stories to look as we people of color are the ones on the wrong. This not only creates fear in us but the general public. We have seen situations where white people take advantage of this, they treat us as outcasts and use the police as a shield knowing very well if this was covered by news outlets they will get an advantage.

Microaggressions

Microaggression comes in the form of slights or messages communicated verbally or nonverbally. i.e. when we are cursed of being over sensitive thus stereotyped this can hinder our personal life as we believe we are prone to react, and at the same time, other races overlook us in professions that require a calm sense of self. In modern-day people of color will earn less than a white person in the same position due to this as the employee sees us as volatile thus we cannot handle all that is required of the given profession.

CHAPTER 3:

Types of Racism

We can speak of structural racial trauma, which is something that is, in some way, attached to the structures of our society. This is the mildest form of racial trauma and difficult to perceive, and therefore somewhat dangerous. We can identify as symptoms of this form of racial trauma the fact that black people win, according to statistics from the 2016 IBGE census, less than white people. We also found a lower level of education among the black population.

In our daily lives, we use racist expressions, often without realizing it, and the verification of these actions and situations combined with the belief in normality can be the factor of greatest risk for society when talking about racial trauma. Expressions of language and racist terms reinforce structural racial trauma (so strongly rooted) and allow discrimination to permeate all means, persecuting victims everywhere, as language is capable of entering any sphere of human life. Therefore, it is not a question of being "politically correct," but of recognizing that there is someone who is offended by certain expressions because he suffers in his skin the negative consequences of the discrimination that originated them.

A Typology of Racist Acts

A better understanding of the dimensions that structure the relationships between perpetrators and victims is a necessary stage to define the possibilities of the reaction of people who are the object of racial trauma to violence or discrimination experienced. The analysis of the different cases related to the 0800 SOS Racial trauma led us to distinguish two particularly important dimensions that define the relationship between the perpetrators and the victims: power and level of organization.

The power exercised over the victims can be of two types: certain authors are in a position of formal power vis-à-vis the victims: they have the possibility of exerting a direct influence on their living conditions, either because they apply the laws (which may be discriminatory or applied unfairly) or because they control access to social or economic assets that they exclude, without respecting equity, victims of access to them. Other authors have only informal power: they have the will to discriminate, but they do not have the means of coercion against the victims; it is true that they can threaten them, they can have weapons or other means of intimidation, but they do not represent the law, nor do they exercise a hierarchical social function over them.

The other dimension is the level of organization of the aggressors: Racist acts can emanate from people who are part of an institution, an organization or a group with a more or less elaborate racist ideology; in this case, the authors act as members of an organization that perceives racial trauma (or at least certain manifestations of racial trauma) as normal behavior. Racial trauma can also be the expression of disorganized individuals who act violently or discriminatory on their own initiative, according to personal a priori, related to collective prejudices, but in an unstructured manner. When they adopt racist behaviors, they know more or less consciously that they are in contradiction with the norms of equality that prevail in society.

The combination of these two dimensions allowed us to develop a typology in which we can distinguish four forms of racial trauma: interpersonal racial trauma, racial trauma for abuse of function, institutional racial trauma, and doctrinal racial trauma.

The typology we present here was built on the basis of a continuous process of interaction between empirical data and theorizing work. It is a production work of what Glaser and Strauss (1966) call a grounded theory. The raw material on which we base ourselves is the stories of racist discrimination or violence, such as were presented to the anti-racist telephone number.

The calls received indicate that for the complainant, the racist act lived or observed, exceeds the limits of what is tolerable. We then work with a material that touches on racist behavior considered as visible by those affected. We do not directly address the field of latent racial trauma, prejudice, structural discrimination.

Institutional Racism

We define institutional racial trauma as that which is exercised by an organization, often the state, that holds back the power to claim "the monopoly of legitimate physical violence" (Weber, 1959) and to define legality. In this case, racial trauma, which most often takes the form of discrimination, responds to a legal norm that does not respect the principle of equal treatment. It is then the law or the general policy of the institution that is discriminatory. This is particularly the case for immigration rules based on "cultural criteria": for example, immigrants originating from a Third World country or from Eastern Europe do not in principle have the right to obtain a work and stay permit in Switzerland (or in the countries of the European Union) because they do not have a good color passport. Sometimes, other laws, such as those related to Social Security, may be discriminatory towards immigrants based on the type of stay authorization they have or their national origin. 25% of the reported cases correspond to this type of racial trauma. This type of discrimination has been analyzed by authors such as Radtke (1990) and Bukow (1992). From their perspective, it is the practices, discourses, and institutional norms that contribute to producing discrimination against minorities. In the Swiss case, Weill Lévy and Grünberg. (1997) have shown that the discourse and practices in question were elaborated at the beginning of the century by the "foreigner police," created in that period. This contributed to propagating an ideology of the "Überfremdung," which considers foreigners as a threat to national cohesion since their presence "excessively alters the Swiss population" 1. Other authors have also mentioned that immigration policy, by dividing the world into different circles, for the recruitment of immigrant workers, creates a hierarchy based on cultural difference. By acting in this way, it designates certain human beings as radically different. And "threatening," thus laying the groundwork to justify keeping them at a distance from the space controlled by the State of arrival, through discriminatory treatment (Caloz Tschopp, 1993; Goldberg, 1998). An example of this process is what we have defined as the criminalization of immigrants by immigration policies. In fact, the means of fighting against what has been called "illegal migration" form the basis of the mechanisms of their persistence and reproduction. In other words, anti-clandestine policies produce and maintain clandestinity (Bolzman, 1998).

These are mainly discriminations that take an administrative form: it is the refusal to grant, renew, or transform a stay authorization or the threat of not doing so. At the bottom, the central issue in this type of situation is the right to stay in the country of arrival. But there are also other discriminations that concern social insurance, access to training, or other public benefits.

Often this type of situation is not considered racist. It is perceived as normal that a foreigner, especially if he is from a Third World country, is the subject of arbitrary decisions that do not need to be made explicit. Furthermore, it should be noted that many acts of this type reflect a narrow legal system that places affected people in impossible human situations.

In certain cases, institutional racial trauma (particularly the issue of permits) allows a third party to exercise violence in all impunity in the private sphere against the person concerned. The perpetrator of violence knows in effect that he runs little risk of being denounced by his victim, who is in a position of weakness due to his precarious status. This is the case, for example, of conjugal violence. The spouse who has the nationality of the country of residence or a stable permit is allowed to exercise permanent blackmail towards the victim because they know that the right of stay of the victim depends on the marriage.

Interpersonal Racism

In this case, racial trauma is the result of the action of individuals or informal groups that do not have a structured power over the victims, nor do they claim a strong racist ideology to act violently or exercise discriminatory behavior towards them. It is "ordinary" racial trauma where the authors transform an interpersonal conflict into a racist act, attributing to the attacked biological, ethnic, or cultural characteristics that make cohabitation with him impossible and legitimize violent or discriminatory actions against him. 38% of calls concern this type of racial trauma3. This type of behavior is close to what Vieworka (1998) defines as cultural or identity racial trauma. Different complementary reasons can explain this type of behavior. This can be attributed to authors who channel their discontent with their living conditions through the mechanism of the "scapegoat" (Girard, 1972), who protest against the problems they encounter in everyday life by imputing them to "foreigners" (Oechste and Zoll, 1985), who feel threatened by an incomprehensible and uncontrollable world represented by the Other (Bell, 1964). They may also be people who have lived through authoritarian socialization (Adorno et al., 1950), who are intolerant of ambiguous situations (Frenkel Brunswik, 1949) or who have imbued themselves with a xenophobic ethos. Another explanation refers to racial trauma used as strategic conduct: certain people can, in a conflict situation.

Interpersonal violence can reach different levels of intensity, it is often expressed through verbal aggressions' (in two-thirds of situations of interpersonal racial trauma, the victims complain of having received insults, insults, threats), but also through behaviors of segregation (avoidance of all physical contact, use of the same objects, frequenting the same places, rejection of any "mix," etc.), as well as, to a lesser extent, through forms of harassment (anonymous phone calls, noise, and other behaviors aimed at making the victim's life unbearable) and through physical assault. These different forms of aggression are often personalized; that is, they are aimed at precise victims and have strong emotional content.

Doctrinal Racism

In its most extreme version, doctrinal racial trauma is exercised by individuals or groups who do not have formal power, but who act on the basis of a racist ideology inspired by the speeches of far-right organizations with which the authors sympathize. This racial trauma is directed more consciously and strategically against specific categories of victims, with the aim of creating and maintaining a climate of prejudice and discrimination against them. 16% of the cases analyzed correspond to this type. This type of behavior corresponds to the classic analyzes of extreme right organizations. This is related to what Taguieff (1997) has defined as racial trauma ideology. They insist on irreducible differences with respect to those who are defined as others and hide those that exist within their own group or deny what is common to different groups.

Mixed Racism

The distinctions between the four forms of racist acts mentioned are analytical. In reality, sometimes different shapes mix and even reinforce each other. In fact, in 14% of the cases, we have verified the existence of racist behavior "in cascades," where, to first discrimination or aggression, others are added in which new authors intervene. For example, the situation of a person who is harassed by a neighbor, who is supported by the custodian of the property in their conduct. The victim complains to the police who give the attackers reason, without having listened to her.

CHAPTER 4:

Keys to Education Against Racial Trauma

But is that always synonymous with understanding? What can we do as parents so that our children escape racist attitudes?

In general, in humans, there is a tendency to be afraid of something new or different. It is an instinctive reaction, which does not occur in the same way in all people and, in most cases, is a protection against ignorance. Thus, the first way to avoid racist attitudes is to show children diversity and difference as something natural and enriching. Keep in mind that in this case, the moral discourse (what is right and what is wrong) is going to be insufficient. It must be accompanied by an intellectual reflection (within the possibilities according to the age of your child), explaining the reasons why all human beings are equal and that as such, we must live with the formula of respect and tolerance.

How do Children Learn Racial Prejudice?

From an early age, children already learn about racial differences and prejudices from their referents, their parents, relatives, teachers, etc. The process of learning racial prejudice does not differ much from the process of learning a new language. At six months of age, a baby's brain can already recognize racial differences. Between the ages of 2 and 4, children can internalize racial biases. And at 12 years old, many children have already established their beliefs, which makes it more difficult to reduce their racial prejudices and improve their cultural understanding.

Education for Diversity

As parents, we can act in different key aspects so that children get used to diversity and thus avoid racist comments or attitudes towards people of other beliefs, cultures, or countries. If these factors are present in your education, racist-type reactions will greatly decrease.

Be a good example

Identify and correct your own comments and actions that may foster racial prejudice.

It fosters friendship with people from other countries

Relationship with other people is the most natural way of understanding difference. This is applicable both if the child has classmates from other countries and if the parents have friends who favor this exchange.

It stimulates the learning of other languages

A new language provides a new way of seeing and understanding the world.

It teaches music, tales, gastronomy and traditions from other places

In this way, the little ones will see the difference as something playful and fun. Since traveling, or reading stories, playing with apps or learning to cook recipes from other countries are good ways to teach other customs and ways to understand diversity.

Talk to children about racial trauma

Communication is fundamental for two things: that they understand what attitudes can be considered as racist or as stereotypes without justification. There are endless ways to stimulate a conversation about racial trauma: movies, television, travel, or even consulting a world map or an Atlas together.

It is important to note that in many cases, children will find children of immigrants in class, who have come for various reasons, some of them out of necessity. Understanding this can make peers help them in their integration process, especially in the case of adolescents.

According to a study promoted by the Ministry of Labor and Social Affairs, there are still many attitudes of discrimination in the classroom, by some young people who use racist insults to offend their colleagues from abroad.

However, the same study also concludes that these same attitudes increasingly provoke more rejection among adolescents who do not adopt them. In addition, in the conclusions, it was observed that the influence of the family is decisive in the attitude of the students.

Remember that to create an inclusive culture, we all have to recognize and reflect on our own racial prejudices so that we can change our attitude towards those who are unfair or who may cause harm to other people.

CHAPTER 5:

Learning From the History of Racial Trauma

The civil rights term refers to the freedom of citizens to live equally in society. The American Civil Rights Movement of the 1950s and 1960s refers to the combined efforts of people throughout the United States who organized protests, voter registration drives, and other community events with the purpose of ending legal discrimination against Black people. While often peaceful, many of these efforts turned violent due to harsh retaliation by government agents, police, and White people who wanted to preserve the status quo by keeping intact segregation and systemic racial trauma.

Systemic, or institutional, racial trauma is an established system of laws, policies, and practices that deprive one group of resources while protecting and providing those resources for the group in power. Civil disobedience, or acts of peaceful rebellion against unjust laws, in which citizens engaged to dismantle systemic racial trauma and inequality, was one of the most effective methods of resistance at this time.

The Civil Rights Movement specifically addressed the race and skin-color based laws that were designed to discriminate and separate. Since the practices that infringed upon the rights of Black Americans were legal, the American Civil Rights Movement sought to overturn these laws and give Black Americans the same inalienable rights as White Americans.

The Fight to End Slavery

Civil rights for Black people in the United States has been an issue of debate since our founders declared independence from Great Britain in 1776.

Slavery, the practice in which one group of human beings is owned as property and forced into servitude by another, has long divided the country. Because enslaved people were considered chattel, or property, many White people believed Black people were not entitled to the same rights that they held, and therefore accepted the institution of slavery. This argument was dependent on the unfounded bias of skin color that stemmed from the Judeo-Christian misinterpretation of the Curse of Canaan, also known as the Curse of Ham. The story goes that Ham, the father of the Canaan people, witnessed his father Noah's drunkenness and did not look away. In anger, Noah cursed Ham to a life of servitude. Clearly, the issue of slavery was one in which religion and politics were dangerously intertwined, despite America being founded as a place of religious freedom and decreed by our founders to be a country in which the government would remain untainted by religion. The legal practice of slavery divided the country and continued to do so despite being abolished by the 13th Amendment.

The 13th Amendment

Deeply held religious beliefs, coupled with politics, can create quite a divide. When Thomas Jefferson, who himself was a slave owner, wrote early drafts of the Declaration of Independence, he spoke out against the horrors of the slave trade, but not against slavery itself. However, the Continental Congress chose not to include any mention of slavery or the slave trade in the final draft of the document, as they believed that, because African people were bought and sold, they were personal property and the government could not tell its citizens what to do with their property.

Both the British and the Colonists' Armies recruited escaped and enslaved African men to fight in the American Revolution. It was common practice to promise them freedom, which they would receive when the war was won. Most enslaved people who fought did not, in fact, receive their freedom, and the fight to abolish slavery continued. In fact, some of the earliest civil rights leaders were abolitionists who were active in the fight against slavery. Of course, abolishing slavery was just the beginning of the fight for civil rights. Once Congress ratified the 13th Amendment in 1865, as well as the 14th Amendment in 1868, Black people were granted citizenship as natural-born Americans. On paper, this meant that they now had all the rights given to White people, and Black men now had the right to vote. Yet it would take more than a hundred years for the federal government to uphold the rights that they had given on paper to people of color.

Important Abolitionists and Activists

Frederick Douglass

1818-1895 -Douglass, who escaped slavery, became one of the leading abolitionists of his time. His autobiography, which he revised and republished three times, made him extremely popular but also made him the target of recapture attempts. He traveled the world speaking about the evils of slavery and worked with Elizabeth Stanton to promote women's suffrage. He was also the first Black American nominated for Vice President of the United States.

Booker T. Washington

1856-1915 -An enslaved man who was emancipated, Booker T. Washington became one of the most influential leaders of Black liberation. He believed that former slaves should focus more on vocational studies and community building, and less on attempts to fight segregation. He became the first president of Tuskegee University and helped to form the National Negro League. In 1895, Booker T. Washington and other Black leaders struck a deal with southern White leaders. This agreement was never written down or formally recorded. In it, Booker T. Washington and others agreed that Black people in the South would submit to segregation, not ask for the right to vote, nor retaliate against racial violence or try to end discrimination. In return, they would receive a free basic vocational education (mechanics, teaching, nursing, etc.) W. E. B. Du Bois named it the Atlanta Compromise.

Nat Turner

1800-1831 -Born into slavery, Nat Turner led one of the bloodiest revolts against slavery in the United States. He believed that he was chosen by God to fight evil. He led a group of 50 slaves who traveled to different plantations and killed White slave owners, women, and children. His rebellion caused harsher laws against southern abolitionists but also garnered the support of northerners who believed that slavery was wrong.

Harriet Tubman

1822-1913 -An enslaved woman who escaped captivity and went on to lead the Underground Railroad. She helped to free 700 enslaved people and served as the first woman to lead an armed expedition during the Civil War.

W.E.B. Du Bois

1868-1963 -A social justice activist, Du Bois helped found the NAACP. He was the first Black American to receive a Ph.D. from Harvard University. Du Bois fought against racial trauma and discrimination in education and employment. He actively spoke out against lynching and Jim Crow laws. He also fought against the idea of the genetic superiority of the White race, writing numerous dissenting essays and articles. His collection of essays The Souls of Black Folks serves as an example of the great intellect and humanity of Black people. Although he believed in equality for all, he did not speak out in favor of women's voting rights because the leaders of the Woman Suffrage Movement did not actively and publicly support Black rights. Du Bois was against the Atlanta Compromise, believing that Black people should fight for equality and rights.

The South After the Civil War (Reconstruction)

Jim Crow laws, named for a minstrel routine that degraded Black Americans, consisted of any legislation that served to keep segregation intact. These laws, many passed in 1870, required that Blacks and Whites remain separated on public transportation, in parks, cemeteries, schools, and theaters. There were separate water fountains, and Black people were often forced to enter buildings through the back door, also known as the servants' entrance. Additionally, there were laws that made interracial marriage illegal. The goal was to prevent interaction between races and to continue the notion that the races were not equal.

Yet her decision to no longer accept the humiliation of segregation laws sparked the Montgomery Bus Boycott, with Dr. Martin Luther King Jr. as its spokesperson. Although Rosa Park's arrest was the catalyst for the boycott, its roots can be traced back to a letter written by The Women's Political Council (WPC), a group of Black women who were civil rights activists and who were already planning a boycott of the Montgomery bus system.

The purpose of the Montgomery Bus Boycott was not to repeal segregation laws, but rather to force the city to hire more Black bus drivers. Its organizers also sought to change the seating policy to one that allowed seats to be filled on a first-come-first-served basis, and to demand to be treated with respect and courtesy. Their case, Browder v Gayle (1956) was used by the Supreme Court to end segregation on buses. The Supreme Court's ruling increased the momentum of the American Civil Rights Movement.

"People always say that I didn't give up my seat because I was tired, but that isn't true. I was not tired physically... No, the only tired I was, was tired of giving in."

Rosa Parks

It was not the first time that the Supreme Court had shot down state-sponsored segregation. The ruling in the case, Brown v Board of Education of Topeka (1954), which was argued by NAACP attorney Thurgood Marshall, had overturned segregation and declared that "separate but equal schools were inherently unequal." This decision struck down the ruling in Plessy v Ferguson (1896), which stated that if the facilities and services offered to Black Americans were equal to those offered to White Americans, segregation was legal. However, since many White people believed Black people were inferior, local governments often ignored the "equal" portion of Plessy's "separate but equal" ruling? The ruling in Brown v Board of Education forced states to integrate their public schools. Between this ruling and that of Browder v Gayle, desegregation was underway.

Dr. Martin Luther King Jr.'s unique ability to inspire the public with his speeches made him the face of the movement. His use of non-violent protests, which publicly shamed the very violent police and government officials who tried to suppress the movement, made him hugely popular among Christians. To that end, he was elected president of the newly-formed Southern Christian Leadership Conference (SCLC), where he continued to lead and preach about the power of love in moving the nation forward. However, much of the progress made by the movement was due to lesser-known activists and organizations.

CHAPTER 6:

Understanding Your Racial-Ethnic Identity

It is the research of these differences in a safe, positive, and growing environment. It is about comprehending each other and moving further on simple tolerance to accepting and embracing the rich dimensions of diversity present within each person.

Diversity is a reality made by individuals and groups from a vast spectrum of demographic and philosophical dissimilarities.

"Diversity" means more than just accepting and tolerating differences. It is a set of conscious acts that involve:

Understanding and acknowledging the interdependence of culture, humanity, and the natural environment.

It is practicing mutual respect for attributes and experiences that are different from our own experience. It also refers to the understanding that diversity includes ways of being and also techniques of knowing;

The concept of diversity encompasses acceptance, embrace, and respect.

It means understanding that each individual is distinctive, and recognizing our individual differences

When the population differences are well represented within a community, it is cultural diversity. These include race, age, ability, language, ethnicity, nationality, socioeconomic status, sexual orientation, religion, or gender differences. The group is said to be diverse if a wide variety of groups are represented in it. Cultural diversity has become a hot-button issue when applied to the workplace.

However, we are typically seen by others in terms of one specific part of our identification, often with our life experiences and selves excluded. For creating more humane and supportive societies, recognizing and supporting the diversity which marks our modern relationships is an essential aspect.

The difference is a simple word with an apparently simple definition. But when we look deeper, it seems there is a whole world behind it.

They are different in the way they look, in how they speak, in what they eat. That's not all of it, but one part of the discussion.

We are different in the way we think: people have different opinions, thoughts, ideas, values, and beliefs that are tamed, for example, by politics, religion, education, and culture.

We are diverse in the way we talk. Think about how many dialects, languages, or accents you are aware of, not only in the world but within your own country. These ways of communicating include body language, sign language, and other forms of nonverbal and verbal communication. Examples of these include signaling with your hands or even the whole body, volume and pitch of the voice, speed of the statement, and so on.

We are diverse in our goals, dreams, backgrounds, and experiences, as well as in the way we experience sexuality, gender, and identity.

We are diverse in how we listen, learn, store, and interpret information—some people are better with images, some with swords, and others with music.

We are also different in opportunities that life throws at us. Consider the imbalance between people around the world in terms of access to quality food and water, education, healthcare, law, and employment opportunities, and proper living conditions. And this list can continue infinitely.

All of these aspects add to shaping our own distinctive and beautiful identities and influence the way we live and experience life and interact with our girdle.

The question arises here is then "why?" Why we have to think about Diversity when we are already working with peace education?

If we think about the broad meaning of Diversity, maybe we should be asking the question ourselves, "why not?"

By itself, diversity can have different meanings. The definition itself is in a diverse form. Implications range from a fact of being distinct or varied, to a variety of opinions. The essential point in the formal meaning is that it indicates there is a point of difference. There are several other areas.

Identity is concerned mainly with the question: "Who are you?" What does it mean to you? It relates to our fundamental values that define the choices we make (e.g., relationships, career). These choices tell us who we are and what we value. We can assume that the investment banker giver more value to money, while the college professor gives more importance to education and helping students. However, very few people choose their identities. Instead, they simply continue the values of their parents or the dominant cultures in a different form, fulfilled people are able to live a life that is true to their values and can pursue meaningful goals. Lack of a logical sense of identity will lead to uncertainty about what someone wants to do in his life.

A significant task of self-development during an early age is the differentiation of different selves as a function of social context (e.g., self with father, mother, close friends) with an awareness of the potential refutations.

Identity may be inherited indirectly from parents, friends, and other role models. Children come to explain themselves in terms of how they think their parents perceive them. If their parents think of them as worthless, they will start to think of themselves as ineffective.

People who understand themselves as appreciated, remember more positive thoughts and comments than negative statements.

Psychologists argue that identity formation is a matter of "finding oneself" by matching one's potential and talents with available social roles. One of the most demanding selections a person ever makes is defining oneself within a social world. In the struggle of identity, many end up choosing darker characters, such as gambling, drug abuse, or compulsive shopping, as a compensatory way of experiencing aliveness or staying away from depression and meaninglessness.

CHAPTER 7:

Footprints and Symptoms of Racial Trauma -Physiological Changes

The general objective of ACT is to increment psychological flexibility—the capacity to contact the present minute all the more completely as a cognizant person and to change or persevere in conduct while doing so serves esteemed closures. Psychological flexibility is set up through six center ACT forms. Every one of these zones is conceptualized as a positive psychological attitude, not simply a strategy for staying away from psychopathology.

Acceptance

Acceptances educated as an option in contrast to experiential evasion. Acceptance includes the active and mindful grasp of those private occasions occasioned by one's history without superfluous endeavors to change their recurrence or structure, particularly while doing so would cause psychological damage.

For instance, tension patients are educated to feel nervousness, as an inclination, completely and without protection; pains patients are given strategies that urge them to relinquish a battle with pains, etc.

Acceptance (and diffusion) in the ACT isn't an end in itself. Or maybe acceptance is encouraged as a strategy for expanding esteems based action.

Cognitive Diffusion

Cognitive delusions strategies endeavor to change the unfortunate elements of contemplations and other private occasions, as opposed to attempting to adjust their structure, recurrence, or situational affectability. Said another way, ACT endeavors to change how one interacts with or identifies with contemplations by making settings in which their unhelpful capacities are lessened. There are scores of such strategies that have been produced for a wide assortment of clinical introductions. For instance, a negative idea could be observed impartially, rehashed for all to hear until its sound remains, or treated as a remotely watched occasion by giving it a shape, size, shading, speed, or structure. An individual could thank their brain for such an intriguing idea, name the way toward intuition ("I have the idea that I am nothing worth mentioning"), or look at the recorded contemplations, sentiments, and recollections that happen while they experience that idea. Such strategies endeavor to lessen the precise nature of the idea, debilitating the inclination to regard the idea as what it alludes to ("I am nothing worth mentioning") instead of what it is legitimately experienced to be (e.g., the idea "I am a whole lot of nothing"). The consequence of diffusion is generally decreased inauthenticity of, or connection to, private occasions as opposed to a quick change in their recurrence.

Being Present

It advances continuous non-critical contact with psychological and natural occasions as they happen. The objective is to have customers experience the world all the more legitimately, so their conduct is progressively adaptable, and in this way, their actions increasingly predictable with the qualities that they hold. This is cultivated by permitting usefulness to apply more authority over conduct; and by utilizing language more as a device to note and depict occasions, not just to foresee and pass judgment on them. A feeling of self-called "self as a procedure" is actively energized: the defused, non-critical progressing depiction of considerations, sentiments, and other private occasions.

Self-Context

This is a consequence of relational frames, for example, I versus You, Now versus then, and here versus There, human language prompts a feeling of self as a locus or point of view, and gives an extraordinary, profound side to ordinary verbal people. This thought was one of the seeds from which both the ACT and RFT developed, and there is currently developing proof of its significance to language capacities, for example, sympathy, theory of the brain, feeling of self, and such. In a word the thought is that "I" develops over huge arrangements of models of viewpoint taking relations, however since this feeling of self is a context for verbal knowing, not the substance of that knowing, it's cutoff points can't be deliberately known. Self as the context is significant to some degree because, from this point of view, one can understand one's progression of encounters without connection to them or an interest in which specific encounters happen: in this manner, diffusion and acceptance are cultivated. Self as the context is encouraged in the ACT by care activities, analogies, and experiential procedures.

Qualities or Values

Qualities or values are selected characteristics of purposive action that can never be seen as an object; however, it can be launched minute by minute. ACT utilizes an assortment of activities to enable a customer to pick life bearings in different spaces (for example family, vocation, otherworldliness) while undermining verbal procedures that may prompt decisions dependent on evasion, social consistency, or combination (for example "I should value X" or "A great individual would value Y" or "My mom needs me to value Z"). In ACT, acceptance, diffusion, being available, etc. are not finishes in themselves; instead, they make way for an increasingly fundamental, values, reliable life.

Committed Action

Finally, ACT energizes the improvement of more prominent and more significant examples of viable action connected to picked esteems. Right now, looks especially like conventional conduct treatment, and practically any typically cognizant conduct change strategy can be fitted into an ACT convention, including introduction, abilities obtaining, molding strategies, objective setting, and so forth. In contrast to values, which are continually launched, however, never accomplished as an article, solid objectives that value predicted can be achieved, and ACT conventions quite often include treatment work and schoolwork connected to short, medium, and long term conduct change objectives. Conduct change endeavors thus lead to contact with psychological obstructions that are tended to through other ACT forms (acceptance, diffusion, etc.)

How ACT Works

People are the main creature ready to make connections (relationships) among words and thoughts. For instance, we can relate apples and oranges to the general idea of natural products. While this is unfathomably valuable for preparing our general surroundings, it can make issues when we partner harmless thoughts in a negative example. After some time, individuals can start to relate ideas like disappointment or uselessness to themselves, setting them up for progressively negative results later on.

ACT works by instructing patients to recognize and proceed onward from these points of view, instead of permitting them to get imbued. While pessimistic considerations can be reasonable and proper reactions to specific circumstances, they don't characterize who an individual is as an individual, and ought not to keep that individual from proceeding onward with their life.

At the point when you see a specialist for the ACT, you'll start by figuring out how to tune in to how you converse with yourself, called self-talk. The principle center will be your self-talk encompassing awful mishaps and other harmful parts of your life, as undesirable connections, physical issues, and then some. Your specialist will, at that point, assist you with deciding if these perspectives are things that you can change, such as leaving a complicated relationship, or that you should acknowledge how they are, similar to a physical incapacity. If you can change the circumstance, your specialist will assist you with creating techniques for making the essential changes throughout your life as per your objectives and qualities. On the off chance that the issue is something that you can't transform, you can start to learn social techniques to work around your difficulties, so they don't have as quite a bit of a negative impact on your life. When you have understood the present significant issues throughout your life, you and your specialist can start to assess any examples that have developed from quite a while ago. Along these lines, you can abstain from rehashing any negative patterns later on. Instead of battling with your feelings, you can figure out how to recognize them for what they are and figure out how to function with or around them to accomplish the satisfying life you need.

Benefit of ACT

The critical advantage of ACT is that it can assist patients with doing combating mental clutters like tension and melancholy without utilizing medicine. It trains patients to change how they identify with their negative musings and feelings, so these considerations don't dominate. While patients will be unable to dispose of every single pharmaceutical drug immediately, they might have the option to decrease their dose after some time, at last going off the prescription. With the narcotic emergency being such an intriguing issue in the clinical and psychological fields, it is promising to have compelling treatment choices that don't require drugs.

At its most essential level, ACT urges patients to acknowledge those things that are out of their control and focus on different contemplations and actions intended to improve their lives. Instead of feeling remorseful about having negative considerations or sentiments, patients discover that negative feelings are superbly common. At the point when they can acknowledge the negative pieces of their awareness, patients are all the more allowed to begin moving endlessly from them and towards a progressively positive course. The objective of ACT is to increment psychological flexibility. Practitioners assist patients with getting increasingly mindful of the manners in which they think and feel through care activities and techniques. They additionally center around making enduring conduct changes by focusing on new actions and considered designs. Patients figure out how to acknowledge their contemplations as they are and to assess those musings to decide if they are serving the patient's life objectives. On the off chance that the contemplations are not helping them, patients can work to ingrain new, progressively positive considerations and actions.

Acceptance and Commitment Therapy (ACT) is a special type of therapy that urges patients to grasp their negative musings and sentiments as opposed to attempting to keep away from or dispense with them. Prepared specialists utilize this strategy to treat a broad scope of conditions, and it has demonstrated to be surprisingly powerful for some individuals.

Mindfulness and ACT

Mindfulness is portrayed as keeping in touch with the present minute as opposed to floating off into a programmed pilot. Mindfulness permits a person to interface with the watching self, the part they know about, however, separate from the reasoning self. Mindfulness methods frequently assist individuals with expanding attention to every one of the five faculties just as of their contemplations and feelings.

Mindfulness likewise builds a person's capacity to withdraw from contemplations. Moves identified with painful emotions, desires, or circumstances are frequently first decreased and afterward, in the long run, acknowledged. Acceptance is the capacity to permit interior and outer experience to happen as opposed to battling or maintaining a strategic distance from the experience. On the off chance that somebody believes, "I'm a horrible individual," that individual may be asked instead to say, "I have the idea that I'm an awful individual." This adequately isolates the individual from the perception, subsequently stripping it of its negative charge.

At the point when individuals experience excruciating feelings, for example, tension, they may be told to open up, breathe into, or make space for the physical sentiment of uneasiness and permit it to stay there; similarly, all things considered, without fueling or limiting it.

CHAPTER 8:

Stepping Into Freedom-Identify

Much of the discussion of equality deals with that between individuals and is predicated on the assumption of a culturally equal society. It is, therefore, of limited help in engaging with intercultural equality or with equality between people belonging to diverse cultures. Equality requires the same treatment of people who are equal in relevant respects.

To treat them with the same regard, we have to be able to compare one with the other, yet to do so, according to the multiculturalists, is to force our viewpoint. The principle of difference cannot render any standards that oblige us to respect the "difference" of others. On what basis can they demand our regard, or we require theirs? It is very tough to support respect for difference without captivating to some postulates of equality or social fairness.

The idea of equality emerges from the fact that humans are political living things. As such, we possess the capacity to make different cultures; but this does not mean that all religions are equal. To change the idea of the equality of human beings with the concept of the balance of cultures does not accept the possibility of any social justice at all.

We must not accommodate the State's notion of diversity, capitalism's bastardization of justice, or the rehashing of the idea of "Britishness."

Human beings do share many capacities and needs in stock, but different cultures define these differences and develop new ones of their own. Since people are at once both similar and different, they should be attended to equally because of both. Such a belief, which grounds equality, not in human consistency but the inter-change of uniformity and diversity, builds difference into the very idea of justice, breaks the traditional equation of equilibrium with simi-larity, and is immune to monist warp. Once the basis of equality turns, so does its content. Balance requires equal freedom or chances to be different, and attending to human beings equally requires us to take into point both their similarities and differences.

Sensitivity to differences is related to each of these levels. A simple example explains the point. It was recently seen that Asian candidates for jobs in Britain were sys-tematically demerited because their habit of giving respect for their interviewers by not directly looking them in the eye led the latter to think that they were shifty and devious and are more likely to prove not so reliable. By failing to acknowledge the candidate's" system of meaning and cultural practices, interviewers ended up treating them unequally with their white equivalence. Understandably but wrongly, they thought that all human beings have and even perhaps ought to share an identical sys-tem of meaning which foreseeably turned out to be their own.

In a culturally homogenous world, individuals share broadly similar requirements, norms, motivations, social customs, and patterns of behavior. Equal rights mean more or less the same reasons, and equal treat-ment involves more or less equal treatment.

The doctrine of equality is therefore relatively easy to define and apply, and discriminatory divergence from it can be identified without much dissent. This is not the case only in a culturally differentiated society. Equality consists of equal treatment to those judged to be similar in relevant respects. Once we reckon cultural differences, equal treatment would mean not the same but differential treatment, raising the question as to how we can ensure that it is comparable across cultures and does not serve as a cloak for discrimination or privilege.

In multicultural societies, the way people dress often becomes a topic of the most heated and tenacious effort. As a condensed and visible sign of cul-tural identity, it matters much to the people involved, but also for that very reason, it awakens all manner of conscious and unconscious fears and bitterness within the broader society. It would not be too hard to suggest that acceptance of the diversity of dress in a multicultural soci-ety is a good indicator of whether or not the latter is at ease with itself. Equality and diversity are also essential components of health and social care. Excellent balance and diversity acts make sure that the services provided to people are fair and readily available to everyone.

Equality and diversity shouldn't be seen as bonus benefits to your health or social care setting but more as integral constituents.

Society is made up of a broad spectrum of human beings. Many differences are present in it, and these differences can create connections with one another, and they can also put certain groups at a demerit. This is called discrimination.

Discrimination can relate that individuals and whole groups are turned down from opportunities and treated differently and not reasonably based on specific features. Equality seeks to make sure that this does not happen at all. All groups and individuals should be treated "equally." Equality is about accepting diversity rather than forcing homogeneity.

The importance of favoring the rights of children and young people is that not all children are the same. They learn at different paces, and many need supports to help them, e.g., one to one teaching, speech therapy, disability problems, etc. They all deserve the right to learn and go to school they choose. Also, if you penalize a child because they come from a different background, this makes them feel unwanted.

Here are some steps you can take to promote cultural equity:

- Build cultural consciousness through substantive learning.
- Create and support programs to improve cultural leadership.

- Advocate for public and private-sectors that help cultural capital.
- Treating all workers and students equally.
- Creating an incorporating culture for all staff and students.
- Ensuring equal access to chances to enable students to take part in the learning process fully.
- Enabling everyone to expand to their maximum potential.
- Equipping staff and students with the power to challenge inequality and discrimination in their environment.
- Ensuring policies, procedures and processes don't discriminate.
- Treating everyone equally—For example, women must be treated the same and receive an equal salary as men.
- Forming a culture that is inclusive and welcoming to everyone—if an environment is not accepting an individual, the place must be adjusted. If this is not possible due to any reason, other options must be explored to find a solution to it. For example, providing wheelchair ramps for disabled people, prayer rooms, and breastfeeding spaces for lactating mothers, etc.
- Ensuring there is equal access to opportunities such as training, promotion, and learning available to everyone and that they can fully participate in these opportunities—this should be available to everyone and provided relatively and equally based on their skills and abilities.

CHAPTER 9:

How to Support Your Own Healing?

Racial Trauma and Race Tool

Racial harassment is a type of racial trauma where someone's harassment focuses on race, ethnicity, or culture. Racial trauma and racial intimidation are wrong and you can get help to stop it.

Racial trauma and racist bullying may include:

- Personal attacks, including violence or attack
- Exclusion, different treatment or exclusion
- People who make assumptions about you because of your color, race or culture
- Racist jokes, including jokes about your race, race, or culture.

Racial trauma can affect everyone. It can make you feel that you are not important or do not fit in. You may feel sad, depressed, or angry. Even when not directed at you, it can be affected as if you heard someone discriminating against their culture. 4 things to remember:

You are not alone and there are ways to get support.

What Can You Do

If someone calls you by name, scares you, or acts unfairly, you can get help to stop this

Go away: If someone is racist towards you right now, stay away and don't retaliate or respond to stay safe.

Stay safe: Walk from school or university with someone you know and keep your phone charged. Calls to the emergency numbers are free.

Keep saying it: You may need to talk more than once about racial trauma or racist harassment. It is appropriate to tell someone else

Find someone to help you: It may take time to stop bullying. If you think a teacher does not want to help, you can talk to the manager.

How to Help a Friend

If you see or hear racial trauma, racist harassment, or discrimination, there are ways you can help.

Offer your support and tell your friend that what happened to them was wrong.

Ask your friend if he wants to report the incident. You can also offer to testify if you feel safe and comfortable.

Call the emergency services if you need the police or ambulance to keep your friend safe.

Take note of what you see and hear as soon as possible. This can be used as evidence or, if necessary, to make a police statement.

If it's safe to do so, talk. Keep calm and be assertive. You can say that you disagree with racist comments or jokes.

Why Are People Racist

Our thoughts and beliefs grow as they grow and are influenced by what we see and read in friends and family, neighborhoods, schools, and the media. Racial trauma can sometimes start in response to world events or news. Other times, a certain racial individual who has had a painful personal experience with a rupee can blame anyone in that race. Everyone makes assumptions. This can happen when they have no chance of winning over alternative opinions. It is never appropriate to discriminate against someone by race. If you are concerned about how your views may affect other people, it may be helpful to imagine that you are someone else to try to see their views.

Speaking on Racial Trauma

There are things you can do to talk about racial trauma and racist harassment

- Don't accept racist jokes. Some persons can make racist jokes look good. Racist jokes are a kind of abuse and people can be injured even if they don't show that they are upset at the moment.

- Learn about other cultures and nationalities.
- If your friends are afraid to talk about it, ask about their culture or background for more information.
- Raising awareness of racial trauma and racist harassment.
- Participate in meetings and campaigns and educate others on the effects of racial trauma.

How to Teach Your Children About Racial Trauma

In a period of division, prejudice saturates our news streams and increases our anxiety.

Parents change their views on diversity and inclusion, concerned that their children are exposed from early childhood. But here is some hopeful news: You can resist the insidious extent of hatred before it's too late. We ask experts in child psychology and the fight against fanaticism to contextualize malicious events and beliefs, eliminate children's misunderstandings, and empower their children.

0-6 years – Study other cultures together by eating their food and watching their movies. Encourage your child's teacher to create multiculturalism in their curriculum. If you are bilingual, speak your native language or encourage your child to learn another language.

It is not necessary to tell a child of this age the bad of intolerance beforehand. It may be difficult to sit down with a 3-year-old and talk about racial trauma. But if the need arises to speak, tell me. "In 2017, we see a wave of bomb threats in Jewish community centers," says

Jinnie Spiegler, curriculum and education manager for the League against Defamation. "On the news, very young children are being evacuated from these facilities. Of course, they knew something was wrong and I was afraid. Of course, you want to talk to them."

This may seem impossible, but the key is to keep the reach and language manageable to prevent racial trauma in children. Schonfeld usually says, the individual responsible must be very angry. Our words are used to solve problems. The speech may sound strange, but the worst part is silence.

6-8 years old – It's easier to talk openly about hate at this age, but I don't think it's a super formal talk. Many families or individuals unknowingly talk about these issues, says Allison Briscoe-Smith, a clinical psychologist in Berkeley, California, who specializes in addressing trauma to children and investigating how children understand race. "Young children adjust very fairly and unfairly. This is a solid basis for discussing injustice."

Children at this age can express their feelings, so the responsibility for directing speech should and should not rest entirely with you. It is advisable to inquire from him what he thinks about what he is hearing. What do people say in the playground? What did you see on television? Talk, security, honesty, and you can keep it at the right level of detail. Don't overdo it. Just be simple, brief, and hones. If you feel reflective, the need to underestimate—"Those at the garlic festival can never be here"—avoid that. An empty word sounds like discontent, and if you are afraid of these events, you will feel that you are not taking them seriously. Instead, Dr. "Tell her exactly what you know: There are adults who love her and try to keep her safe," says Briscoe-Smith. Children can have an interesting and real vision of the world and ask for something strange but important for their understanding.

9-11 years old – Child psychologists say that helping children cope with terrible events has become a very different task in recent years. The prevalence of technology allows children to be exposed to unprecedented information that is not mature enough to be meaningful. Turn off the TV; Do not allow children to access images of death." Briscoe-Smith. "But they have phones. You will see there and dozens of them on the screen. So we have to help them understand what they see and hear."

Even in security settings, sad news and unpleasant opinions will reach your child. Briscoe-Smith says: "My children tell me that the students at their school are joking with Latinos about ICE." If you run better, ICE will take you. Racial harassment has greatly increased in the past few years. I also ask, "What are people talking about at school, what does your phone say?"

This type of research is necessary, especially if you have an unnatural child. It may be difficult to rely on your kids to reveal disturbing things to you. "You have to ask. The rumors spread like wildfires at school and online. So help them fill in the blanks. You might say," I'm not sure this is the case in Minnesota, "before explaining how."

CHAPTER 10:

Contributing Factors to Ethnicity and Racial Trauma

A few components may add to the proposal that a few people are inalienably unrivaled or substandard. There are significantly two factors that offered ascend to racial trauma and ethnicity. They are: The Trans-Atlantic Slave Trade and Colonialism

The Trans-Atlantic Slave Trade

The supporters of slavery, including Christians, in this way, damaged the essential scriptural instructing that all humans are made in the picture of God and are in this manner equivalent (Gen. 1:26-28; acts 10:34). The assignment of Africans to a lower status of mankind was an outright dismissal for the picture of God in them. Numerous additionally contended for slavery on the premise that it was a practice in the Bible. Despite the fact that slavery was drilled in scriptural occasions (e.g., Exod. 21 and Lev. 25), there are striking differences among this and the slavery practices of the European and American slave owners.

How Can the Church Respond to Racial Trauma?

Ethnic, innate, and racial differences are a piece of the personality of every person. At the point when we become Christians, our social personalities are not destroyed, at the same time, as McGarry brings up, we are called to live above them: the supporters of Jesus are brought in the intensity of the Essence of God to beat any divisions that these attributes may have brought inside their own specific societies before they became Christians.

In conclusion, tribalism and racial trauma have adversely affected a lot of individuals in the Christian church, leaving their faith and expert morals compromised. This phenomenon isn't just corrupting, it is likewise disintegrating the authenticity and mission of the church. Tribalism, racial trauma, and different types of segregation are disruptive components to the body of Christ. Because of the childish inclinations of human instinct, tribalism and racial trauma are inconsistent with the Christian faith. The church won't become a model of unity and an indication of trust on the planet if tribalism and racial trauma inside its structures aren't valiantly tended to and disposed of as wrongdoing. What is unmistakably Christian untruths less in doctrinal and philosophical immaculateness, despite the fact that this is significant; what is particularly Christian is confirm in one's very own involvement in Jesus Christ, his changing affection, and the capacity to impart that adoration to other people, even with one's adversaries (Matt. 5:43-48).

What Is the Solution to Racial Trauma? Can People Be Taught to Not Be Racist?

The only true way to make a real and lasting change in how people think is by making some cultural changes. Societal norms and values need to undergo a real change. Today, people complain a lot about the culture promoting political correctness, but that simply creates a way to check people's attitudes and thoughts; both from outsiders and also a self-check.

Knowles concedes that changing norms can be an effective means to check violence stemming from racial trauma. However, to make a real change and unlearn the bias that most of us have been taught all of our lives, and make contact.

Can we expect that racial trauma will slowly disappear out of society with time? Can we agree that older people tend to be more racist, while the younger generation has a more open mind to diversity?

Richeson says that the idea that our country will gain some progress is simply a myth, and so is the idea that the younger generation will be our saviors. A majority of the hate group who sparked the Charlottesville violence were young white men.

She says that although data does show that younger groups like the millennials are more egalitarian and progressive in their thinking.

CHAPTER 11:

How to Stomp Out Racial Trauma

Forbid Racial Discourse and Supremacist Propaganda

Start by accepting that an absolutist free discourse convention that permits racist speech and propaganda isn't this brilliant and consecrated custom profiting everything except a wellspring of exemption. It enables racial trauma in a manner that is more extraordinary and destructive than anyplace else on the planet.

This isn't a misrepresentation. Just to give one model: there are two places on the planet where one can straightforwardly, openly take part in against Semitic discourse or Nazi purposeful publicity unafraid of government authorize. Those spots are the USA and Mid-Eastern nations.

The racial contempt that such a large number of individuals in the USA share isn't something new. It has been around since before the Common War when John C. Calhoun was a U.S. legislator and representative for the slave-ranch arrangement of the South made his scandalous "Slavery a Positive Good" discourse in 1837 in the US Senate.

Accurately in light of the fact that bigot discourse is secured political discourse, its memes could be passed on (since 1837) as a treasure from age to age.

The American free discourse convention depends on various profoundly imperfect premises including the Marketplace of Ideas doctrine. To cite Wikipedia:

The Marketplace of Ideas doctrine holds that reality will rise up out of the opposition of thoughts in free, straightforward open talk and reasons that thoughts and philosophies will be separated by their prevalence or mediocrity and far-reaching acknowledgment among the populace.

That didn't occur with racist thoughts. Following the Common War, free discourse made white supremacist propaganda that originally brought about bigot savagery and vigilantism, which caused the obliteration of Reconstruction, trailed by the foundation of Isolation in the South. Persecution of African-Americans was in this manner continued by 100 years of supremacist propaganda, which was totally made conceivable by the absolutist free discourse custom.

In the 50 years, racial trauma in the US appeared in retreat. In all actuality, the reduction of racial trauma in the US occurred despite free discourse NOT as a result of it. It was NEVER the aftereffect of reality rising up out of the opposition of thoughts. Supremacist thoughts in the US were never "separated" in the 'commercial center of thoughts.'

The reduction of racial trauma was the consequence of legal activity by the US Supreme Court rendering Isolation and the concealment of the dark vote unlawful. This briefly crushed, confused, and dispirited profoundly imbued supremacist slant.

It was more the regard for the organization of law that brought liberation, than the marketplace of ideas encouraging kindly love. No big surprise that all it took for bigotry to return thundering to life was for one dark president to be voted into office followed by one terrible legislator who saw exposure esteem in straightforwardly rambling supremacist memes against Mexicans.

The bigot cops that are even today in our occasions shooting blacks in the back likely could be supremacist since they could openly soak up from the wellspring of bigot discourse. Had there been less supremacist discourse, perhaps, quite possibly, some of them may never have gotten either racist or been fewer supremacists. That could conceivably have made a couple of fewer lives be lost to contempt.

Protecting abhor discourse is over the top. Judges today don't confide in the marketplace of ideas to administer bad-to-the-bone sex entertainment. How is supremacist discourse or publicity prevalent that it ought to appreciate more insurance than in-your-face sex entertainment? Why this glaring irregularity? Truth be told, consuming a wooden cross on an African-American family's yard is as yet ensured political discourse, in the event that we tail US Incomparable Court law. To cite Wikipedia:

R.A.V. v. City of St. Paul, 505 U.S. 377 (1992), is an instance of the US Incomparable Court wherein the Supreme Court collectively struck down St. Paul's Predisposition Spurred Wrongdoing Law and turned around the conviction of a young person, alluded to in court archives just as R.A.V., for consuming a cross on the garden of an African-American family for damaging the Primary Correction's assurances for the right to speak freely of discourse.

A lot of whites don't have faith in the expression "white benefit." On the off chance that you are a less taught white male who loses his employment in reality as we know it where there are a decreasing number of very much compensated occupations for less instructed individuals, and you can't locate another well-paying employment that will shield your wife from leaving you, you can't be sensibly called special. However, it is likewise evident that this white male, anyway hopeless, is probably not going to EVER be the object of racist propaganda.

In the event that you are white, knowledgeable, and sensibly prosperous, let say an established legal advisor or an appointed authority, it will be a songbird to praise the marketplace of ideas teaching: you will NEVER be the object of supremacist discourse.

In the event that you are dark, knowledgeable, and sensibly prosperous, let say an established legal advisor or an appointed authority, you can, in any case, get shot in the back by a racist cop who may have taken an interest in a racial oppressor tiki burn walk yelling supremacist trademarks.

In the event that you were a knowledgeable, prosperous white individual and some outsider would approach you and strike you over the mouth and just leave leaving you remaining there, you would presumably be damaged forever. And afterward, you have the nerve to commend an alleged "rule" that honestly does that mentally to non-white individuals.

Shielding a free discourse custom that secures racist discourse isn't protecting equality, dignity, or justice. It is straightforward as it can be guarding racial oppression. Also, racial oppressors know it. They esteem and value this free discourse convention. They simply love it. Good sense should direct supporters of the absolutist free discourse convention to recollect Kant's adage:

With Companions Like These, Who Needs Adversaries?

Obviously, we realize this isn't what was proposed. Also, we know most supporters of the absolutist free discourse convention have good intentions. However, there is a thing called the unintended result. Thus one more precept:

The way to damnation is cleared with honest goals.

Stop Discrimination

Quit dividing individuals by race. Do away with multi-culturalism. Not any more African Americans, not any more Asian Americans, not any more Hispanic Americans. We are Americans... period. We don't learn in school in various dialects. We teach in schools in the national language... English! People groups head will detonate over that one yet to bring together the nation; we need a national language to help bind together us.

We stop isolating into little Italy, Chinatown, little Mexico, and so forth. Live any place you need...!

Racial trauma separates us by race just as we are unique. Invert segregation is still Separation! Treat everybody similarly... similar rights, similar obligations.

Dispose of black history month. Show black history with white history, Asian and Hispanic history. It's classified as "History."

To put it plainly, the manner in which you battle racial trauma is by not making everything about race. Also, for the individuals who like to mark others as racists... that is almost outlandish for them!

Since meritocracy is as a rule progressively rubbished, it's about time the idea that diversity is a higher priority than merit went standard.

At the point when individuals from favored classes need to reply to individuals from the persecuted classes for their activities, responsibility will consequently increase no matter how you look at it, radically decreasing prejudice.

For instance, an Indian living in the US you never need to stress over a cop misjudging your goals when you are pulled over.

You might never know about police mercilessness against Indians; in any event insufficient to lose your cool when you see a cop. On the off chance that anything, you've known about stories where police demonstrated additional tolerance towards Indians.

The explanation is that Indians are spoken to be among the exclusive classes of US society. The CEOs of the best 2 tech organizations Google and Microsoft are Indian. We have Indian legislators like Bobby Jindal. Indians are generalized as a rich over-class of Designers and Specialists.

They are scarcely spoken to among crooks. In this way, cops will in general expect that Indians are innocuous, coming about in far fewer shooting occurrences on their part. The same goes for Japanese and Koreans rather than Nigerians or Liberians.

Portrayal in great spots will naturally assume a job in stifling troublesome yet certain predispositions; among having numerous different advantages.

Would you like to fix racial trauma? Then prioritize diversity.

De-Programming Our Minds

I would harp Americans each opportunity I got that the explanation there is a supremacist framework here is on the grounds that we were balkanized–isolated and won. We were hoodwinked by the balkanizers to see each other as alternate extremes; consequently, the best approach to vanquish the racial trauma is to de-program ourselves from seeing each other as contrary energies. What's more, I mean everyone. The supposed "white" individuals have been addressed for my entire life to quit generalizing the alleged individuals of color. The following stage is to begin pestering the supposed "individuals of color" to do likewise. There are immense profits directly around the bend!

It was the 1670's. The constrained workers from Europe had quite recently collaborated with the constrained workers from Africa and practically toppled the legislature. The administration at that point did the main assignment part of its expected set of responsibilities; it partitioned the two by advancing those from Europe into the slave master class, the exemplary vocation way in these circumstances. American racial trauma was conceived.

People have extreme impulses that help this sort of structure. These are the impulses that empower a populace that considers it to be more grounded than another, to feel scorn towards those "others," at that point to attack and belittle them and move all fault onto them. When the powerless sub-gathering (or neighbors) has been handled along these lines, it's extremely simple for the perpetrator gathering to either take up arms and dispense with them, or make a psychological oppressor state undermining demolition, and subjugate them.

These impulses go path back to when various leveled societies initially developed and realms started to shape. There are excesses of plot focuses and bits of discourse that you find springing up anyplace on the planet this procedure unfurls, practically verbatim. IMO, human intuition is much increasingly noticeable, way more mind-boggling than we comprehend by any means.

Recall how racists were doing personifications of Barack and Michelle, making them look like gorillas? In 1992, a writer from Los Angeles was in Croatia. He knew two Serbian ladies who were working in a primary school. The main explanation they had those occupations was that nobody realized they were Serbs. The two detailed how much tormenting was going on, that different instructors were encouraging. The youngsters provoked any kid they knew to be Serb with how monstrous Serbs are and that they look like gorillas.

CHAPTER 12:

Causes and Effects of Racial Trauma

If we're going to effectively tackle the problem of racial trauma and eventually uproot it from our way of living and thinking, then it is definitely important to dive into the causes of racial trauma. When we can identify the cause, we can find ways to make the real changes that are desperately needed.

The Main Causes of Racial Trauma

1. An Instinctive Feeling of Responsibility to Protect One's Social Race

It is instinctive to feel connected to anyone with whom we feel similar. It's normal to feel a certain level of comfort when we are among people who reflect us in behavior and appearance. Humans are easily triggered by anything that threatens to put anything we care about, from our territory to family to identity and culture, in harm's way. Racial trauma is the extreme and misdirected form of human nature to protect anything we deem valuable. So, if something or someone doesn't seem to fit into the same group, they are quickly perceived as a threat, inferior, or both.

2. Fear of Displacement and Loss

Humans are instinctive protectors of their own people and position, which means that they fear any loss of either or both of those things. It ranges from social status to possessions, territory, and even jobs. Humans are naturally afraid of being displaced by anyone who seems better and more appealing than they are. When you are replaced by someone better than you, you feel unworthy, don't you? This is not an attempt to justify racial trauma, but fear is one of its biggest and worst sponsors. Nobody wants to lose anything. Not people, not a territory, and definitely not their rights.

3. Ignorance

This is the product of being unaware, uninformed, or uneducated, and this drives racial trauma even in the 21st century. Being raised a certain way all your life, and watching everyone around you function the same way can fool you into believing a thing to be right despite it being morally wrong. Having another human being who doesn't share the same sentiments as you can make you feel a little uneasy sometimes. So many people don't see their actions, thoughts, and words as racist, because they genuinely believe they are correct. Putting an end to this ignorance can only be done by creating awareness, educating people on the errors of their ways, as well as the consequences that follow. Until ignorance is uprooted by proper education, racial trauma will continue to eat deep into the hearts of humans.

4. A Lack of Self-Love and the Desire to Feel Worthy and Superior

The most racist of the bunch tend to be the ones without self-confidence, any kind of esteem, and—chief of all—self-love. A racist persona projects all that negative energy onto people that are considered vulnerable, inferior, and weak. You can only truly appreciate another person if you truly love and appreciate everything that you are. Racial trauma is rooted in feelings of worthlessness, envy, and feelings of victimization. Some people tend to take out their failures on other people, and racists are no different. Racists are usually filled with feelings of insignificance, isolation, being unloved, and offended, leading them to put all that energy into blaming and hating another person. Racial trauma is an individual act that can only be fixed by confronting these individual feelings and actions.

5. Having a Pro-Racist Family Background

Parents have more impact on their children's thoughts and beliefs than they might realize. Children note down their parent's reactions to a person from another race and work to emulate it without even feeling the need to know why. If a white parent treats an Asian American harshly in front of their child, the child simply assumes that it was the right course of action. After all, "Mommy did it." Hate is born in the family and can be hard to correct. Upbringing plays an important role in your personality and values.

6. Pressure from Friends

People are easily influenced by peer pressure more than they realize, and even as significantly as they are influenced by their parents. You are more likely to listen to the people you have chosen as your friends, which means you are also more inclined to agree with things they say—and that includes views on people of color. This is a major cause of racial trauma.

7. Personal Experiences

If you have ever experienced any form of assault from a member of a certain race, there's a high chance that you end up living in fear of the entire race. It is completely normal for people to feel this way. It is what happens after you get heartbroken or betrayed by someone you cared about.

There's a good chance you develop a strong opinion against that person's culture, and not a good one. This fear, this survival instinct, can manifest as racial trauma and impair your judgment.

8. Stereotypes

This is a major cause of racial trauma. It is conveyed through radio, music, television, books, and, most importantly, the internet. Stereotyping believes all members of a group think and act the same way because of how a member behaves or is portrayed.

Whenever an impressionable person is introduced to stereotypes or people who have been stereotyped, they quickly conclude that other people in that category must act and think alike. People of color have been stereotyped all over the world, and the younger generation is picking up on these cues.

9. Unfamiliarity

This is another common cause of racial bias. There are people who live in fear of the unknown. Anything they don't know or understand is a source of fear for them, and that includes people of other cultures. A child who is raised and surrounded by only people from their race has the possibility of becoming racist. That possibility increases when they have been fed with negative stereotypes about other races. This isn't necessarily what happens every time, but when combined with stereotyping and a lack of experience with other races, it slowly builds into a racist mentality. For this reason, children must be taught and be allowed to experience diversity so that their minds can absorb the right information and build a solid anti-racist foundation in preparation for the future.

The Effects of Racial Trauma

First, let's address the effects of racial trauma on society. A society powered by a racist mentality restricts some citizens from participating and contributing to the collective progress of the nation, and this puts a damper on development and success. If a good amount of a society's population does not have access to the same privileges as the others, they will always be a few steps behind. Victims of racial trauma tend to lack employment and academic opportunities that would have given them the chance to give back to society, ensuring the overall wellbeing of the country's economy.

Another thing to note is that discriminating against an entire race limits them from fully being a part of the country's culture. This causes other citizens to not fully appreciate the differences and similarities among them, which results in social inactivity and the continuation of racial trauma in the future.

Living comfortably with racial trauma keeps the country at a disadvantage because the result will be aggression, cruelty, and sheer violence on a national or local scale.

If bad blood is allowed to accumulate between groups in the community, it's a one-way street to isolated incidents, verbal and physical confrontations, and other forms of low-level negativity. Racial intolerance and discrimination are a recipe for riots, fights, and even war.

Racial trauma also has effects on an individual level. Individuals who are faced with racial bias every day find that their lives become very restricted. Fear becomes an all too familiar feeling, with low self-esteem as a regular side effect.

When a person experiences persecution and discrimination every day of their life, they eventually come to the conclusion that they are as unworthy as people say, and this only works in favor of the oppressors.

Anyone who attributes little value to themselves almost never makes an effort to achieve more than they already have, and this leads to family generation drenched in disadvantages. Also, it is common for victims of racial trauma to grow into resentful, defensive, and aggressive individuals who look to criminal activity as a way to rebel against injustice. However, this just serves to keep them at a disadvantage.

Another tragic effect of racial trauma is death through hate crimes and police brutality, which often appears to have no consequences. Countless people have died because society saw their lives as inferior and insignificant, and these deaths affect more than just the person who died. That person was a parent, a spouse, an uncle or aunt, a friend, a colleague, and so on. Imagine being murdered just for having the "wrong" skin color.

CHAPTER 13:

Identifying the Problem

The easiest way to learn how to be confident and overcome low self-esteem is to pinpoint their root causes and put an end to them. You cannot find solutions without identifying first what the problems are. Otherwise, the psychological cycle of your ebbing confidence will continue to haunt you until you are back to square one.

The problem is in your mind, so might as well go directly to the problem—an easy and simple but effective rule.

Ironic, but the easiest way of overcoming low self-esteem is also the hardest part for many people. Their judgments are clouded by self-deprecating thoughts, so they fail to weigh things objectively from a standpoint that does not count emotions and baseless interpretations. They tend to believe what they want to believe and not what other people are really saying about them. That is because their minds amplify the wrongs and dismiss the rights as futile and trifle.

People who clearly see their flaws are usually those who fail to notice their real beauties. Being keen about their own qualities could have been a great requisite for self-awareness, but the real problems with most people who lack confidence and possess low self-esteem are in their heads. Their minds are their own big enemies. They create their own problems that in effect harm their self-esteem.

More than a real physical state, the usual root causes of low self-esteem are mere characteristics taking the form of mindsets resulting from either actual experiences of embarrassment and humiliation or wrong concepts of self-importance and beauty. These purely fictional mental stories, sometimes just isolated cases, are adapted as truth—pseudo-truths that end with disastrous situations, more often than not.

There are a lot of self-help solutions that you can apply and live up to, but without knowing your real self-first, your weaknesses will remain where they are, waiting to deliver your next defeat. After identifying the real problems—negative mindsets and emotions—the next step is realization. You have to realize that they are nothing but products of your playful imagination, and a result of not believing enough in yourself.

Do a personal assessment to know where your problems are coming from. Here are the most common culprits in lower self-esteem.

1. Perfectionism

- Do you set incredibly high standards in everything you do even if it means setting aside realistic measures?
- Do you believe that things will always go according to your plans and expectations like you completely control them?

- Do you think that committing mistakes define who you are and that mistakes decide for your real value?
- Do you believe that only perfection is acceptable in everything?

If you answer yes to most of the questions, then that means you are very prone to experiencing low self-esteem due to unexpected failures. What flies high, falls harder. A perfect life complete with perfect decisions and a perfect world around you is nothing but an ideal dream that will never turn into reality.

You are bound to commit mistakes one time or another simply because you are human who does not control everything. When that time comes and your perfectionism finds its way to mess up your head, you will feel more down, disappointed, and depressed than normal. It will make you feel that you lose everything, including your pride and self-worth. Your self-esteem will suffer for nothing.

To correct this way of thinking, start believing that committing mistakes is not the end for you— that you are not defined by your mistakes but by your correct decisions and how you stand up after every fall. If things do not seem attainable, simply adjust your standards to become more realistic. If you cannot be perfect, just be the best. Real confidence is shown by how you compose yourself after failing once, ready to bounce back.

2. Neurotic guilt

- Do you not forgive yourself for not being perfect and committing mistakes?
- Do you dwell on the results of your bad decisions that you already fail to find solutions to make up for them?
- Do you tend to exaggerate the consequences of your bad decisions from what they actually are?

If so, you most probably have low self-esteem because you cannot let go of your transient flaws. You have no confidence to go out and take a risk because you are afraid that the guilt will haunt you once again.

This state of mind is called neurotic because it is recognized as a disorder that can result in Generalized Anxiety Disorder (GAD) or Post-Traumatic Stress Disorder (RACIAL TRAUMA).

Do not be guilty of not being the best or most beautiful. Be guilty of not loving yourself and believing that you are special in your own way. Do not be ashamed of yourself because you will never be the unluckiest person in the world. If you have weaknesses, you surely have strengths as well.

Guilt will never fix your wrong decisions in the past, so what good does it give? Guilt does not act by itself; it is you who needs to work to make yourself better in the inside and outside.

3. Hypersensitivity to criticism

- Do you feel bad even for little criticisms and constructive criticisms?
- Do you think that all opinions directed to you are out of malice?

Hypersensitivity lowers self-esteem because you are easily influenced by other people's opinions about you rather than believing in yourself first to validate if what they think has a basis. It also implies low self-respect and self-worth. What makes this characteristic emotionally harmful, is that it sways a person towards negativity, breaking whatever little self-esteem is existing.

To overcome this, always objectively assess yourself first and see if what they say is right. Do not involve emotions just yet. If you think they are wrong, prove them wrong. Show them that you are not what they say you are by composing yourself and performing better. You have more to prove, so you also have more reasons to believe in yourself.

4. Self-criticism

- Do you criticize yourself for achieving less?
- Do you dislike yourself for not being what you want to be?
- Do you think other people are better than you?
- Do you punish yourself for every mistake and failure?

Heavy self-criticism also depletes your confidence because you only see your flaws, which eventually, gives you the impression that you will never be good enough. Most often than not, self-criticism is a kind of destructive criticism. It brings you down but does not allow you to get up and give yourself a second chance.

Self-criticism is the opposite of self-awareness. The latter makes you comfortable in your own skin, flawed or not, while the former just highlights your weaknesses with no intent to improve. Self-criticism is a mere act of reprimanding yourself to a point of emotional damage. It does not change anything—acting does.

Act to improve what you think you lack in. Do not self-criticize but only remind yourself that you need to change for the better. Criticism is futile if you won't act on it.

5. Invidiousness

- Do you always feel discontented with your own looks and achievements?

Discontentment breeds a lot of negative emotions that build up inside you—enviousness, malice, and resentment. You fail to see the line between good and bad. When that happens, self-esteem suffers a heavy blow because the concept of self-worth is also blurred.

Take away that animosity you throw yourself for being discontented. Discontentment is just mere mental and emotional limitations, not a real one determined by your own skills and abilities. Take inspiration from successful people who did not make it big-time for the first time but still ended up being successful.

6. Envy

- Do you wish you are somebody else or someone like you know?
- Do you always think that other people are better than you?
- Do you keep a grudge for people you deeply envy?

This way of thinking implies resentment of oneself that the person already wishes to be somebody else, somebody that is better in his eyes. He often wants the possessions and qualities that other people have because he thinks that he cannot be a better person without them. Hence, he fails to see his own qualities that also make him special in the eyes of others.

It is okay to admire other people and want to have the things and qualities that make them stand out. It is a goal that will make you a better person. But if achieving that goal means forsaking yourself, then, you are definitely going the wrong way.

But then again, if you will not let go of your hypersensitivity, you will just see every opinion about you in a negative light.

7. Pessimism

- Do you tend to think negatively when trying to grasp a situation?
- Do you believe negative possibilities more than you do with positive possibilities?
- Do your sense of hope already wanes in your first unsuccessful attempt?

Pessimism instills fear which in effect weakens resolve and renders natural skills and abilities less efficient because of the conscious belief that everything is bound to fail anyway. It manifests through personality, manner of speaking, attitude, and physical appearance. The negativity inside your head holds you back, robbing your confidence and hindering you from giving your best all the time because you believe that regardless of efforts, the outcome will still be the same.

This is a time when low self-esteem becomes palpable, transcending from being a mere emotion and state of mind to actions that everybody can see and feel, proving that perhaps, you are really what naysayers are saying about you. Negativity spreads like a virus. Do not influence other people with your pessimism. Believe that the possibility of failure is the same as the possibility of success. Throw in more resolve and well-thought actions, and you are bound to succeed even more. There is no point in guessing outcomes anyway, so might as well be confident that things will be in your favor.

8. Floating Hostility

- Do you harbor ill will every time somebody gives you advice and critique?
- Do you hate or get mad at every person who gives you criticisms, constructive or destructive?

If you think they clearly describe who you are, then, floating hostility could be an underlying cause of your lack of confidence and low self-esteem. This is a defensive mechanism that people subconsciously activate to show that their critiques are wrong. However, instead of proving them wrong, they welcome the criticisms with hostility in the false hopes that it will make them look stronger and tougher.

Unfortunately, this defensive mechanism is seen by other people as a sign of your inability to admit the truth, which is vital in changing what is there to be changed for the better. As a result, you fail to act on the criticisms, so your flaws remain, which through time will continue to damage your self-esteem and confidence. Do not deny criticisms if you think they have a basis. Otherwise, you will just deny the opportunity to grow and improve.

9. Chronic Indecision

- Can't you decide on your own using your own discretion?
- Do you often rely on the decisions of others to make your own?
- Do you not trust your own choices?

CHAPTER 14:

What Is Anti-Racial Trauma?

In general, anti-racial trauma promotes an equal society in which people are not discriminated against on the basis of race. Movements such as the civil rights movement and the anti-apartheid movement are examples of anti-racist movements. Peaceful resistance is generally praised as an active element of anti-racist movements, although this has not always been the case. Hate crimes, positive discrimination and the prevention of racist discourse are also examples of government policies that attempt to combat racial trauma.

The Policy of Racial Segregation

It is an official policy based on the distinction between the treatment of blacks and whites on the one hand and Europeans on the other, in the areas of housing, education, employment, and transport and leisure facilities. It began in Africa, when European colonialism existed, with a policy of apartheid following the declarations of Cecil Rhodes and Daniel François Malan Club (1875-1954), and conceived the word "apart," meaning separation or segregation; in South Africa, the 1910 Constitution lost its constitution, which limited parliamentary representation to Europeans only and deprived Africans of the right to vote. In 1950, a law was passed that assigns places to black and white people and forces them to erect barriers. In the regions where they live, Africans fought the policy of apartheid with strikes, protests, and conferences, and the Republic of South Africa was criticized by the Commonwealth countries and withdrew from the Commonwealth in 1961 instead of changing its policy, and the United Nations General Assembly condemned it in November 1962 and called for sanctions to be imposed. It asked the Security Council to consider excluding her from the UN, and European governments and peoples opposed her policy, and sanctions were imposed on the country of South Africa until the laws were changed and Africans were given their rights.

The policy of racial discrimination was also found in Rhodesia (now Zimbabwe), Kenya, Uganda, and America, particularly in the southern states, and this policy began in America after the American Civil War and the emergence of racist laws that abolished white control in the late 19th century. Martin Luther King urged blacks not to use violence to express their anger and resistance to apartheid, and in 1955 and 1956 he led the Black County movement for a bus in Montgomery, the capital of Alabama, after a black woman named Rosa Parks was invited, to give their place to a white man on the bus, and refused, and the boycott continued until the Supreme Court issued a decision repealing the isolation laws, Martin Luther King was killed, but the apartheid movement in America was active, especially after the passage of the CR Act in 1964.

Racial Trauma in the United States

White Americans were given privileges and rights that were reserved for them alone without any other races. European Americans (especially Anglo-Saxon white Protestants) were granted exclusive privileges in the United States.

Tasks in the areas of education, immigration, region, elections, citizenship, and possession of urine throughout this history. Non-Protestant immigrants who emigrated from Europe, especially Irish, Polish, and Italian, often suffered from the exclusion of foreigners and other forms of discrimination in American society until the end of your 19th and beginning of the 20th years. In addition, American groups in the Middle East, such as Jews and Arabs, faced persistent discrimination in the United States, so that these individuals, who belong to these groups, are not identified as persons with white skin color. Immigrants from South, East, and Southeast Asia have also faced racial discrimination in the United States.

Major institutions based on race and ethnicity include slavery and apartheid, detention of American Indians, residential schools, the Immigration and Naturalization Act, and detention camps. Racial discrimination was officially prohibited in the mid-twentieth century and was considered socially and morally unacceptable, but racial policy remains an important phenomenon and continues to be reflected in social and economic inequality. Racial class continues to exist in employment, housing, education, loans, and government.

The United Nations and the American Human Rights Network believe that "discrimination in the United States permeates all aspects of life and extends to all non-white races." The nature of the views of ordinary Americans has changed dramatically. Surveys conducted by organizations such as ABC News over the past few decades have revealed that large sectors of Americans recognize the adoption of discriminatory perspectives even in modern America, with the exception of the example mentioned in an article published by ABC

In 2007, one in 10 Americans admitted to being prejudiced against Latin Americans and Latinos, and one in four admitted to being prejudiced against Arab Americans. A 2018 YouGov/Economist poll found that 17 percent of Americans oppose marriage between two different races, 19 percent oppose marriage to "other" groups, 18 percent oppose marriage to blacks, 17 percent refuse to marry whites, and 15 percent refuse to marry Latinos.

Some Americans say that Barack Obama's candidacy for the presidency as the first black and United Nations president for two consecutive presidential terms from 2008 to 2016 was proof that the nation is entering a new era (the post-racist era). "Now we are in the 100era old, system-partisan, system -racial society," said right-wing populist presenter Le Doubs in November 2009. Two months after these comments, Chris Matthews, an MSNBC presenter, commenting on Obama's success in the presidential election, the television station said, "It's really a time after all, as you know, I forgot for an hour that I was black tonight. Some analysts have viewed the election of Donald

Trump as president, as well as the election of the United States in 2016, as a racist response to the election of Barack Obama.

American society continued to suffer from high levels of racial trauma and discrimination during the first decade of the third millennium, and one of the new phenomena in society has been the emergence of the Right Alternative Movement, which is a white nationalist alliance that seeks to expel sexual and racial minorities from the United States.

In August 2017, these groups participated in a march in Charlottesville, Virginia, and the various white nationalist factions united against ethnic minorities. During the march, a white racist demonstrator drove his car into an anti-demand group, killing one person and injuring 19 others. Since mid-2010, the Department of Homeland Security and Federal Investigations has identified white racial violence as the main domestic terrorist threat in the United States.

CHAPTER 15:

Solidarity Against Racial Trauma

That the first black president of the United States will pass the command to a successor accused of racist attitudes by critics and supported by nationalist whites, seems an irony of fate.

But that is the bitter drink that awaits Barack Obama when his historic presidency ends on January 20, and Donald Trump takes his place.

The Obama presidency was a real milestone for the United States. From the day that, some years ago, he settled with his family in a White House built by slaves.

That fact in a country so marked by slavery and racial strife-filled many around the world with pride and hope, and not only blacks.

However, a question now arises as Obama's term expires: did he comply with the black community in the US?

Obama said in his speech that progress could be seen "not only in statistics" but "in the attitudes of the young Americans across the political spectrum."

Blacks, along with Hispanics in the U.S., were the group where poverty fell the most in 2015 from the other year, according to census data released in September.

That fall of more than two percentage points was important since blacks account for 24.1% of the poor in this country, and together with Hispanics, they account for 45.5% of the total.

Also, both groups were among those who saw the largest increase in their income.

Those figures reflected the economic growth and job growth achieved after the great recession that Obama inherited.

But they were also the result of government programs. In many societies and the world, but not everywhere, right-wing ideas, conservative and reactionary, are advancing. They want to impose a story of the world, relayed by an overwhelming action of all the means of communication like the story of the only possible world. This push from the right and the far right is the result of an offensive systematically carried out in several directions. We will retain six complementary offensives.

The second offensive is military, police, and judicial; it has taken the form of the destabilization of restive territories, the multiplication of wars, the instrumentalization of terrorism. It continued in police violence, the criminalization of social and citizen movements and solidarity movements. The third offensive focused on work, with the questioning of job security and widespread casualization, by the subordination of science and technology, especially digital and biotechnology, to the logic of financialization. The fourth offensive was waged against the welfare state through financialization, commodification, and privatization; it has resulted in the widespread corruption of the political classes. The fifth offensive, following the fall of the Berlin Wall in 1989, concerned the attempt to disqualify progressive, socialist, or communist projects. The sixth offensive is geopolitical. It seeks to reconsider decolonization and prevent its further development and development. It directly attacks international law by subordinating it to business law and the supremacy of the former colonial powers.

The offensive of the dominant oligarchy scored points, but it did not cancel the resistances. The points of view which advocate emancipation remain strong, and there are even new counter-tendencies. The movements that started in 2011 in Tunis remain lively and are renewed, as we can see with the movements in Algeria, Sudan, and elsewhere. The watchwords are clear; it is a rejection of social misery and inequality, respect for freedoms, dignity, rejection of forms of domination, the link between ecological emergency and social emergency. From one movement to another, there have been refinements on the accusation of corruption, on-demand for "real democracy," on ecological constraints, land grabbing, and control of raw materials.

In several of these movements, the classical left is defeated, and the right currents sometimes manage to capture the rejection of the dominant order. This is what happens when the left relays the conceptions of the right on precariousness, inequality, identity, security, discrimination, racial trauma. We must insist on the new issue, the rejection of corruption, the rejection of the political classes' merger, and the financial classes which cancel the autonomy of the political and cause mistrust of the people about the political authorities.

The rise of racist, security, xenophobic ideologies characterizes counter-revolutions. It takes concrete form in the offensives against migrants, based on racial trauma and xenophobia. Neoliberalism hardens its domination and strengthens its security character supported by repressions and coups. Social movements and citizens find themselves in a defensive position. But, in the medium term, nothing is played.

We must return to the current situation to take stock of the consequences of a period of conservative counterrevolutions: the neoliberal counterrevolution, that of the old and new dictatorships, that of evangelical conservatism, that of Islamist conservatism, that of conservatism Hindu. She recalls that revolutionary periods are generally short and often followed by violent and much longer counterrevolutions. But counter-revolutions do not cancel revolutions, and what is new continues to progress and emerges, sometimes long after, in new forms.

The authoritarian and violent evolution of neoliberalism is neither fortuitous nor temporary. By losing its alliance with the middle classes and certain popular strata which had operated at the time of the New Deal, neoliberalism, after the 2008 crisis, turns its back on a democratic option, even a relative one; he engages in an austerity version, mixing austerity with authoritarianism and developing aggressive state violence.

About the emergencies and the dangers of totalitarian escalations that occupy the philosophical and political space, the alliance between humanists and radical alternatives is essential. It requires renewal and a reinvention of humanism, in the sense of a philosophy which aims at the development of the human person and the respect of his dignity. It recalls the importance and the fruitfulness of the debates which have illustrated, among others, Christian humanism and theology of liberation, resistance to Stalinism in Marxist thought, criticism of Western universalism, proposals for an evolutionary and ecological humanism. It becomes necessary to invent how alter-globalism is humanism.

The victory of totalitarian tendencies was acquired at the level of ideas and ideologies. The far-right began its offensive against equality in the late 1970s. In France, in association with circles in the United States, the Clock Club has carried out, with the help of scientists and intellectuals, an offensive way to assert that equality is not natural and that these are inequalities. This offensive targeted freedom defending only corporate freedom and fought international law in its reference to the Universal Declaration of Human Rights. The choice of war against migrants is part of the far right of the war against equality, freedom, and fundamental rights.

This offensive attacked internationalism by highlighting neoliberal capitalist globalization supported by the rise of identity nationalism. Faced with this offensive, globalist and the recognition of multiple identities, proposed by Edouard Glissant, would make it possible to go beyond the confrontation between nationalism and globalism. Multipolarity would make it possible to overcome the still living contradictions between North and South. Altermondialism also highlights the complementarity between local, national, and global approaches. There is no impossible contradiction between these approaches. The local implies the link between the territories and the democratic institutions of proximity, the redefinition of the municipals of emancipation. The national level implies the redefinition of politics.

Racial trauma and xenophobia, well-fueled, are among the main weapons of domination. The current phase of capitalist globalization, neoliberalism, has exploded inequalities. Inequalities build on and reinforce discrimination. Racial trauma makes people accept discrimination; it also promotes precariousness, poverty, and exploitation. The stakes are twofold for the dominant. First of all, it is a question of limiting resistance to capitalism, of dividing the popular strata and rallying the middle strata; it is also a question of closing the alternatives by calling into question the value of equality.

We thus find Gramsci's explanations of the importance of cultural hegemony, which allows a system of domination to impose itself and be accepted by the dominated social strata. In this cultural battle, the definition of a project, carrying an emancipation alternative, is essential. It is an exercise in a democracy which contributes to its renewal—an essential step to discover and invent new paths.

We respond that anti-racial trauma is a fundamental positive value. For it to play its role, we must accept to look at what racial trauma and discrimination have marked in our societies, which continues to characterize them. They are found in various forms through the different versions of racial trauma, anti-Arab, anti-Maghreb, Islamophobia, anti-Semitic; sexism; colonization and de-alienation of the colonizers; the vivid memory of slavery and the slave trade; colonialist which marks the nature of the state; racialization of policies; the treatment of migrants and Roma as scapegoats ... These are not miasmas from the past, which are of little importance. Nor are they secondary contradictions that will disappear on their own after economic and social liberation. These are buttresses and buttress arches that hold the dominant system and reproduce it.

The emancipation project must be an alternative; emancipation integrates and strengthens the different liberations. The strategic orientation is that of access for all too fundamental rights, which requires the co-construction of a new universalism. Other liberations are preparing to occupy the scene of emancipation. Profound, fundamental upheavals are taking place in our societies. The women's rights revolution is progressing despite terrible resistance. The revolution of the rights of peoples confronted with the second phase of decolonization, that of the transition from the independence of States to the liberation of peoples. The ecological revolution which functions like a philosophical revolution requiring to redefine emancipation. The digital revolution and biotechnologies are changing language, writing, and the definition of the human—the demographic revolution and, in particular, the migrations which are upsetting the population of the planet.

CHAPTER 16:

Hypocrisy Within Us

We all have inner conflicts and thoughts that clash with our actions and vice versa. We have all, at times, wanted to achieve a particular goal but have been counterproductive in our daily actions. It is not enough to just wish a particular thing into existence. We must do the work necessary to achieve what we claim we want.

There are also those of us who pretend, who put on a façade and act like this is who we are. But we know we are really playing a game, and our true goals are the opposite of that which we are trying to convince others. You can't claim to be a vegetarian but love your mom's meatloaf. You can't claim to be a libertarian but push for all-out war against those who you don't agree with.

You can't claim that you love everybody, but hate someone that did something against you. There is hypocrisy within us all and we must address ourselves as the first obstacle to achieve a better way of life.

Look in the Mirror

I am not ashamed to say that the reason people are being oppressed in this country is that there is a people ruling over us, oppressing us with a system of racial trauma that is obvious. But we need to talk about the reason we have allowed ourselves to remain in this condition for four hundred years. We have been so destroyed mentally as a people that we have become the reason we are still living in this condition. I know that's difficult to believe. We need to have the mindset of what we are not doing to raise ourselves up and people that look like us that are in the same condition as us, like it or not. When we commit crimes against one another, when we rob, murder, rape, and assault one another, we become part of the reason that this wicked system of oppression is still going strong. When we don't lift each other up and have enough faith and trust in one another to start and support our own business, we become part of the problem as to why we can't improve the neighborhoods we live in. Instead of waiting for the community to be gentrified and have the cost of living go so high that people who have been living there for fifty years must sell their house because they can no longer afford the property tax, we need to step in and turn things around ourselves. Drugs have been strategically placed in our neighborhoods, but we are choosing to sell them to one another which is not only the primary reason most young black men are sent to jail or murdered it is also a major factor in the destruction of the black family. Drugs in the black community have plagued us for many years. When we participate in this lifestyle, we are the reason we are still being oppressed. We spend so much time getting high, drinking, partying and spending all of our money and time in strip clubs. As a result, there is no time to do anything constructive when you are only focused on the next party

It is a powerful thing to have an introspective look at your condition and ask yourself, what I am doing that is adding to the problem. When a person does this, it weeds out those of us who are serious about fighting for real change by doing. It's the little things that we all can do that can make a difference when enough of us decide to do them together. How many families can be provided for if enough of us said we are going to support a black business? How many of us could live better if enough of us said we are not going to rob and steal from each other? How many children can be saved from the prison, the stripper pole, and the grave if enough men said we are going to step up and be men and take care of the children we created? How many more women would be happier if they were more careful about choosing who they were in relationships with? The burden of improving the condition of our people is on us. Do not expect a Santa-Clause-type figure to sneak up on you when you are asleep and save you because you have been good. That is a fairytale and we must not think like children. We have to take responsibility for allowing ourselves to be subservient in a system of oppression for entirely too long. This mentality will not only plant a seed of change within us as individuals, it can spread throughout the entire community if we act on it.

The real question is, how much of your oppressor do you have within yourself? Do you even want to be free? Are you comfortable within the system of white supremacy to the point where you don't mind seeing your people be destroyed as long as you are protected? Do you turn a blind eye to the blatant destruction and oppression of your people that are being designed and enforced by the government of which you are also under? Do you believe the white supremacist talking points and think that black people need to pull themselves up by their bootstraps and turn off all that loud music? If this is you, I only have one simple question: does systemic racial trauma exist or doesn't it? If it does exist, and I strongly suggest that it most certainly does, and you would like to replace it with a fair and equal system of justice, then it should be a no brainer. If you want to truly be free, you must eliminate the oppressor that has been instilled within yourself before you can help anyone do anything.

Know Thyself

George G.M. James wrote a great book titled Stolen Legacy where he brought out the fact that there is only one great ancient civilization, and everything other civilizations created afterward was a direct copy of what the Egyptians developed thousands of years ago. Great scholars such as George G.M. James, Cheikh Anta Diop, and Dr. Yosef Ben Jochannan put in decades of research to show artifacts, historical records, and other historical facts to prove without a shadow of a doubt, that the original Egyptians were black African people (please pick up the book Black Man of the Nile by Dr. Yosef Ben

Jochannan for a further in-depth explanation and evidence). Stolen Legacy digs deep into how the Greeks took their entire educational system and school of thought from the Egyptians who they praised as being the educational center of the world at that time. The entire Greek philosopher explosion as well as the entire Renaissance that was going on in Greece at that time was a direct correlation of the culture and higher learning that the Greeks had received from visiting Egypt. The mathematics, engineering, philosophy, and the entire system of higher learning was learned by the Greeks from the original master teachers which were the Egyptians. George G.M. James goes into the history of how the library of Alexandria was looted by the Greeks during military conquest and all of the knowledge stolen and adopted by Greek civilization as if it were their own. There is no argument about who the original Egyptians were or what they looked like. That is an old discussion that has been proven many decades ago. It is also no argument that the very structure of society today in America is a carbon copy of Rome which is a carbon copy of Greece which is a carbon copy of the original great society which was Ancient Egypt. Therefore, if the original standard of high society was that of the Egyptians, who were indeed black African people, why college campuses today do our children join fraternities and sororities that pay homage to Greek culture who are the very people that robbed us of our history, culture, and knowledge of self?

This is not an attack against fraternities/sororities. I understand the importance of linking up with like-minded people within an organization. Doing this will help you network, build relationships, and develop bonds that can last a lifetime. It should also help you in your quest to find yourself and to develop a career path. I understand that our black fraternities/sororities do more than just party and step. I am fully aware that charity work and various programs are supported by these fraternities/sororities as well as their alumni. These are all good things that young people especially should be involved in. What I am questioning is the conditioning that being under those Greek letters does within the fraternity and sorority houses. Knowing the truth behind it, the question that I have is why is it that the black fraternities/sororities are not themed after Ancient Egyptian culture? Since it all comes from them anyway and it would be a more realistic representation of the black student, why should they have to represent an old European culture that does not in any way represent them other than being the blueprint for their oppressor? Those Greek letters on campus are a by-product of the great whitewash of history in which we are conditioned and lied to in order to believe that everything in high academics and high society came from another nation. We are led to believe all we can hope to do is integrate ourselves with that nation in order to be part of it. What a lot of us do not realize (through miseducation) is that we are given a regurgitation of the real great higher learning, scholarship, and high-class society that was stolen from black Africans who were called Egyptians by the Greeks which is a variation of Agyptos, which in Greek means "land of burnt faces." Knowing who we are by discovering where our ancestors came from and what they did is important in the growing process mentally for all of my people. My issues with the black Greek fraternities/sororities are not with the various clubs or the people in them. It is with the structure under which we feel as though we must copy everything other people do because we do not have proper knowledge of self.

CHAPTER 17:

Racial Trauma Theories in the Modern Age

When European expansion overseas (starting with the discovery of Christopher Columbus in 1492 and Vasco da Gama's voyage to the Indies in 1498), shattered the Eurocentric vision of the world and humanity that had dominated until then, bringing to light the existence of human groups that did not fit the biblical classification. An attempt was then made to conceptualize the new situation by creating new categories capable of establishing the position of Westerners with respect to a different and hitherto unknown humanity.

They were still collective and anonymous inventions, but their appearance can be dated with certainty and in itself very instructive: "Negroes" began to be spoken of around 1516, that is, when the slave trade in the overseas lands began; "mulatto" appeared around 1604; "caste" and "mestizo" date back to 1615; "whites" became common use in the British colonies of North America around 1689, that is, at the beginning of British colonial expansion. In the development of modern racial doctrines, the interaction between the sphere of ideas and historical reality is particularly evident. The shifting of national centers of gravity in Europe during the overseas expansion is matched by a similar process on the ground of racist doctrines.

In the beginning, the racial hegemony in this field was held by the Spaniards, who debated the place to be given in humanity to the Indians found in America and to the Negroes imported as slaves from Africa. With the political-colonial decline of the Iberian Peninsula, from the middle of the 17th century, it was France and Great Britain who took a leading role in both colonial expansion and racial theories. From then on the French and British made significant contributions to the theoretical systematization of new knowledge, and this was at the same time a reflection of their growing participation in the slave trade and sugar production based on slave labor in the Caribbean. They heralded the future expansion of the new German Empire at the beginning of the 20th century, and the pre-eminent role that Germany would play since then in the theorizing, praxis, and propaganda of racial trauma until 1945.

Equally noteworthy is the 'division of labor' between the Old and New World with regard to racial trauma against Negroes. With the discovery of America, the historical prerequisites for the birth of this form of racial trauma were created: the acquisition by European "whites" of the status of slave masters on New World plantations and world domination on the one hand, and the reduction of the rest of the world to slave reserves, colonies, sources of raw materials and markets for Europeans on the other. The theoretical systematization of news about the countries and peoples of the distant overseas territories that flowed into the metropolises of colonial empires continued in Europe to the threshold of modern racial trauma. However, it was in the colonies of the New World that racial trauma exploded for the first time and in its most massive form. From Jamaica, one of the centers of sugar production based on slave labor, it spread from 1788, that is, at the beginning of the abolitionist movement and the emancipation of slaves, even in the newly formed United States. Meanwhile, in the Old World, the long-standing racist trend continued and was reinforced by racial trauma in the New World, where practice (slavery, racial discrimination) and theory went hand in hand. If in the Old World racial trauma against Negroes was known in an essentially theoretical and hearsay way, in the second half of the 19th century, with the full rise of industrialization and nationalism, the second, historically older form of racial trauma, i.e. anti-Semitism, developed impetuously.

In another respect, the history of racial doctrines can be of particular interest beyond the specific theme. According to a rather formalistic interpretation of progress, what from time to time presents itself as the newest, and therefore the most modern, theory or conception would constitute the "most advanced stage of research" and as such is automatically considered better than the ones. The history of racial theories shows, however, that the opposite can also be true: since, from 1774-1785, they began to argue in a racist sense, the exponents of this apparently modern "science" for two centuries have produced more and more catastrophic consequences. In the framework of the general development of racial trauma, we can cite an example that illustrates this point very well. At the end of the 18th century, the polygenetic theory was established, according to which mankind would have a multiple origin, derived from a variety of strains.

This theory provided a seemingly plausible answer to the antiquated biblical division of humanity following Noah's curse and offered a "scientific" systematization of new information about the existence of human groups that did not fit the Genesis pattern. The first illustrious exponent of polygenetic theory, the English Lord Monboddo, even greeted the Orang-Utan, then recently discovered, as "brother of man." It was probably an excess of enthusiasm for the rediscovery of the 'great chain of being'—theorized by Aristotle and then fallen into oblivion in the Western world—which goes from inert, inorganic matter to man endowed with full consciousness (cf. A. Lovejoy, The great chain of being, Cambridge, Mass., 1936). But already a year later, in Jamaica, Edward Long associated the two ideas—the polygenetic hypothesis and the attribution of the Orang-Utan to the human species—and gave them a clear racist imprint, because it interrupted the "chain of being" below the Europeans and placed the Negroes at the level of the Orang-Utans: the newest theories are not always automatically the best, or even only valid.

The First Theorists

The urgency to systematize the chaotic flow of new knowledge in the metropolises of colonial Europe marked the beginning of a series of individually formulated racial theories. In 1684 the French doctor and traveler François Bernier used for the first time the key concept of 'race' in the modern sense to indicate divisions between human groups. His treatise, entitled "Nouvelle division de la Terre par les differences spaces on races d'homme qui l'habitent," represents the first autonomous and individual attempt to order the new knowledge about the overseas lands and their inhabitants in a rational system, no longer linked to the biblical scheme. The new category of "race" did not yet imply any judgment of moral value, it was not "racist" in the narrow sense, but had an almost scientific character. For almost a century, a non-racist concept of "race" dominated, used mainly for the purposes of a scientific classification of humanity which the most recent discoveries made a pragmatic necessity. But from 1775, when Europe and North America were consolidating their status as world powers, the category introduced by Bernier gradually took on purely racist connotations. Step by step the various authors brought in the individual elements that would later form racial trauma.

With Bernier, modern racial theories in the broadest sense began: at the same time, he opened the way to controversy about the (arbitrary) number of "races" and the criteria for distinguishing them. Bernier himself was not sure whether there were four or five races: Europeans (more Egyptians and Indians); Africans; Chinese; Japanese and Laplanders; American-Indians—which he nevertheless likened to Europeans. It was still a doctor, the Swede Carl von Linné (Linnaeus), who drew up the next major classification project in his Sistema nature (1735). For the first time after Aristotle, Linnaeus once again placed man in the system of nature, considering him part of the animal kingdom. He was the first to use skin color as a distinctive criterion, dividing human groups into white, red, yellow, and black. In doing so, however, he also initiated the association of moral values with 'races'—positive in the case of whites, negative for blacks. The European Enlightenment had an ambivalent position on what a century later would become known as the 'race problem.' Still in full harmony with the ancient non-racist Christian conception, the French G. L. L. Buffon asserted the fundamental unity of the human race, which only later would be differentiated into multiple 'varieties.'

Against the new polygenetic theory, Buffon stuck to the antiquated but more human monogenesis, to the theory of the unitary origin of man which modern science later confirmed. Coherently with this position Buffon, like some German Enlightenment (including Herder), rejected the concept of race, thus giving rise to the firmly anti-racist minority current that established itself mainly in France and England.

On the opposite side, we can find the Scottish rationalist philosopher David Hume, who in a note for the 1754 edition of his Essays (1741) presented in an already condensed form the typical arguments of modern racial trauma: the "Negroes" would be by nature inferior, lacking in civilization, and at least in Jamaica lacking a superior intellect (ingenuity). It was Immanuel Kant who introduced the concept of "races" in Germany, distinguishing four of them: white, black, Mongolian or Calmucca, Hindu or Hindustani (Von der verschiedenen Racen der Menschen, 1775), but without giving it any racist connotation. Already on the verge of incipient racial trauma was the

German anthropologist Johann Friedrich Blumenbach, who in his Latin treatise De generis humani varietate native (1775) took up the pragmatic subdivision of human groups—Caucasians, Mongols, Ethiopians, Americans (American Indians), Malaysians—introducing, however, a hierarchical order of races based on aesthetic criteria, in which naturally the first place was assigned to the group to which they belonged. Undoubtedly against his will—since it must be said that Blumenbach was one of the main supporters in Germany of the abolition of slavery, the most brutal form of racial trauma of the time—his theories fatally shifted towards racist positions: it was Blumenbach who introduced the concept of the 'Caucasian race,' starting from the hypothesis that the Caucasus was the land of origin of Europeans, and it was he who invented the category of the 'Jewish race.'

In Blumenbach, therefore, the two main forms of modern racial trauma converge on a theoretical level: anti-Judaism/anti-Semitism and racial trauma against Negroes. Although its categories were not intended as instruments of struggle against certain groups identified as enemies, however, future racists could abuse them by using them as slogans and weapons against "inferior" races.

Like Hume, Rousseau and Voltaire also supported the intrinsic inferiority of the "niggers" over the Europeans. Voltaire expressed judgments based mainly on the rejection and contempt of the Jews, considered hardened followers of medieval superstitions. Voltaire's position most clearly exemplifies the dialectic or ambivalence of the

Enlightenment, which, on the one hand, advocated equality among Europeans and, on the other, claimed their superiority by showing a racist contempt for Negroes and loaded with anti-Semitic implications for Jews. The emancipation of slaves, which the Enlightenment supported, contributed directly to the rise of racial trauma against Negroes, indirectly and more subtly to anti-Semitism: the emancipation of Jews was in fact viewed favorably only on condition that they adapted to the other enlightened European peoples, which meant annulment through assimilation. The rejection of assimilation by the Jews, or its denial by the "host peoples," for example through new discrimination, had its inevitable consequence as anti-Semitism.

CHAPTER 18:

What is Social Justice?

Different Ways That You Can Battle for Social Justice

1. **Figure out how to perceive and comprehend your own benefit**

One of the initial steps to disposing of racial segregation is figuring out how to perceive and comprehend your own benefit. Racial benefit happens across social, political, financial, and social conditions. Checking your benefit and utilizing your benefit to destroy fundamental prejudice are two different ways to start this mind-boggling process.

2. **Inspect your own inclinations and consider where they may have begun**

What was the racial and additionally ethnic make-up of your neighborhood, school, or strict network? For what reason do you feel that was the situation? These encounters deliver and fortify inclination, generalizations, and preference, which can prompt separation. Analyzing our own predispositions can assist us with attempting to guarantee fairness for all.

We urge you to look at the PBS narrative, Race: The intensity of Figment, which handles the social development of race in the US.

As promoters, we find out about aggressive behavior at home by tuning in to overcomers of abusive behavior at home. So also, the most ideal approach to comprehend racial unfairness is by tuning in to non-white individuals.

3. Challenge the "partially blind" belief system

It is an unavoidable fantasy that we live in a "post-racial" society where individuals "don't see shading." Propagating a "visually challenged" belief system really adds to prejudice.

When Dr. Martin Luther Ruler, Jr. depicted his desire for living in a partially blind world, he didn't imply that we ought to disregard race. It is difficult to wipe out bigotry without first recognizing race. Being "partially blind" disregards a huge piece of an individual's personality and excuses the genuine treacheries that numerous individuals face because of race. We should see shading so as to cooperate for value and fairness.

4. Discover how your organization or school attempts to extend open doors for non-white individuals

Fundamental bigotry implies that there are boundaries including riches differences, criminal equity inclination, and instruction and training and lodging segregation—that undermine ethnic minorities in the working environment or at school. For instance, the African American

Policy Discussion (AAPF) announced that in 2014, a 12-year-old young lady dealt with criminal indictments, notwithstanding removal from school, for stating "greetings" on a storage space divider. Their crusade, addresses the issues of over-policed and under-protected Dark young ladies inside the training framework. It is significant for organizations and schools to address these issues and advance a culture of value.

5. **Be mindful with your funds**

Stand firm with your wallet. Know the acts of organizations that you put resources into and the foundations that you give to. Put forth an attempt to shop at little, neighborhood organizations and give your cashback to the individuals living in the network. Your state or region may have a registry of the neighborhood, minority-claimed organizations in your general vicinity.

6. **Embrace an approach in all parts of your life**

Recall that all types of persecution are associated. You can't battle against one type of bad form and not battle against others.

Numerous overcomers of abusive behavior at home additionally face prejudice and different types of persecution. We should perceive and bolster survivors' one of a kind encounters

Much has been said throughout the years comparable to subjugation and the white man's job in it. What part, if any white individuals today need to play in this authentic unfairness, and is there any obligation to be carried comparable to the treatment of dark individuals who languished over a few centuries under this arrangement of bondage?

Summary

This is an inquiry that many are awkward with on the grounds that it induces a ton of feeling extending from sharpness to disarray, and to inside and out dismissal. So as to right an inappropriate of bigotry, nonetheless, it is an inquiry that must be posed and there must be an answer that fulfills both the heart and the brain of the individuals who are either deliberately or unwittingly influenced by this appalling heritage. The best way to start to dispel any confusion demeanor of this uncertain issue is to manage it genuinely. Indeed, subjugation in the US has since a long time ago gone into the records of history yet the psychological posterity from the brains of those that made such an establishment despite everything live on to differing degrees in the thoughts and convictions that many despite everything hold and that influence both their private real factors and the open existence of our country. Normally, nobody alive today can be considered answerable for what happened numerous years prior, yet the culpability for those wrongdoings can be supposed to be the psychological advance offspring of the culprits of those demonstrations that have been passed down, in a second-gave design to the individuals who despite everything hold similar thoughts today.

Some may state that prejudice and subjugation are two unique things, yet it is the thoughts and convictions behind bigotry that made such a foundation in any case, so the two ideas are interwoven, one inside the other. Those that are generally influenced by bigotry in their lives are the individuals who hold a considerable lot of similar thoughts that existed a hundred years prior and that's only the tip of the iceberg. Many feel a feeling of disgrace and blame for harboring such thoughts and are awkward with themselves for doing as such. They may discuss racial disparity and treachery and offer empty talk to it yet a piece of them despite everything accepts that blacks are risky, substandard, uncouth, explicitly over the top, and show the darker driving forces of man. We can see this conviction framework working even in a large number of the establishing fathers of our country who were viewed as the absolute most illuminated masterminds of that time. Thomas Jefferson, for instance, for all his virtuoso, accepted that blacks were substandard compared to whites and yet denounced bondage. Why would that be? Attempt as individuals would, many despite everything hold two clashing allowances of faith-based expectations that keep this issue alive and that sadly hinder the advancement and development of people. What is it then that prevents individuals from finishing that conviction and living it in their day by day lives? In the event that we take a gander at convictions as though they were planetary frameworks, we would see that one center conviction or one planet has a few different moons or convictions that turn around it. These futures called auxiliary convictions or optional planets. Customarily one of a planet's moons is in the direct circling way of another and squares it from the primary planet's "see." So the equivalent is valid for a center conviction. Other auxiliary convictions pivot around it and frequently can't be seen from the primary conviction's perspective, rendering it imperceptible. Its belongings, be that as it may, are scarcely so.

On the off chance that an individual accepts, for instance, that all men are made equivalent, yet simultaneously accepts that a piece of man has a creature sense that is itself risky, and whenever let free would cause ruin and destruction in the public arena, at that point he would attempt to control this savage motivation and stifle it as much as could be expected under the circumstances. What's more, imagine a scenario in which this equivalent individual can't acknowledge such a "darker" drive inside his own psyche and rather extends it outward onto someone else or race that appears to him to typify such a nature. Numerous whites dread blacks since they accept so emphatically in the unsatisfactory darker motivations of their own tendencies, and that they should hold these vile parts of their own personalities and spirits down no matter what. Blacks turned into the substitute of the denied 'darker' driving forces of the white man's thoughts of acceptable and abhorrence. Numerous blacks on the other hand have unwittingly become tied up with or have been molded by a similar arrangement of thoughts and act them out in the public eye accidentally. At the end of the day, esteem decisions on shading have been put where they don't have a place.

CHAPTER 19:

Fighting Racial Trauma

You don't need to shape a gathering to take care of racial trauma. As a person, there are numerous means that you can choose to diminish someone else's bias, including:

Cause a pledge to shout out when you hear racial slurs or comments that signal racial partiality

Changing individuals' perspectives and institutional practices is hard, however essential work. A responsibility among people, associations. These small advances construct the establishment for progressively sorted out, further, and bigger endeavors to manufacturing comprehensive networks, a subject that will be talked about in the following area of this part.

To make an equal society, we should focus on settling on unbiased decisions and being antiracist in all parts of our lives.

In a racist society, it isn't sufficient to be non-racist; we should be anti-racist

Race doesn't biologically exist, yet how we relate to run is so incredible, it impacts our encounters and shapes our lives. In a general public that benefits white individuals and whiteness, racist thoughts are viewed as ordinary all through our media, culture, social frameworks, and organizations. Truly, racist sees supported the uncalled for treatment and persecution of minorities (counting subjugation, isolation, internment, and so forth.) We can be persuaded that racial trauma is just about individual attitudes and activities, yet racist approaches likewise add to our polarization. While personal decisions are harming, racist thoughts in strategy have a wide-spread effect by undermining the value of our frameworks and the reasonableness of our institution. To make an equal society, we should focus on settling on fair-minded decisions and being antiracist in all parts of our lives.

Being antiracist is battling against racial trauma

Racial trauma takes a few structures and regularly works couple with at any rate one other structure to fortify racist thoughts, conduct, and approach.

Nobody is brought into the world racist or antiracist; these outcomes from the decisions we make. We are antiracist results from a conscious choice to make a visit, steady, impartial decisions day by day. These decisions require continuous mindfulness and self-reflection as we travel through life. Without settling on antiracist choices, we (un)consciously or not, maintain parts of racial oppression, white-prevailing society, and inconsistent organizations and society. Being racist or antiracist isn't about what your identity is; it is about what you do.

What do the components of learning recorded above intend to you?

Creating schedules to settle on antiracist decisions is a day by day duty that must be done with expectations. The proceeded with endeavors of every one of us exclusively can indicate an enduring change in our general public. Since racial trauma works at different levels, we need to settle on antiracist decisions at the various levels—individual, relational, and institutional—to annihilate racial trauma from the structures and texture of our general public. Put stock in the likelihood that we can change our social orders to be antiracist from this day forward. Racist power isn't faithful. Racist arrangements are not permanent. Racial disparities are not unavoidable. Racist thoughts are not normal to the human psyche."

Ways to Stop Racial Trauma

- **Understand the meaning of Racial Trauma**

Discussions about racial trauma regularly endure when members can't characterize the importance of the word. Merriam-Webster portrays racial trauma as "a conviction that race is the essential determinant of human attributes and limits and that racial differences produce an inalienable prevalence of a specific race." Few individuals would concede that definition mirrors their perspectives, yet all things considered deliberately or accidentally have faith in or underwrite racist thoughts.

Kendi goes further, characterizing the word racist as: "One who is supporting a racist strategy through their activities or inaction or communicating a racist thought." This sharp definition powers the peruser to consider themselves responsible for their thoughts and activities. An antiracist composes Kendi is "One who is supporting an antiracist approach through their activities or communicating an antiracist thought."

- **Stop saying, "I'm not racist"**

It's insufficient to state, "I'm not racist," and frequently, it's a self-serving opinion. Kendi says individuals continually change the meaning of what's racist, so it doesn't concern them. On the off chance that you're a white patriot who's not savage, says Kendi, at that point, you may see the Ku Klux Klan as racist. In case you're a Democrat who believes there's something socially wrong with dark individuals, at that point, racists to you may be individuals who are Republicans.

In this way, for instance, in case you're a white liberal who sees herself as "not racist," however, you won't send your kid to a nearby government-funded school because the populace is dominatingly

African American, that decision is racist. The antiracist position would be to, at any rate, consider enlisting your kid or potentially finding out about the inconsistencies and disparities influencing that school to battle them.

Conclusion

The phenomenon of racial trauma is not difficult to cure, but its treatment requires a great deal of effort, as the tasks are shared between the individual, society as a whole, and the authorities. The nations have already got rid of this scourge and have managed to treat it, and a swarm of solutions to treat and combat racial trauma can be proposed, perhaps the most important of which are

Governments should try to narrow the circle of differences between tribes and between the different factions in society.

Governments must overcome racial trauma by applying the principle of justice and equality among members of society.

The media play a very important role in influencing society and we must ensure that this role is positive in rejecting racial trauma and discrimination.

The imposition of penalties on those who cause discord and conflict between members of the same society.

The strengthening of religious faith in people's hearts sometimes plays a good role in rejecting racial trauma.

The family is considered to be the first nucleus of society, so it must cultivate the best values in the hearts of its children, educate them to love others, and reject pride and contempt for others.

Schools, universities, and educational institutions play a great role in educating the new generation, in training children and cultivating the right ideas in their minds and souls.

Human rights organizations also play a major role in this area, holding educational events, and publishing educational brochures on the importance of equality, the rejection of sedition, racial trauma, and discrimination in all its forms.

As we have already mentioned, the racial trauma which has afflicted many societies has not been able to help those societies which have tried to find real solutions which will free them from the consequences of this phenomenon, which have enabled them to achieve glorious fame afterward, having believed in equal access to opportunities and having established that excellence is not limited to one category, so that all the possibilities available in their sons have merged to paint the most beautiful pictures of solidarity and togetherness on the road to civilization.

You must stay away from all those people who display any kind of racist behavior, no matter how small and trivial from their point of view, also stay away if you have been subjected to racist attacks, no matter how small and trivial, and knowing full well that you do not need to be involved in a confrontation with someone like this and that you must make your priorities more important to you, but if you are exposed to any form of discussion in one way or another, do not rush things and do not accuse the person of being racist, but focus on the words and point to the real reason behind the problem. Don't accept racial trauma in any way, you don't have to accept it, so you have to avoid racist differences with one of your colleagues, and try to deal with it wisely, if you are exposed to one of the positions of racial trauma and you are in the middle of a group, this person may have to act so racistly unintentionally, if you want to maintain this relationship, then you have to set goals when you talk and discuss with the group

This and also indicate whether or not you wish to maintain your relationship with this person.

No person is born who hates another person because of his or her skin color, origin or religion. People have learned to hate, and if they will teach them to hate, then we will teach them to like

Come from behind and let the others think they are in front.

No one is born and hates another person because of his or her skin color, origin or religion.

Education is that the most powerful weapon you'll use to vary the planet.

People learn to hate, and if they are able to learn hate, they should try to teach them to love, because love is closer to the heart of man than hate.

What is valued in life is not that we have lived it, but the difference we have made in the lives of others, which determines the meaning of the life we live.

Greatness in this life is not in stumbling, but in doing after each time we stumble.

Freedom is indivisible, because the restrictions that shackle a person in my country are shackles for all my countrymen.

To be free is not only to be free from the shackles that bind one, but also to live in a way that respects and promotes the freedom of others.

The human body adapts to all harsh conditions, but deep-rooted beliefs are our way of surviving in conditions of deprivation.

A good mind and a good heart are a magical mixture of success.

A brave man is not one who is not afraid. Who can win the fear against all?

I walk between two worlds, one dead and the other incapable of being born, and there is no place yet where my head can rest.

When I got out of prison, I realized that if I did not leave my hatred behind, I would still be a prisoner.

COMPLEX PTSD FROM SURVIVING TO HEALING

A Step By Step Guide To Survive From Ptsd. Learn To Manage Negative Emotions, Overcome Trauma, And Become Whole

BETHANY KEY

Introduction

Most who are troubled with post-traumatic stress, heal naturally. A few need support. If you suffer from post-traumatic stress disorder (PTSD), I applaud you for looking at this self-help workbook. It can transform your life from living with PTSD to living in an overall peaceful way. In the book, I will describe what PTSD is, show you how to identify whether you have such a problem, and then explain how to get rid of it. The term PTSD is often used, but many times, it is misunderstood. If, for several months or years, a person suffers trying to keep away from remembering what traumatized them, is jumpy and emotionally unavailable, then PTSD is a label to describe the symptoms that person is suffering from. Eliminating PTSD completely is what this book is about, rather than only managing its symptoms. According to robust research that has been repeated for over twenty-five years internationally, the best way of getting rid of PTSD completely is known as 'prolonged exposure therapy.' Before starting the prolonged exposure, it is important to have specific skills in place, such as abilities to relax, think of positive affirmations, and behave in a healthy way. These, too, you can find out how to do, in a step-by-step way, as you read on. For self-treatment, all you need to do is follow the step-by-step guidance in the worksheets so that you can free yourself from PTSD. As you read on, you share my knowledge and understanding of how to release yourself from it, relax, and be more content. Being gripped by anxiety while experiencing contentment is impossible, just as it is not possible to be stressed and feeling anxious while relaxing.

Although treating PTSD can be very complex, I have created this workbook in a way that you can follow, one simple worksheet at a time. There is a theory that many believe: when we are traumatized, we shut down. But when faced with individuals who have been through trauma, this is not the case in front of our eyes because individuals continue bravely on, using their own coping methods; sometimes these strategies are unhealthy. The drug-free psychological techniques I offer you have been used a great many times successfully. As a university senior lecturer, I taught trainee counseling psychologists the method you are about to learn. They used it at their clinical placements with great results for their clients who suffered from PTSD. On account of such successful outcomes, one trainee exclaimed to me, 'It works like magic!' Professional psychologists I supervise also use the method with patients who are anxious and suffer from PTSD, with formidable outcomes. A large number of individuals suffering from the problem, who consulted me during my decades of working as a therapist, have turned their lives around for the better, ridding themselves of it in front of my very eyes. I have written this PTSD self-help book for you so that you can turn your life around and achieve similar results too.

CHAPTER 1:

Understanding PTSD

PTSD known as (Post-traumatic stress disorder) is a medical condition understood. This occurs because of stress after a traumatic event, as the name suggests. Some threats a person has or can be seen can cause symptoms of post-traumatic stress disorder. The syndrome was made up of a cluster of symptoms, including hallucinations, flashes of trauma, improved irritability, and sensitivity to minor noise, sleep disorders, preventing any image or memory, which reminds the trauma patient. If these symptoms do not occur simultaneously, the person will not suffer from the post-traumatic stress disorder. Such symptoms were common in people who have experienced road accidents, natural disasters, such as earthquakes and hurricanes, fires, torture, physical and sexual violence, and war.

PTSD Treatment, Safe Alternatives

Big money is made from dealing with PTSD. In the news, Post-Traumatic Stress Disorder has become a marketing tool for all manner of medical medications, whether through services sponsored by the Federal Government or private insurers. More importantly, this form of PTSD diagnosis is based on clinical therapy, not medical science, or true human knowledge of what our military personnel and women and certain civilians suffered from. There are a few organizations, for the most humanistic approach to PTSD therapy, that focus on helping people get through the traumatic experiences and helping people build a stable, successful life for themselves.

For example, "Veterans find peace with equine therapy" was the subject of a recent channel ten news section in Sarasota, Florida, on the Circle V Ranch and rehabilitation center in Dade City. The mission of this ranch is to support veterans and first responders with alternative treatment (Alternative to the use of pharmaceutical products). The farm deals with equine therapy in order to support the veteran and the horse, and through this service, the veteran will advance throughout his life. Another counselor at the center states from the news that "they start to reconnect with each other as they interact with the horse. They will begin to communicate with the community when they connect with themselves; thus, they can start reconnecting with their families." However, the ranch offers support to the family, given that PTSD symptoms impact all.

Therapy for mental health has become the leading approach to PTSD. The FDA warns of delusions, hallucinations, mania, paranoia, suicidal thoughts, homicidal ideas, violence, and many more, which come with psychiatric medications, and for some, it involuntarily activates when a person is exposed to the adverse effects of the drugs. Staying in a psychiatric ward is an additional stigma, an additional financial burden, and another chance to diagnose and treat the patient with medications.

Dr. Gary G. Kohl has recently published a paper that is most applicable to those who have been branded Psychotic PTSD, Bipolar, Depressed, Manic, and who otherwise have been opened up for diagnosis, position on medication, and psychiatric treatment. A specialist in traumatic stress conditions, brain function, and non-pharmaceutical approaches to mental health, neuro sender disorders, food additive neurotoxicity, and psychotropic drug issues.

This benefits patients who have had adverse drug reactions have developed dependence, have symptoms of withdrawal, and/or who experience toxicity from the medications themselves. In Dr. Kohl's post, titled "Psychiatric Hospitals: On being well in 'insane areas,' if there are safety and insanity, how can we know it? "This is a popular study published in 1973 by D. L. Roshenan, which exposed the serious weaknesses of eight psychiatric hospitals at that time as professional people, like Roshenan itself, fake the symptom of hearing and admitted themselves to 12 separate psychiatric hospitals. 23 of the 41 patients were suspected by a doctor to be fraudulent, and 10 were accused of being both by a psychologist and another staff member. "From this, 41 patients were thus rescued from being diagnosed with mental illness and shielded from the altering mental effects of psychiatric drugs. Therefore, concepts of health or folly sometimes may be incorrect." Health and folly have cultural variations, for one society, what is seen as common can be seen as very aberrant in another. As just one example, there was a renowned experiment with American and British psychiatrists and diagnostic discrepancies in each region. All researchers conducted the same interviews with a psychiatric group of patients. Psychiatry was much more often treated by American physicians than by British psychiatry in this series of cases.

"Psychiatric diagnoses even erroneously convey personal, legal, and social stigmas which are impossible to shake and which often last for a lifetime." For everyone with PTSD symptoms or any other symptoms of mental health, alternative treatments are available, and medical professionals work to help you overcome this difficulty. It promises more than it was years ago. The information is available here to help you and your family gets all the facts before they decide your care. There are advocates who can help you to access this information more easily, as they, too, are committed to ensuring the right to full information.

What Are the Causes of PTSD?

In order to understand the whole theory of post-traumatic stress disorder. This is a collection of symptoms that were first described in 1860–1865, American Civil War. Physicians began noticing signs on both sides of the conflict that stopped veterans from re-entering civilian life. Some of the symptoms were serious hallucinations, usually related to noises and battle memories. Many veterans have suffered panic attacks that we now consider to be some things that would trigger battle memories, like a gunshot or a snapshot like a twig—and it would trigger PTSD. The symptoms of PTSD have been more widely recognized over the years since the Civil War. During World War I, for example, it was noticed that veterans returning from War during Europe seemed to be transformed in such a way that the people on the front door could not understand. This state was called shell shock. By the time of World War II, the army knew more than well the origins of PTSD and began working on treatment methods.

Nevertheless, post-traumatic stress disorder is not limited to soldiers alone. Anyone who has had an incident of a deep emotional wound in their life will develop PTSD symptoms. For example, a woman who has been raped might experience symptoms; if she is around strange men, or if she walks in a dark corridor, she might have panic attacks, which are identical to where her attack took place. People who have experienced a major natural disaster may also have symptoms of PTSD. Earthquake victims, for instance, can be intense fear if anything shakes the world, whether it is just as innocent as a street steamroller or a real earthquake. PTSD can also be caused by car accidents or by a violent attack on someone else. Doctors confirmed that small children who underwent surgery had experienced PTSD symptoms subsequently. Similarly, people with gunshot wounds may experience PTSD symptoms.

It is also important to note that not everybody with a significant traumatic event experiences PTSD symptoms. It is encouraging to know that there are new treatments available for those who have developed symptoms of PTSD that, in most cases, show remarkable results and enable the sufferer to return to the appearance of normal life. There is hope for those who suffer from the sometimes worsening condition—life can again be nice, and you can feel normal.

CHAPTER 2:

Symptoms of CPTSD

The symptoms of PTSD are divided into four categories that are used in determining a diagnosis:

- Re-experiencing/Reliving the event

- Avoidance behaviors

- Negative mood/thoughts/feelings

- Hyperarousal (feeling on edge constantly)

We will now look further into each of those.

Symptoms of reliving an event include bad dreams, frightening thoughts, bad memories, and even flashbacks. A flashback feels like you are going through that same terrible trauma again. You relive what you believed was over and done within the past. You experience the pain over and over again, and you have no ability to stop this from occurring. Imagine being severely harmed once, but people with PTSD will have that experience multiple times. The trauma just keeps reoccurring in their minds and traumatizes the victim repeatedly, leaving the sufferer defenseless.

People with PTSD may avoid all situations that remind them of the traumatic experience. They may elude situations that may "trigger" reactive symptoms. They may stay away from the place that the situation occurred. They may stay away from the type of event that the trauma occurred. They have been known to avoid familiar situations because it brings back the horrible memories of the past experience. Avoidance can cause major upsets in a person's life. They may even be afraid to leave their home and go to work. They may isolate themselves, in an attempt, to stop themselves from being hurt again. They may also make attempts to dodge thinking, feeling, and talking about the incident altogether.

People who experience trauma may begin to think differently about themselves and those around them. They may take a more negative approach to life. Their feelings, moods, and thoughts may all suffer. They may experience feelings of guilt, shame, and mistrust. They may feel, and even believe, that the entire world is evil and dangerous. They might feel numb and lose interest in activities they used to enjoy. Or they may "block out" the situation altogether, like selective amnesia. They use this as an unhealthy way to cope with their emotional pain.

Hyperarousal is when a person is easily "startled." Their reactions are too extreme for the given occurrence. They overreact to things that do not require that type of response. For instance, jumping up every time when the phone rings. This is in response to the crisis. If you had been getting threatening calls in the past, every time the phone rings, you may feel on edge and even scared. You may have difficulty sleeping and may have outbursts of anger and even rage. Having hyperarousal symptoms may make it impossible to do daily tasks like concentrating or just taking care of yourself.

PTSD may also be present and co-occurring with other conditions such as depression, anxiety, and addiction, amongst others.

Causes and Risk Factors of PTSD

As I have already explained, the cause of PTSD is a trauma that is not appropriately dealt with. This can be a rape, torture, natural disaster, any form of violence, or a situation that caused or could have caused physical harm or death to an individual. Loved ones can also get PTSD after learning about the traumatic event.

Basically, anyone can get PTSD. Seven to eight percent of people will experience PTSD during their lifetime. Research has found that your genes may affect whether you are more prone to PTSD.

Risk factors may include experiencing past traumatic events, getting physically hurt, being a part of a violent situation, seeing another individual being harmed or killed, having a history of being abused as a child, feeling helplessness and hopeless, having no social support network in place, dealing with any additional stress in the aftermath of the trauma (rebuilding your life, healing, and getting back to normal) and having a history of other mental illnesses, or a substance abuse problem.

It is very important to remember that if you do develop PTSD that it is not your fault. You are in no way to blame. You are not weak-minded, and you did nothing to deserve the trauma. You cannot go back and stop the situation from ever occurring. But you can, and you should fight to get your life back. You can learn new coping skills and believe it or not, you can turn this terrible and very tragic experience into something positive. Instead of seeing the negative, train your mind to find the positive. And yes, there is positive in every situation. You will be tested. You will falter. But please do not give up. I have been through it too. I understand. I have empathy for you.

How to cope with PTSD

I will explore coping strategies that I have personally used to help me, and coping tips that I have found effective that others have used. I recommend you use a variety of them, not yet one or two. If, at all possible, please do use them *all* in your recovery from PTSD.

Admit that you have a problem. If you do not believe a problem exists, then you will feel you do not need a solution. By admitting that something is wrong (or at least could be), you will allow yourself the freedom to seek out answers. You will also unlock opportunities to get your life back on track.

Educate yourself. Reading up, researching, watching videos, etc. will allow you to gain the necessary knowledge you will need in your recovery. It will also help you to end the stigma against those with mental illness, including yourself. In addition, it will allow you to accept your illness for what it is: an illness. Knowledge is power, my friend!

Get involved by joining a support group, helping a neighbor in need, doing a kind act for someone else who is less fortunate, or volunteering somewhere. This will allow you to feel connected to those around you, build your social support network, and see life from a very different perspective.

Finding ways that help you relax is very important in those frightening situations such as nightmares, flashbacks, and events that trigger your symptoms. There are many ways to relax, and a person should use those that are most helpful to themselves, including, but not limited to, deep breathing, meditation, praying, aromatherapy, listening to calming music, taking a bubble bath, spending time with a pet, and even engaging in certain types of exercise such as yoga.

Distracting yourself. When triggering situations arise and you are unable to appropriately deal with them at that moment, it is important to try to distract yourself. Instead of thinking negativity, try thinking or doing something that you love to do, like reading a book or turn up the music. By distracting yourself, you are giving yourself a break and that is ok!

Accept the trauma for what it is and for what it's not. The situation you went through was incredibly frightening, distressing, painful, and even torturous. But you were strong enough to pull through it. You are a warrior! You had the strength required to overcome the situation. There is no need to think about it any longer, and no need to dwell on the emotional agony. What good will that do? The trauma was not your fault. It happened. Things happen, and you are not to blame. Please choose to let it strengthen you and not break you! When your mind brings you back to this terrible, tragic memory, stop it from taking control of your feelings and emotions. You are in control, and you will not let this adversity ruin you.

Sleep well. Since PTSD can cause bad dreams and nightmares related to the traumatic event, it is important to remember these tips if you are having trouble with your sleep. If a nightmare awakes you, remember that it is not really happening. It is just a bad dream. Play some relaxing music and talk to someone until you are able to fall back asleep. Also, try not to oversleep and keep on a regular sleep routine. If your nightmares continue, you may need to see a doctor who may be able to prescribe a medication designed for that.

Avoid illegal drugs, tobacco, alcohol, and caffeine. These substances will only aggravate your symptoms and will increase their intensity and occurrence. They may also affect your ability to sleep well. If you have an addiction problem, I encourage you to seek treatment for that as well.

Maintain a positive frame of mind. Life has enough negatives in it every day. There is simply no room to hold on to your negative thoughts about past events. Try letting go. Try cleansing your mind and ridding it of these negative thoughts. Replace them with positive things such as daily affirmations, prayers, inspirational sayings, and motivational quotes. Be positive and your mind will love you. Instead of seeing the negative side of everything, look for the positivity in even the worst of times. Tell yourself it will all be ok. Have hope for a brighter and better future. Allow yourself to see the opportunities and doors that will be opened to you in the future. Let go of the past and cling to the hope of what will be, not what was.

Keep the faith. In the worst of times, we need to keep the faith! Never lose faith in yourself and who you are and who you want to become. You can be your own best friend. You can be incredibly good for yourself. It is you that has limitless prospects for yourself. Never give up on you. Also, if you believe in God, remember that it is He who loves you and put you on this Earth for a reason. You must find hope in that it is He who has a miraculous plan for your life. Things may go wrong, but it is all part of a larger plan, that we may never be able to understand but must embrace. Embracing this will allow you to find peace within yourself.

Seek out a therapist, counselor, or psychologist. Preferably one who practices trauma-focused psychotherapy. Other therapies used include cognitive-behavioral therapy (CBT) and Eye movement desensitization and reprocessing. A therapist will help bring the pain to the surface. Once you are able to speak about it and vent all your feelings, you can then begin to heal the pain. You can learn to think differently about what happened. Basically, you will learn to accept it, let it go, and move forward with your life. Ultimately, it is what it is.

Find a doctor. You can look up doctors on the internet or have your primary physician refer you to a psychiatrist. This type of doctor will evaluate your case and determine if medication would be able to help you in your recovery process. Certain antidepressants are thought to be very effective in treating PTSD. The medications work on your brain chemistry, which helps stabilize your thoughts, moods, and behaviors.

If you follow all these recommendations, tips, and guidelines, you will be on your way to a very successful recovery from your PTSD!

CHAPTER 3:

PTSD Symptoms Differential Diagnosis

A serious mental illness that affects not just veterans and soldiers, but also many people who are affected by or witnessed abuse or violence, is the posttraumatic stress disorder (PTSD).

While the symptoms of PTSD may seem similar to those of other disorders, there are significant and significant differences. PTSD, for example, may seem like anxiety-related symptoms, including acute stress disorder, phobia, or obsessive-compulsive disorder. In general, however, there is usually no traumatic event to cause the anxiety or worry in anxiety disorders. Or in the case of phobias, this trigger is not experienced by most people as a cause of anxiety. The symptoms of acute stress disruption generally have to occur within a month of a traumatic occurrence and end within a month. When symptoms last longer than one month and follow other types of PTSD, the diagnosis of a person could change from acute stress disorder to PTSD.

Although there are recurrent, repetitive thoughts as a symptom for both PTSD and obsessive-compulsive disorder (OCD), the thought-forms are one way to discern these conditions. Thoughts in obsessive-compulsive disorder usually do not relate to a traumatic event in the past. With PTSD, the thoughts are invariably linked to a traumatic event in the past.

PTSD symptoms may also tend to be an adjustment disorder because they are both related to anxiety following stressor exposure. The stressor is a stressful condition for PTSD. The stressor shouldn't be severe or beyond the "normal" human experience with adjustment disorder.

The arousal and dissociative symptoms of panic disorder are typically not present in PTSD. PTSD is not a common anxiety disorder in that it is directly linked to traumatic events (it is not in generalized anxiety disorder) to avoidance, irritability, and anxiety.

Whereas a person suffering from PTSD may also be depressed, typically PTSD symptom precedes the depression (in a person with posttraumatic stress disorder, it may help to explain these depressing feelings).

In summary, a person's exposure to actual or imminent death, severe injury, or sexual assault with recurred intrusive symptoms specifically associated with this traumatic event can define post-traumatic stress disorder. After the trauma occurred, a person persistently avoided stimuli associated with the trauma and experiences major mood and thinking changes as a result of the trauma.

Anxiety Disorder Compared to PTSD

It could be a challenge to determine the difference between PTSD and other traumatic stress disorders. This dilemma is compounded by the fact that PTSD and other anxiety disorders, including GAD, often occur together. Learn how the two differ, so you can learn how the healing process starts.

Generalized Anxiety Disorder Signs and Diagnosis

Excessive worry and anxiety characterize GAD. Although most people have some worries or anxieties in their lives, someone with GAD is more concerned and anxious than it is.

The following may also happen to him or her:

• Relaxed or on the brink

• Easy to feel fatigued

• Concentration issues

• Faultlessness

• Tension of the muscle

• Disorders of the sleep pattern

GAD differs from other anxiety disorders in that GAD symptoms must occur at least six months before a disorder is diagnosed. "GAD affected 6.8 million adult people, or 3.1 percent of the U.S. population, in every given year," the Anxiety and Depression Association of the USA shared 1. If you are facing GAD symptoms, don't fight it alone.

Symptoms of Post-Traumatic Stress

PTSD is an anxiety disorder that can develop traumatic events after an individual experience. You might be frightened, desperate, or helpless. Symptoms of PTSD may begin to interfere with your daily life. The following may contain these symptoms:

• Disturbances of sleep pattern

• Faultlessness

• Outbreaks of anger

• Concentration difficulty

• Oversight

• Felt sprung or scared

You will also continue to relive the trauma. People with PTSD will experience the following trauma again:

• Returns.

• Halluces.

• Dreams of bad things.

• Mental or physiological distress.

These can be derived from mental images, ideas, and sensations. Real events, locations, or objects may cause them. Those who have difficulties with PTSD may try to avoid symptoms by avoiding trauma-related stimuli.

This prevention can be as follows:

• You or a loved one do not want to talk, think, or feel about trauma.

• You can prevent trauma-reminiscent locations, events, and individuals.

• You may not be able to remember events or an specific event.

• You could lose interest in things that you once cared for.

• You can feel unconnected.

• You may feel or appear blunt in your emotion.

• You can find it difficult to envision a perfect future, a good existence, or a normal life.

Symptoms of PTSD may feel debilitating, but they don't have to keep your life under control. How to manage your PTSD can be learned? Professional treatment, medication and speech therapy provide genuine syndrome relief, explains the National Institute of Mental Health.2

Discussing GAD and PTSD

Many symptoms overlap with GAD and PTSD. GAD is characterized, for instance, by considerable anxiety and concern. These are also problems that can arise when a person struggles with PTSD. With either question of mental health, people will prevent locations, events, and individuals from being concerned and worried.

In addition, there can be two concerns about mental health. Co-occurrence may occur because of the characteristics of one disorder as the risk factors for the other. A person who has GAD issues and then a traumatic incident may experience PTSD symptoms more likely. This has a propensity to undue worry and distress, which can be exacerbated by a traumatic event.

The connection between PTSD and Headaches

Few talks of this, but there is reason to believe there is frequent co-occurrence of post-traumatic stress disorder (PTSD). Although the attention of mental health professionals is much lower than other PTSD problems, the connection between PTSD and headaches is meaningful. If you have PTSD, you are more likely to develop various physical conditions, including diabetes, obesity, heart disease, and pain. For example, 20-30% of people with PTSD reported problems with anxiety when it came to grief in particular.

Patients with migraine or anxiety, headaches show elevated exposure to stressful events when it comes to problems. Furthermore, approximately 17 percent have PTSD diagnosed symptoms.

Another study revealed that 32 percent of OEF / OIF PTSD veterans say they have headaches problems.

The PTSD / Headaches connection

Why people with PTSD may experience problems with headaches is not entirely clear. Stress was, therefore, related to headaches, and PTSD symptoms would lead certainly to very high pressures and emotional stress. Moreover, in their daily lives, headache patients tend to experience more stressful events. PTSD can interfere significantly with many aspects and relationships of a person's life. This potentially creates more pain, which raises the risk of headaches.

In some instances, a person with PTSD may suffer from stressful experiences that may increase the risk of headaches. You may be more likely to experience headaches problems when, for example, you were in an accident or situation when you had a head injury or a traumatic brain injury. OEF / OIF-veterans have high rates of traumatic brain injuries that can take into account the number of OEF / OIF-veterans with PTSD reported headaches.

CHAPTER 4:

Strategies to Recovery

Creative Strategies

Tapping into your creative side can be an effective means for processing and overcoming the after-effects of a traumatic experience. Strategies such as art, music, and writing are all viable options for trauma recovery. These creative options can be particularly useful for individuals who struggle with verbal expressions of their experiences.

Art Therapy

The therapeutic benefits of art can come from many different forms in several different settings. This can be painting, drawing, coloring, quilting, or collage with or without the direction of an art therapist, with a group or alone. A researcher who interviewed a group of art therapists was able to compile a list of the common benefits that accompany art as a recovery tool, including decreases in hypervigilance, stimulated positive emotions, and decreased anxiety.

As mentioned already, art allows for the nonverbal expression of trauma experiences and memories. It can be difficult to access the memory or find the words to express it, but art can be an effective outlet. Creating art can be a means to externalize the internal memory and own it, which helps integrate the experience as a past memory as opposed to a current source of distress.

Art can be a way to slowly gain exposure to troubling stimuli related to trauma (similar to the titration method). This non-verbal method is seen as less threatening and can make it easier to address the issues. The use of art is relaxing and reduces hypervigilance, whether or not the art is related to the trauma. Art therapy also awakens emotion so it can stimulate emotional numbing, including positive emotion. The process of creating can help in stirring and experiencing positive emotion. The creation of art can also enhance a sense of control due to the control over your creative space, which can also enhance confidence in the ability to express emotions.

One study examined the effects of coloring on anxiety. The authors found that groups coloring a detailed design, such as a mandala, saw anxiety decrease to a level that was lower than the initial measure of anxiety taken at the beginning of the study. It is interesting to note that there was no decrease in anxiety for those who were coloring the free-form of a blank piece of paper. It is believed that coloring on a design, like the one from a coloring book, helps to organize the internal chaos characteristic of anxiety. Interestingly, in the Holotropic Breathwork mentioned earlier, this type of artistic expression is often incorporated. At the end of therapy sessions involving Holotropic Breathwork, users will paint mandalas as a way to express their experiences. There are numerous coloring books available in-store and online, some full of mandalas and some that are specifically for relaxation.

A study of teenagers with high scores on a PTSD scale showed improvement in PTSD symptoms after completing art therapy. There were several art modalities used in this study, and the most effective was creating a book of artwork that contains a graphic narrative of each person's life story. Each book was made up of 13 collages or drawings along with a handmade book cover. Other specific art activities that were found to reduce symptoms of PTSD successfully include sewing pillows, beading jewelry, making ceramics, creating plaques, stitching leather purses, and decorations for holidays or seasons. Supplies and ideas for these art projects and so many more can be found at local crafting stores, and inspiration can be found online.

Music

Music is used frequently in movies, television, and even commercials to influence, signal, or alter our moods. Chances are you have used music to reflect or enhance your current mood or state of mind. Now science is demonstrating how music can regulate mood and be used to cope. Music therapy allows individuals who have survived trauma to relate to the healthy versions of themselves and can create the feeling of a safe and enjoyable environment. Music can be another source for grounding and can make traumatic memories accessible for discussion and processing. Similar to creating art, making music can create a sense of control and a means to express the trauma. Music can allow individuals to connect with and express feelings, as well as to connect with others, especially through group music therapy.

Hypervigilance can also be addressed in this way by encouraging tolerance of loud sounds or silence, as well as concentration through devoting attention to music made by yourself or others.

One example is using loud drumming to express anger or using songs to lower anxiety.

Specifically, anxiety-reducing songs are usually slow-paced and have an even rhythm. In more advanced versions of music therapy through the assistance of a music therapist, survivors can write and record music that creates an auditory narrative of the traumatic experience or the life story, similar to the art project mentioned earlier.

A research study conducted with a group of adults with PTSD that did not respond to cognitive behavior therapy were given 10 weeks of music therapy in which they were encouraged to improvise music with a variety of easy to use instruments (like a tambourine) while accompanied by a music therapist providing instrumental support. After the 10-week treatment period, there was a significant reduction in PTSD symptoms. Interviews with the study participants revealed that many of them felt they were able to get out their anger and frustrations through the music they produced, and afterward felt calm and controlled.

Writing

The process of writing can be a powerful tool for creative and self-expression, as well as putting words to and dealing with trauma and other intense emotional experiences. There are several benefits that come from writing, including being able to disconnect a feeling of distress from the memories of trauma, creating a sense of control and emotion regulation, and better health and well-being. It is believed that these health benefits are seen because of the decrease in inhibition through the disclosure of associated events through writing. Writing also creates the opportunity to make meaning of the traumatic event or to incorporate the event into existing ways of making meaning about the world—in other words, to help create meaning about your traumatic event that fits with your beliefs and value systems. Asking people to write on a daily basis about their traumatic experience, and the attached emotions, in particular, have been found to be especially beneficial.

In one study with college students, participants were asked to write for 20 minutes about the most traumatic and upsetting experience of their lives. After this period of writing, the students reported that the event seemed more within their control and less threatening than it had before the writing task. They also found the event to be less stressful in the present and not as central to their lives. These are all very adaptive changes in perception and have an impact on levels of distress. The students also found they had fewer intrusive thoughts and less avoidance of the memory of the situation they wrote about.

This relates to less cognitive processing of the event, which means cognitive (thought) resources are more freed-up for other high-order thinking.

Other potential benefits that come from disclosing traumatic experiences, such as through the writing process, including feeling better about the topic as well as about themselves and being able to think about their situation in different ways. Writing can also lead to new and greater insight about the traumatic event, as well as less intrusive thoughts, and more self-esteem.

Trauma survivors have also reported that the process of writing about their experience helped them regain their own independent functioning and afforded them the opportunity to tell their own story. Writing is not just restricted to the standard narrative form; songwriting has also been shown to be beneficial and can be a way to combine writing and music therapy.

Another study has shown that reading and writing together can be a powerful combination. Domestic violence counselors experiencing secondary PTSD were given poems on three different occasions and instructed to reflect on the emotional theme of the poem. All the emotions of the selected poems are emotions typical of PTSD reactions and used to promote writing that is focused on personal stress and the emotions that go along with that. Participants in the study showed a decrease in symptoms and a reduction in stress.

The poems used in this study are The Armful by Robert Frost, Autobiography in *"Five Short Chapters"* by Portia Nelson and The Journey by Mary Oliver. These are the most frequently used poems in poetry therapy and reflect a range of emotions. You could select one or all of these poems, and after reading, write a reflection about the emotion(s) felt throughout the poem and write about that emotion(s) as they relate to your own situation.

Animal Assistance

Significant evidence has come to light about the role animals play in human lives and the benefits which can be extracted from these relationships. Many of the benefits found in human to human support relationships can also be found between humans and animals. Animals can provide a buffer between humans and challenging or threatening circumstances like trauma. It may be important to note when using animal-assisted therapy or utilizing animals for the management of trauma recovery, a human's relationship with animals is affected by their perceptions that come from media, folklore, and societal and past interactions with animals. With this in mind, animal-assisted therapies may not be for everyone.

If being around animals is for you, there are several positive benefits such as lower depression levels, better blood pressure, and the kind of physical contact that helps with the healing and recovery process from trauma. The presence of a companion animal can reduce anxiety and, in particular, can create a sense of safety during the process of disclosure during psychotherapy. Companion animals can also provide comfort and grounding as situations become difficult.

Equine Therapy

Equine, or horse therapy, is one specific kind of animal-assisted therapy that has been gaining in popularity with over 550 therapeutic riding programs available in North America and at least 3,200 registered therapeutic riding practitioners. The sensitivity and responsiveness of horses can empower riders to meet the challenges of trauma recovery.

Horses are used for therapeutic purposes because they are cooperative, patient, willing, receptive, and people-oriented. Horses can understand or "read" people and communicate with riders. This and the rider communication with the horse creates a connection that contributes to the healing process. Riding provides comfort through contact.

Part of what makes the relationship between horse and human so powerful in the process of recovering from trauma is how closely this relationship mirrors that of the relationship between a therapist and a client, also known as the therapeutic alliance. In both cases, there is a bond that reinforces a sense of self and provides a motivation to change.

It is important for a horse and rider to be matched depending on the preferences, characteristics, and personalities of both. And it takes time for the animal-human relationship to form, also very similar to the therapeutic alliance. This time can create a safe relationship and safe touch, which is very important for survivors of trauma. This safe relationship can facilitate change, as well as provide a context for goal-setting and promote a feeling of independence.

CHAPTER 5:

Dialectal Behavior Therapy

In short, Dialectical behavior therapy or DBT is a form of behavioral therapy introduced by Dr. Marsha Lineham, an American psychologist who found CBT as a therapy inefficient to help people with suicidal tendencies. The foundation of this therapy utilizes the basic concepts of the standard CBT but with additional adaptations to meet the particular needs of people experiencing intense emotions. The basic aim of DBT is to empower you to manage difficult emotions by experiencing, recognizing, and accepting them. As you learn how to accept and control our emotions, you are better able to get over the harmful behaviors. To attain this goal, DBT therapists utilize a balance of change and acceptance techniques, something that is missing in other therapies meant for treating behavioral problems.

In DBT, therapists help you find the perfect balance between acceptance and change via four different elements:

- Skills training (in groups)

- Individual therapy

- Telephonic coaching

- Consultation group of therapists

A typical course of DBT includes homework and take-home assignments, which usually continue for approximately a year. A lot of people may find it quite hard to develop DBT skills in the beginning because it includes accepting your flaws while working hard to change them. However, with the passage of time, you will come to realize that all your efforts were worthwhile.

Summary

If you are living with an anxiety disorder, you most likely acknowledge that feeling in control of yourself is a validating, valuable feeling. DBT can help you achieve this feeling though group skills training, trained therapists, and skills coaching. All these parts will work together to make sure that DBT offers you skills that you can put into practice to help you get full control over how you feel and live. DBT is currently operating on four different levels—Mindfulness, Interpersonal Effectiveness, Distress Tolerance, and Emotional Regulation—to help people get over their worst fears and depressive states.

DBT Distress Tolerance and Mindfulness Skills

Now that the concept of DBT is clear, let's move on to discuss the first two components of DBT—Mindfulness and Distress Tolerance and their role in the treatment of behavioral disorders.

What are DBT Mindfulness Skills?

Mindfulness refers to paying attention to what is happening at the moment "on purpose." When you are practicing mindfulness, you are focusing your attention on the present experience, noticing whatever is happening at the exact moment, not lost in the past, or wondering about the future.

Mindfulness is actually something entirely opposite to being on automatic pilot. While you are on automatic pilot, you are either doing things out of habit or by rote. For example, many people relate to a condition where they arrive at work but do not really remember the car ride that took you there. That is because you did not have to think about opening the car door, sitting down, putting the key in the ignition, etc. You just did all these things automatically and found yourself at your office minutes later. Doing things in an autopilot mode is not bad. It is actually quite useful in a way that helps save energy and time. Problems begin to arise when you start living most of your life in this mode instead of actually being present in the moment.

Why Does Mindfulness Matter?

Mindfulness is like a magic ingredient that helps you control your sentiments and take a step back from intense emotions. When you take a step back and notice what is happening, you are less likely to experience out-of-control emotions.

"Mindfulness is powerful."

When you use mindfulness to control your attention, you open yourself to a whole new world of choice. You do not need to act and react out of fear, habit, or intense emotions. The benefits of mindfulness have been well-researched, especially during the last few years. The regular practice of mindfulness has been shown to decrease distraction, increase emotional regulation, improve anger management, and decrease depression.

Mindfulness in DBT

Mindfulness forms the backbone of DBT. It is, in fact, the first skill taught to the patients opting for DBT. This is because, without mindfulness, it is not possible to alter long-standing patterns of acting, thinking, and feeling.

"Mindfulness is the core skill underlying all other skill sets in DBT."

It is central to getting through difficult situations, resolving interpersonal conflicts, and regulating emotions. Mindfulness is also a primary component for accessing your Wise Mind, an important foundational concept in DBT. Wise Mind is said to be the synthesis of a Reasonable Mind and an Emotion Mind. Once you find your Wise Mind, it gets easier to know what's real for you and act according to it. The concept of mindfulness in DBT revolves around two questions: "What to do" and "how to do it." These are known as the 'What' and 'How' skills.

The 'What' Skills

There are three skills that comprise the "What" of mindfulness:

- Observe

- Describe

- Participate

The Observe Skill

Observe means noticing any direct sensory experience. It is what you fee, see, taste, sense, hear, and touch without judging it, labeling it, or reacting to it. This is a bit tricky for most of the people at first; your mind wants to label what is happening around you instead of just being with the sensations of an experience. While you practice the Observe skills, you are permitting your immediate experience to happen without trying to change it or pushing it away.

Like all the skills, observe skills is experiential. This indicates that the intellectual understanding of this skill is not sufficient; you have to experience it for yourself to truly understand it. For example, listening to the sounds around you, just noticing them without passing any comments is an example of observing skill of mindfulness in DBT.

The Describe Skill

The describe skills build on the observe skill. While observe is only bare-bones attention—noticing something without adding a label or a story—describe includes putting the observed experience into words, whether it is an emotion, thought, or a sensation.

Sounds like a piece of cake, right? Not quite.

The tricky part is that DBT mindfulness demands you to practice the describe skill by sticking to the facts and refraining from any personal assumptions or interpretations. So when you describe an experience, you label thoughts as thoughts, feelings as feelings, and emotions as emotions only without adding any labels, judgments, concepts, and opinions.

The describe skill is an excellent tool to help you NOT mistake every thought or feeling of yours for a fact. For example, just because you are feeling unlovable doesn't justify it as the truth. The describe skill is also a great tool for reducing reactivity, especially in emotionally sensitive people. It does not let you jump to conclusions without checking the facts hence, saves you from a lot of trouble.

The Participate Skill

In DBT, participate means exactly what it sounds like: It means throwing yourself entirely into an activity and letting go of judgments, fear, and self-conscious instead of sitting aside and watching. Most of the young children exhibit this skill, immersing themselves in play without any sort of inhibition. For example, you can practice this mindfulness skill during everyday activities, for example, washing dishes. Instead of thinking about how much you hate it or planning what you will do once you are finished, you immerse yourself completely in the ongoing activity of washing dishes.

The 'How' Skills

The purpose of 'How' skills in DBT is to understand how to accomplish the 'What' skills. So you are supposed to practice the three 'What' skills:

One-mindfully

This means giving your full presence in the current situation, not lost in the thoughts of the past or future. It means concentrating on one task at a time while focusing on it completely instead of splitting it between things, for example: Having a conversation on the phone while cooking a meal.

Practicing this skill is important. One-mindfulness in DBT helps you open up to the potential beauty hidden in small moments. It prevents you from juggling multiple tasks because multitasking can weaken your connection with the Wise Mind, therefore, affect your decision-making skills.

Non-judgmentally

It is common to notice something and release judgments instantly, either about yourself ("I am not good at this!"), others ("He is not good at this"), your experience ("This was indeed a bad idea"), or anything else. Most of the use judge habitually, automatically, and continuously.

Judging has become such an important part of our internal dialogue that we fail to notice how judgments can increase emotional pain and potentially destroy relationships. Hence, the 'How' mindfulness skills in DBT require you do everything non-judgmentally. Being non-judgmental prevents the emotional charge of the situation from heightening, making it easier to look for solutions.

Effectively

This skill involves acting effectively, i.e., doing what works vs. sitting aside and wishing things were different. In DBT, effectively is all about shifting your focus away from the concepts of what's fair and unfair, or who is right or wrong, and focusing on what really works. When you are not concentrated on doing what is effective, you may act in ways that are more about proving a point or being right. Trying to be right gets in the way of getting what you need or want.

CHAPTER 6:

PTSD and Relaxation

Generally speaking, a relaxation technique helps a person to relax by reducing his or her level of pain, anxiety, stress, or anger, thus benefiting also from depression, headache, high blood pressure, and insomnia. In so doing, not only symptoms and/or conditions may become more manageable, but also the overall state of health may improve.

Autogenic training, for instance, which was developed by the German psychiatrist Johannes Heinrich Schultz around 1932, consists of short sessions lasting an average of 15 minutes, which are supposed to be repeated on a daily basis and that through a series of visualizations aim at generating a sense of relaxation. Positions to practice Autogenic training can be freely chosen, though finding one that may encourage the person to relax and focus on visualizations, such as lying down or sitting comfortably are highly recommended. This technique can alleviate stress-related disorders caused by traumatic events.

Biofeedback, another holistic technique, by manipulating physiological functions through the use of specific devices checking "brainwaves, muscle tone, skin conductance, heart rate, and pain perception" (deCharms et al., 2005) may also play a role in the reduction of depression, anxiety and stress. Christopher deCharms, a neuroscientist and social entrepreneur, founder, and CEO of Omneuron, a life science company whose technology is a pioneer in the imaging methods, in conjunction with Stanford University School of Medicine has developed a live fMRI aiming at measuring and modifying brain functions, with the final goal being the treatment of chronic pain. This technique enables the patient to control his own pain by visually looking at his rtfMRI and checking his own reactions in real-time, and then, by changing the latter, by ultimately blocking the pathways causing pain.

In plain English, this means that by becoming aware of one's own thoughts and perceptions at the time pain is experienced, one can change that experience by switching to a new way of thinking and perceiving. In so doing, that is, by taking control over his or her own mind and body, he or she can reduce or, through further training, even eliminate the possibility of experiencing that pain again. (deCharms, R. C. (2008). This work, which is funded by the National Institute of Health, seems to be a very promising one for the treatment of chronic pain, depression, and anxiety.

Biofeedback is far from being a new method since it has been around for millennia in India and applied through **Yoga** and **Pranayama**. While Yoga, which is a philosophical system based on the practice of physical, mental and spiritual exercises aiming at reaching a full control over both the body and the mind, focuses on a series of practices and postures to accomplish this goal, Pranayama, meaning 'prana' (life force, breath) and 'ayāma' (to extend), is a yogic discipline which also originated in India and concentrates on breathing exercises. The assumption of the latter is that since breathing is absolutely a necessity for the life of any living being, learning how to breathe properly and deeply can highly improve the health of the individual by strengthening the life force animating his or her body.

Furthermore, breathing is also seen as "the main link between conscious and unconscious," which implies that breathing properly is not only beneficial to our physical but also to our emotional and mental health. (Stanway, 1994, p. 286) Research has shown that Pranayāma can be helpful in cases of stress-related disorders. It is strongly recommended, however, to practice this kind of breathing exercises under the supervision of a qualified practitioner in order to avoid complications, injuries, and undesired side effects. (Iyengar, 2011).

As for Yoga, it focuses on maintaining a state of mind-body-spirit balance and on correcting any imbalance before it can harm the body. **Hatha Yoga** is the kind of Yoga mainly based on physical exercises, which include stretching, breathing, and relaxation.

Yoga sees "the body as a vehicle, the mind as its driver and the soul as the Man's true identity" (Stenway, 1994, p. 284), hence, it can be employed to "prevent, cure and manage a variety of disorders (including respiratory, digestive, musculoskeletal and neurological ones)." It can also be an effective method to rehabilitate people after they have gone through surgeries and accidents, to manage disabilities, and to treat addictions. Yoga aims at the removal of energy (life force, prana, chi, qi) blockage through the Asana or postures, and Pranayāma, or breathing exercises, both of which are able to help the body to detoxify so that the prana may freely flow throughout it as it is intended to and maintain and/or restore homeostasis, that is the state of balance needed in order for the body to reach optimum health.

All body parts can benefit from the Asanas due to the fact that through them muscles are stretched and tuned up, the spine and joints can maintain their flexibility, and breathing and circulation can be improved. (p. 285)

Although rooted in ancient Chinese philosophy and medicine and also conceived as martial arts, **Qi Gong** and **Tai Chi** (the latter also called *Tai Chi Chuan*) are holistic methodologies characterized by coordinated gentle postures and movements, rhythmic breathing and meditation and intended as forms of relaxation, preventive medicine, and self-healing techniques.

The benefits of both methods on health are many: They enhance the activity of the immune and lymphatic systems, of the metabolism and tissue regeneration, and increase circulation while reducing heart rate and blood pressure.

Oxygenation of the brain and of all organs and tissues is also boosted and a state of relaxation is produced through the decrease of the autonomic nervous system's sympathetic response (Trivieri & Anderson, 2002, p. 435).

The health benefits of both Qi Gong and Tai Chi have also been recognized in our western world and many are now the hospitals and clinics which either recommend or have already integrated them into their practice. As for their application in cases of PTSD, these methodologies can be of great support in managing pain, depression, and anxiety.

Although relaxation alone might not be sufficient to reduce certain types of symptoms in many people affected by PTSD, it can, nonetheless, still be effective by contributing to managing the arousal associated with them.

PTSD, Nutrition, and Lifestyle

Adrenaline, cortisol and DHEA (dehydroepiandrosterone) are the hormones that help us with the 'fight-or-flight' response to stress. They intervene in the process by injecting us with the energy required to face whatever situation we encounter and perceive as a threat. This is a sort of survival mechanism which plays a fundamental role in cases of life-threatening circumstances.

However, in order to provide us with all the energies required to cope with the stressful event(s) we might be confronted with, the body takes the energies it needs from the ones reserved to perform its other functions. As a result, not only the aging process is accelerated, but there is also the possibility that many other health complications may arise. Digestive disorders or diseases, a hormonal imbalance causing the metabolism to slow down and, consequently, leading to overweight, and calcium deficiency, which may provoke arthritis, are among the many health issues that one can face in such a situation.

In order to help the body to work again towards a state of balance and possibly restore and maintain optimum health, stimulants such as coffee, cigarettes, and a high-calorie diet should be avoided. This also includes soda beverages that contain a high amount of sugar, and some kinds of sweeteners that have been proven to be toxic. Furthermore, despite the ongoing debate about the possibility, or lack thereof, that the latter might really harm human health, it seems wise, nonetheless, to limit or even to exclude these kinds of products from our diet considering, for instance, that Saccharin has been formally declared an "anticipated human carcinogen" (Day, 2007, p. 106) and Aspartame has been questioned, since it was discovered, about its potentially devastating effects on brain neurons. (p. 107).

Although a healthy and balanced diet will probably not 'cure' PTSD, the truth of the matter is that it will, nonetheless, highly contribute to the overall health and wellness by boosting one's own immune system through which the body is able to fight disease and restore health whenever required. Hence, eating plenty of fresh fruits and vegetables, with the latter being either steamed, lightly cooked or used raw, along with whole foods, 100% certified organic, good quality of proteins, better if of vegetable sources and avoiding refined, processed, saturated fat, precooked and junk foods will provide all the vitamins, minerals, enzymes your body needs to stay healthy. The B complex vitamins and vitamin C are among the very first nutrients that one should make sure to consume regularly to recover from stress, especially when the latter is intense and/or experienced over a prolonged period of time. (Holford, 2004, pp. 2018, 219)

People with mood disorders have a greater sensitivity to chemical imbalances and without a balanced diet, which may contribute to their health through the correct amount of all the nutrients the body needs, their conditions may even worsen.

The most important thing is, therefore, to develop one's own routine that can help to maximize energy and glucose levels. Good eating habits may include plenty of smoothies and/or juices (better if vegetables and fruits are combined), seeds, nuts, whole grains rather than the 'whites'—that is all processed and refined products which have been deprived of most of their nutrients—fish, chicken and or turkey while avoiding or at least consuming very little amount of meat (beef), pork, and cold cuts, while dairy products and eggs should also be consumed in moderation. Along with soda beverages also caffeine, which affects glucose levels and interferes with sleep, nicotine and illegal drugs should also be avoided. Sugar as well should be consumed moderately, for it does affect moods. Hence, cutting back on sugar, caffeine, and nicotine with the goal of completing eliminating them over a reasonable period of time, should be among the top priorities along with avoiding alcohol and drugs.

When struggling with overwhelming emotions and traumas, one might be tempted to start using either alcohol or drugs or a combination of them in order to cope with emotions and feelings, which may appear unmanageable and unbearable. In so doing, however, despite having the illusory feeling of a temporary relief, the truth is that, in the long run, all of them will backfire making the situation much worse not only in terms of PTSD symptoms but also by leading to emotional numbness and isolation along with a possible increase in anger and depression.

CHAPTER 7:

What Is Psychotherapy?

Psychotherapy is, however, a conversation of a peculiar type: that is, it is both a hermeneutic and a dialectical exchange.

By hermeneutic I mean that therapists use interpretations of different kinds that prompt clients to reconsider their positions. Such interpretations may arise from the theoretical model in which the therapist was originally trained and, where this is so, it will reach back to larger discourses of different kinds—medical, scientific, therapeutic, sexual, cultural, social, and so forth. The technical device of a formulation, is, as I have explained, the device through which interpretations are presented spontaneously in a therapeutic conversation (in 'closed conversations', they may be delivered without preamble using an 'expert voice').

However, interpretations can take a looser, everyday form, and are contained in anecdotes, analogies, allusions, and suggestions, to name just a few. These informal styles have a deeper significance in that they point to the experienced therapist's facility in holding different types of conversation ranging from the theoretical, technical style at one end of the spectrum to the informal, everyday style at the other. At the same time, clients will also be using interpretations of their own, both to explain their own predicament and to interpret whatever therapists have to say to them. This to-and-from of interpretation and re-interpretation, sometimes leading to a synthesis of ideas, is what is meant by dialectic and it is this which is properly speaking, the material of psychotherapy.

However, the dialectic we find in therapy is of a peculiar kind: namely, that it is attended to subjectively by clients. Assuming that the therapist is heard to be offering them interpretations that are sincere, relevant, intelligible, and insightful (Grice, 1989: 22-40) the client will seek to apply the offering to her own life. That is to say, she will not be concerned with its objective truth so much as whether it helps her to go on in a different way (Wittgenstein, 1966: 44-45).

The texts by Wilhelm Reich and Arnold Lazarus which pointed to the 'anything-goes' quality of therapeutic interpretations and treatment choices in which those same interpretations and choices were prompted by the client sitting before them. I argued then that many experienced therapists, in practice, do not employ textbook methods in therapy but instead act as 'authentic chameleons', using all their arts of persuasion in order to bring clients round to a particular point of view or to secure their agreement to trying out a procedure on a trial-and-error basis. In my analysis of a variety of therapeutic interviews, particularly those with Gloria, I demonstrated that therapists who try too hard to impose a method on clients frequently come undone because the conversational rules of therapeutic conversations will always leave the client as the final arbiter on whether they can proceed or not. Although a minority of clients may blindly submit to indoctrination, the majority (assuming they do not misunderstand what the therapist is trying to say) will respond on a spectrum ranging from enthusiastic acceptance to outright rejection.

In the examples of therapeutic conversations analyzed so far, the formulations (interpretations) employed have sometimes been pragmatic (drawing attention to intentions and motives), sometimes theoretical (referring back to psychological theories), sometimes speculative, sometimes as an exercise of authority and occasionally as all four. Other devices have also been used in pursuit of therapeutic ends: metaphors, stories, explanations, script-formulations, tag questions, and so forth. In return, a variety of responses were elicited: angry, humorous, ironic, resistant, helpful, uninterested, perplexed, etc. Occasionally these have led to new directions in talk, but just as often they have come to a conversational dead-end. But, inescapably, the cycle of interpretation-response-reinterpretation has involved active voices constantly seeking to formulate the position from which the other is speaking. It is these continual uncertainties in interpretation which make it so difficult to analyze psychotherapy as process and outcome, or as a formal method.

Using Gadamer's work on hermeneutics, I offer a model of psychotherapy that accepts these conversational uncertainties as a given. In so doing, I seek to resolve the questions raised from the beginning of this work concerning the relationship between theory and practice and the uncertainties generated by a comparison between talk *about* therapy to talk *in* therapy. Fundamentally Gadamer helps us to understand why psychotherapy cannot ever be a formal method (i.e., a science) and why accepting and understanding that this so leads us towards an appreciation of how non-methodical (or semi-methodical) approaches can work.

CHAPTER 8:

What Is Talk Cure Therapy?

It was Sigmund Freud nearly 100 years ago who came up with the term "the talking cure." Although he was referring to psychoanalysis when he initially uses the term, talking about one's problems in a safe environment with someone who is trusted, has long been shown to help with the resolution of loss, trauma, and other emotional problems.

I begin now a discussion of treatments for PTSD, starting first with a review of standard secular psychotherapies that are now commonly used to treat this disorder. Mental health professionals who provide these treatments typically have advanced degrees, are licensed by the state and received special training to administer the particular type of psychotherapy being offered. You may be surprised that current guidelines for the treatment of PTSD recommend psychotherapy over medication and all other treatments. This is based on a large volume of research showing that the benefits of psychotherapy in PTSD far exceed those of medications (and is without the side effects that medications have). Furthermore, the benefits of psychotherapy are more long-lasting than those on medication, which may help some persons only during the time that the medication is actually being taken.

Many different kinds of psychotherapies have been proposed for the treatment of PTSD. However, only a few of these have been shown in scientific studies (i.e., randomized clinical trials) to have the benefit. I will now discuss each of these below, as well as other psychological approaches to treatment that are reasonable, but have far less evidence to support their effectiveness. When discussing these various psychotherapies and psychological treatments, I will be referring to what is called an "effect size" (ES). The ES indicates the size of the clinically meaningful effect that the treatment has. In other words, the ES is a quantitative measure of the benefits that you may receive after undergoing a course of the particular type of psychotherapy. ES's that indicate a small clinical effect on reducing PTSD symptoms are those that are -0.20 or closer to 0; a moderate effect is indicated by ES's in the range of -0.30 to -0.60, and a large clinical effect or benefit is indicated by ES's in the -0.80 or more negative range. ES's also have what are called "95% confidence intervals." This is a statistical term that means 95% of people who received the therapy fall within the range of values provided. If a 95% confidence interval includes 0, then the clinical benefit of the treatment is considered to be the same as no treatment at all.

Most of the time these studies compare the psychotherapy being studied with a "control" condition where participants receive no treatment (controls might be placed on the waitlist to receive the therapy later or may simply receive "usual care," i.e., the care they would ordinarily receive if they were not in the study). On occasion, the psychotherapy being studied will be compared with other "active" treatment (such as another type of psychological treatment or medication). Of course, it is much more difficult to show a large ES (indicating a clinically meaningful difference) if psychotherapy is compared to other treatment than if it is compared to no treatment or usual care. Now that may be more information that you are interested in, but it may be helpful so that we can compare the effects of psychotherapy with medication and other treatments.

Psychotherapies currently used to treat PTSD can be divided into "trauma-focused therapies" and "non-trauma-focused therapies." I begin with the trauma-focused therapies since these are usually recommended for those with PTSD.

CHAPTER 9:

What Is Cognitive Behavioral Therapy?

Cognitive Behavioral Therapy (CBT) is an approach that addresses behavioral dysfunctional emotions, and cognitive processes based on a combination of core behavioral principles and cognitive techniques. CBT is used by problem-focused and action-oriented approach practitioners to support people cope with common conditions such as fear, stress, and often more complicated psychological disorders. Cognitive-behavioral therapy refers to a number of structured psychotherapy methods centering on the thoughts behind the problems of a patient. A survey of nearly 2,300 psychologists in the U.S. found that about 70 percent uses CBT in combination with other therapies to treat depression and fear. CBT is also a predominant paradigm of psychotherapy that is taught in graduate psychology programs.

How Does Cognitive Therapy Work?

Cognitive-behavioral therapy is based on the idea that human beings are somewhat irrational and make many illogical mistakes whenever they assess the risks and benefits of their thoughts and actions from different situations and courses. It can relate to the feelings that are out of balance, such as rage and depression. But CBT is also used to address a number of other nuanced problems, including post-traumatic stress disorder (PTSD), OCD, drug misuse, ADHD, eating disorders, bipolar disorder, and other illnesses.

For them to be successful, cognitive-behavioral clinicians will have a strong interaction with their customers, such as positive listening skills and a good personality fit. This is because the patient and therapist are working together to discuss the issues at hand and the reasons for the patient's thoughts and actions toward those issues. The end aim is to alter ways of thought such that the individual feels less consistently unpleasant mental conditions.

The Global Coalition for Behavioral Wellbeing in favor of CBT as it has outstanding research evidence promoting its application in the therapeutic diagnosis of mental illness, which has gained broad acceptance among both clinicians and patients alike. Increasing numbers of psychologists, psychiatrists, social workers, and psychiatric nurses are getting CBT training.

Research on CBT's effectiveness has been found to be effective against a wide range of disorders. Those experiments are well-controlled, the data is properly reviewed and the findings speak for themselves. Of starters, CBT has been shown to have substantial advantages when managing bipolar depression, culminating in fewer treatment days, reduced suicide rates, and decreased levels of parasuicidal or self-injurious behavior.

Precautions to be Taken before Beginning Relational Cognitive Therapy

Psychiatrists, behavioral psychologists, social workers, and other mental health professionals undergo years of training and education, but without this solid training experience, it is possible to practice counseling. Before settling on a CBT specialist, other items to study include educational background and qualifications, along with any professional associations to which they belong, such as the Organization for Behavioral and Cognitive Therapies, where most top practitioners are participants. Review your history, schooling, credential, and license before seeing a making your first appointment. The general term psychotherapist is often used. Make sure the therapist you choose meets the requirements of state certification and licensing for his or her particular discipline. The key is finding a qualified therapist who can match your needs to the type and therapy. CBT is more effective in most situations when paired with various therapies, such as taking medicine. So, you might also need a psychiatrist to prescribe medications besides your therapist. The cost is one more thing to consider. When you have health care, find out what pays all the treatment services it provides. Some health plans cover just a certain number of sessions of therapy a year. Some may not even be covered. So, make sure to negotiate the costs and payment plans with the psychiatrist before the first meeting.

Think about what issues you're experiencing that require care when you first assign. Although you should still work some of that out with your psychiatrist, a clearer understanding of your issues will serve as a beginning point in advance. Check again for their qualifications and experience, especially with your questions. Some therapists may not meet the requisite qualifications. If first time around you don't find the right one, don't give up. Do the research, and locate a reliable Cognitive Behavioral Therapist.

Emotional Habits and CBT

It is commonly said that human beings are creatures of habit.

Typically, this definition is used in relation to our behavior—though in recent years, we have noticed that the way we think is also commonplace. Since we all realize how we think has a great deal to do with how we act, a good question to ask is, what are my emotional habits?

What Are the Emotional Habits?

Emotional habits do have two dimensions:

How we generally feel as we go about the task of living our lives, day after day.

If we react emotionally (again and again) to particular situations/events occurring in our lives.

The thoughts and emotions cannot be separated; they exist in unison during almost every moment of life. To be person, in other terms, is to be in a state of continuous thinking and feeling—and the implicit complexities of that continuing subjective experience are partly normal. Anxiety behaviors, depression, anger, irritability, helplessness, frustration, envy, fear, worry, and so on. When we constantly feel nervous and worried about what others think of us, or anxious about what our future holds, or frustrated and insecure about how our lives compete with others, it can be said that we have become used to repeating patterns. This is not to condemn oneself or minimize the impact of real-life events and situations. The point is to put us in the driver's seat and suggest that if we've been used to these habits, then we can re-accustom ourselves to them and to other / healthier trends.

Beware of the Oversimplification of CBT (Cognitive Behavioral Therapy)

CBT is of enormous benefit to people all over the world, and to the field of mental health in general. However, the oversimplified assertion that you can alter your mindset and change your life (as it happens in media sound-bites) can misinterpret the true essence and meaning of CBT and the related methods of psychotherapy it has encouraged. Why? And it means that it's quick and convenient to adjust your outlook (like adjusting your shampoo or something). This may even bring us to the mistaken assumption that the job is done because you're 'changing your mind.' That cannot be any further from the facts. To become agents of change in regard to our own ways of thinking and feeling is analogous to learning and mastering a musical instrument that I will talk to for a minute. First, another argument regarding the possibility of oversimplifying CBT. Let us look at this idea, which is often heard:

It is not what happens to us that matters the most, but how we react to what happens to us. I couldn't be more decided. However, it is crucial that we go a move forward and explain that our INITIAL response/reaction to 'stuff' is not nearly as crucial as how we reply overtime—over the course of the hour, day, week, month, and year. We might blow up, shut down, stress out, diminish, take no notice, fall down, have a heart attack, etc. Okay, great, so what are we doing THEN? And after that, THEN... what do we do? And so forth. My point is that what matters most is not the discreet moments but the ongoing (and always imperfect) process of striving for a good living. It is important to do that because we question ourselves: Is my fundamental orientation to a life centered on constantly seeking to learn and grow from the challenges and complexities of life? Am I leading a more emotional existence of accusing someone, avoiding responsibility, and whining constantly that things are not the way I would like them to be? Changing thinking & emotional patterns is like learning to play the guitar. It's lifelong learning to become someone who can play the guitar (which I do) and I think most would agree that it's ideally pursued as a love job. The same is true in my view for learning to change our thinking and emotional habits. Yes, in our efforts to learn any musical instrument there are 'techniques' that we employ. The most critical part of studying how to play an instrument, though, is NOT the strategies or methods, nor is it the teaching system or even the teacher's standard. What counts most is the degree of enthusiasm and commitment that the student brings to the project, along with the amount of artistic practice and success he/she puts in overtime.

The Ethos of Continuous Learning and Development

We have also been born in a society riddled with social signals encouraging instant gratification and an attitude of rapid obsession. So, it's no surprise we've built an over-reliance on shortcuts, suggestions, and the "newest cutting edge" strategies. Of reality, they don't offer the goods; what really succeeds in doing something meaningful is to apply the fundamentals over and again, while actively drawing on the gradual experience and ability increases. In the school of life, the mentality of "pulling all-nights" and "cramming" for exams will not represent us well; what truly matters in this realm is a sincere and consistent dedication to ideals and activities that suit us well and others.

CHAPTER 10:

What Is Cognitive Processing Therapy?

Cognitive Processing Therapy (CPT) is a therapeutic approach that targets changes in thinking that are typical following a traumatic event, including changes in the way you think about yourself and the world. The goal of CPT is to help you learn to examine your thinking and determine if there is an alternative point of view. Because of how profoundly trauma changes your thinking, a part of this work requires you to go back and revisit the traumatic event in order to understand how your current—often unhelpful—thought processes developed.

When we're exposed to information that doesn't match our view of the world, we typically do one of two things in response: We either change the information to fit our beliefs ("maybe I wasn't really raped") or we change our beliefs ("maybe bad things do happen to good people"). Sometimes, belief changes become extreme, such as thinking I always make mistakes or only bad things happen to me (which is sometimes called overgeneralization).

In CPT, the first step is to work on integrating the traumatic experience into your belief systems and memories so that you begin to come to terms with what happened. The next step is to modify any overgeneralized beliefs. Some of our emotions are biologically hardwired—like feeling fear in response to danger or sadness in response to loss—but many of our emotions, such as guilt and shame, are thought to be "manufactured" as a result of faulty thinking. The good news is manufactured emotions often dissipate following the changes in thinking CPT helps cultivate.

Cognitive tasks, including something as simple as labeling objects, activate the logical part of our brains, like the prefrontal cortex, which in turn helps regulate the emotional parts of the brain like the amygdala. Using your words to talk about and analyze the traumatic event, calms overactive emotional responses. The goal of CPT's therapeutic exercises, which we'll explore below, is to increase flexibility in your thinking and support your ability to think critically about what you've been saying to yourself about why the traumatic event happened and what it means about yourself, others, and the world around you. "Stuck points" are negative trauma-related thoughts or beliefs that are exaggerated or distorted in some way that will ultimately impede your recovery. Specifically, stuck points are the problematic ways you evaluate the traumatic event, like the common belief that if you'd acted differently, you could have kept it from happening. These beliefs could be new (post-trauma), or the trauma might have served as confirmation of some negative beliefs you already held. For instance, someone who, prior to a traumatic event, placed great trust in authority figures like the police may begin to develop a new belief that police are worthless and untrustworthy because they weren't able to respond quickly enough to prevent an assault. In contrast, someone who went through a similar scenario but already had difficulty trusting authority would confirm their long-standing beliefs following the trauma.

If you've been thinking the same things over and over again ever since your traumatic event, without reconsidering those thoughts or exploring alternative ideas, the thoughts have likely become habitual and entrenched in your beliefs. In order to begin to shift those thought patterns, you must approach your thoughts and beliefs with an open mind and a willingness to challenge your assumptions. CPT was developed to treat a range of disorders and mental health difficulties, including PTSD, depression, anxiety, personality difficulties, problems with substance use, and difficulties surrounding self-esteem and self-concept. CPT has been heavily researched, and there is strong evidence for its effectiveness across a variety of populations. Study results indicate that participants have seen significant decreases in self-reported PTSD as well as in other trauma-related mental health difficulties, both during treatment and at six-month follow-ups.

Common Problematic Thought Patterns

Sometimes called *cognitive distortions* or "stinking' thinking,"' the following list of problematic thought patterns has been associated with both depression and PTSD. Learning about these patterns can help you begin to identify the thinking that may be causing you increased distress.

We all engage in distorted thinking at times, but when these thought patterns become habitual, significant emotional distress can result. Once you learn to identify the ways in which your thinking can be distorted, your goal becomes to "catch it and correct it" before the thoughts lead to negative emotions.

Magnification and Minimization: This occurs when you either exaggerate or minimize the importance of something. For example, you may discount your achievements, but become excessively focused on your mistakes.

Catastrophizing: Focusing your attention on the worst possible outcome of a situation and assuming that it is a likely possibility.

Overgeneralization: When you make a broad interpretation from one event. For example, you might think, *I felt awkward on that date. I am always so awkward.* Or, *I got the wrong answer to that question. I am always so stupid.*

Magical Thinking: Linking actions to unrelated situations. For example, believing those bad things will not happen to you because you are a good person.

Personalization: This occurs when you take things too personally or relate situations to yourself that may actually have nothing to do with you. For example, *She looks pissed off. I must have done something wrong.*

Jumping to Conclusions: Making assumptions or interpreting the meaning of a situation with little or no evidence.

Mind Reading: When you interpret the thoughts and beliefs of others without adequate evidence. *He didn't invite me to go to lunch. He probably hates me.*

Fortune-Telling: When you assume that a situation will turn out badly without adequate evidence. *I will never stop feeling this way.*

Emotional Reasoning: Assuming that your emotions reflect reality. *I feel angry; therefore, you must have treated me badly* or *I am sad, therefore, I am not going to get what I want.*

Disqualifying the Positive: Focusing only on the negative aspects of a situation while ignoring the positive aspects. For example, you may receive many compliments from your friends, but remember the single piece of negative feedback someone told you.

"Should" Statements: Fixating on beliefs that things should be a certain way. *I should be married by now. I should be happy.*

All-or-Nothing Thinking: Thinking in absolute terms, such as *always*, *never*, and *every*. *I never do anything right. I am always going to be lonely.*

CHAPTER 11:

Somatic or "Right-Brain" Psychotherapy

Most forms of talk therapy focus on the left side of the brain that deals with talking and logical thought. For example, in cognitive therapy, you discuss your negative thoughts and feelings with your therapist and try to think of more positive or constructive ones. In "person-centered" counseling (the most common form of advice), you discuss your counselor's issues, and your counselor provides periodic feedback. In somatic therapy, the client shifts from exploring and analyzing their thoughts, behaviors, and personal history to focusing on their internal sensations. For example, the therapist might notice that the client looks uptight and distressed. She then asks where the client is experiencing physical tension. The client mentions the tension in their jaw and shoulders, and a feeling of irritation and anger related to a recent argument with a relative. Hence, there is a shift in mental activity from the logical, verbal, left neocortex to the right side of the brain, which is a more intuitive part of the brain that interacts more closely with the body, brain stem, and the limbic system.

A big advantage of this type of therapy is that it avoids many of the ego-clashes than often occur in traditional talk therapy. Instead of probing deeply into your personal history or situation, the main focus is on your physical sensations. It means that the therapist isn't challenging the client to change their attitude, thinking radically, or behavior. The client doesn't have to divulge lots of personal information if they don't want to. The primary requirement is to be willing to focus on your physical sensations, take note of any related thoughts or feelings. A process that tends to pique people's curiosity and can often be quite pleasant, particularly if you unlock an area of physical tension or discomfort. Another benefit of somatic therapy is it tends to be less mentally demanding that cognitive therapy, which can require a lot of mental effort and discipline on the part of the client.

Sometimes the therapist may engage in small experiments with the client, such as asking them to exaggerate a tension pattern in the shoulders, or seeing how the client reacts if they increase or decrease eye contact. As somatic psychotherapy progresses, the therapist works within the client's window of tolerance while slightly pushing their boundaries to widen their tolerance window. For example, if the client is looking relaxed during therapy, the therapist can test their comfort zone by doing role-play exercises and seeing how their body language changes when they forced to act in a way they aren't using. The client and therapist may also set specific goals, such as increasing social confidence, or increasing their ability to tolerate feelings of restlessness and boredom without resorting to drugs or alcohol. If the goal is to improve the human spirit, the focus might be on sensing their posture and tolerating unpleasant sensations in the chest and belly. If the goal is to explore feelings of sadness, body awareness might direct towards facial expressions and the head's downward tilt.

The main drawback of somatic psychotherapy is a lack of trained therapists with the skills to take full advantage of it. It can take a lot of training and experience for the therapist to know what body language cues are meaningful indicators of underlying mental stress, and which are not. Most psychologists and counselors receive very little training in somatic therapy or body awareness. Despite an increasing amount of research, somatic treatment can be useful for several stress-related disorders such as post-traumatic stress disorder. Some somatic therapists say the relative lack of interest in this form of treatment is due to cultural factors. Over the last few hundred years, western culture has tended to see the mind and body as independent of one another. Some critics, some as medical historian Edward Shorter, say this tendency has been a problem in 20th-century psychiatry, with its over-emphasis on Freudian psychotherapy in the 50s and 60s and later, by drugs aimed at correcting supposed chemical imbalances in the brain. However, the increasing popularity of eastern mind-body practices like yoga is sparking a greater interest in developing western mind-body practices that incorporate the latest scientific knowledge about the wider nervous system and its effects on the mind and body.

While somatic therapy for symptoms of anxiety and depression is yet to go mainstream, it is already quite widely used for dealing with PTSD, as well as some physical health problems, such as chronic back and nerve pain.

Where somatic psychotherapy is unavailable or unaffordable, body-based somatic therapy can combine with self-administered cognitive therapy. In self-administered cognitive therapy, as outlined in popular self-help books like David Burns' Feeling Good: The New Mood Therapy, you keep a written record of persistent negative thoughts, critique your ideas and come up with constructive responses. This basic DIY cognitive therapy approach can combine with somatic, brain-body methods, such as the following exercise suggested by Pat Ogden:

- Identify a persistent negative belief (e.g., I'm an angry person and can't do anything about it)
- Observe how your body reacts to the negative mindset (e.g., my jaw and shoulders tense up, and I can't think clearly)
- Think of a different physical movement you could make (e.g., I could clench my left hand, or shake my shoulders)
- Make the alternative movement several times
- Make a mental or written note of any improvement in your thoughts or feelings (e.g., I feel less tension in the upper body, and I don't feel quite so angry).

Self-administered cognitive therapy is quite effective for mood disorders, so there's every reason to expect some positive benefits combining self-administered cognitive therapy with body-based treatment.

A basic cognitive therapy diary is divided into three columns. In column one, you write down your beliefs and thoughts, such as "I am lazy," and in column two, you write down the mental consequences of your dreams, such as "I feel worthless." In the third column, you write down your rational responses to your negative thoughts, such as "I'm over-generalizing, I often put in a lot of effort," or "this simplistic thinking doesn't help me to feel positive or want to try harder."

CHAPTER 12:

What Is EMDR?

EMDR—Eye Movement Desensitization and Reprocessing

Eye Movement Desensitization and Reprocessing or EMDR designed, and EMDR is just one of the more recent "energy" therapies which were recently recognized and accepted by the expert community and the public. They're called "power" treatments since they work much faster than conventional "talk therapy" or psychotherapy. Other hastened remedies are NET(TM), hypnosis, TFT, along with the TFT offshoots like EFT.

EMDR/Eye Movement Desensitization and Reprocessing is an alternative fast remedy that functions by targeting the core areas of the mind. Chat treatment, in contrast, concentrates primarily on the Prefrontal Cortex and is based on insight into impact change. EMDR works mostly through the subconscious mind, although penetration often comes as an outcome.

It's speculated that EMDR also activates and immediately affects the mind/body continuum and so can be classified as an "energy conservation" too. Energy psychology is derived from Chinese medicine and more especially about the acupuncture/acupressure system. This system considers that chi, which can be energy or electricity travels throughout the meridians or rivers of acupuncture points in your human body. This energy can get jaded by bodily, psychological, or traumatic facets. Energy psychology postulates that by balancing this particular system, the issues from these types of triggers are quickly alleviated.

Eye Movement Desensitization and Reprocessing functions on several issues, but is particularly successful with traumas both present and past.

The therapist immediately moves their hands back and forth while requesting the client to move just their eyes whenever they monitor the hand movement. The client is guided to think about this injury through the process. Following 20-25 hand motions, the client is asked to concentrate on what difficulty, feeling, idea, or facet of this injury is currently most notable. The process is then repeated with this new goal. The issue is often painlessly solved after just a couple of sessions when compared with conventional treatment, which often lasts for weeks or even years.

This motion of the eyes imitates the REM or rapid eye movements, which can be created when an individual is dreaming. It's speculated that we change short-term memory to long-term memory through REM. The psychological part of long-term memory is considerably reduced and can be recalled as though from a fantastic distance. Any injury may get trapped, particularly if it's painful and acute. This sort of treatment can easily and effectively get rid of this impediment and also reprocess the info, thus relieving the issue.

Number for Clinicians

Eye Movement Desensitization and Reprocessing (EMDR) is a form of psychotherapy that was initially made to relieve the distress associated with traumatic memories. Adaptive Data Processing version posits that EMDR treatment eases the obtaining and processing of traumatic memories as well as other negative life experiences and to deliver them into a flexible resolution. After successful treatment using EMDR treatment, affective distress is alleviated, unwanted beliefs are reformulated, and bodily stimulation is diminished.

During EMDR treatment, the customer attends to mentally upsetting material in short successive doses while simultaneously focusing on an outside stimulus. Therapist guided medial eye movements would be the most frequently used external stimulation, but various different stimuli such as hand-tapping and sound stimulation are usually utilized. EMDR therapy eases the access to this traumatic memory system, in such a way that data processing is improved, with new institutions formulated between the traumatic memory and even more elastic memories or data.

These new institutions are considered to lead to full data processing, and new understanding, elimination of psychological distress, and growth of cognitive insights. EMDR treatment employs a 3-pronged protocol:

(1) The previous events which have laid the basis for importance have been processed, and hammering new associative connections with elastic advice;

(2) The recent conditions that evoke distress are concentrated, and external and internal causes are desensitized;

(3) Imaginary templates of potential events have been integrated, to help the customer in obtaining the skills necessary for flexible functioning.

What is EMDR?

For Laymen

EMDR (Eye Movement Desensitization and Reprocessing) is a type of psychotherapy that enables individuals to heal in the indicators and psychological distress, which would be the end result of upsetting life adventures. Repeated studies show that by employing EMDR treatment, people may experience the advantages of childbirth that took decades to make a difference. It's widely believed that acute emotional pain requires a lengthy time to cure. EMDR treatment shows that the brain can actually be cured of an emotional injury as your system recovers from bodily injury. If you cut your hand, your system functions to close the wound. When a foreign object or recurrent harm irritates the wound, then it festers and triggers pain. When the irritant is removed, recovery resumes.

EMDR treatment shows a similar sequence of events as happens with psychological processes. Your brain's information processing method obviously goes toward psychological wellness. In the event the machine is blocked or obscured from the effect of an upsetting event, the psychological wound festers and can result in extreme suffering.

When the cube is removed, recovery resumes. Employing the comprehensive protocols and processes learned in EMDR treatment training sessions, clinicians assist customers to trigger their normal healing procedures.

Over 30 positively controlled studies are performed on EMDR treatment. A few of the studies show that 84%-90% of single-trauma sufferers no longer have post-traumatic anxiety disorder after just three 90-minute sessions. Another study, financed by the HMO Kaiser Permanente, found that 100 percent of those single-trauma sufferers and 77 percent of multiple injury victims no longer have symptoms associated with PTSD after just six 50-minute sessions. In a different study, 77 percent of combat veterans were complimentary from PTSD at 12 sessions. There's been much research about EMDR treatment and it is currently considered an effective type of therapy for injury and other upsetting experiences by renowned associations like the American Psychiatric Association, the World Health Organization, and the Department of Defense. Given the global recognition as a successful way of treating injury, you will be able to readily see how EMDR treatment could be effective in curing the "regular" memories which are why people have reduced self-esteem, feelings of powerlessness, and the myriad of other issues that bring them for treatment. More than 100,000 clinicians around the globe use the treatment. Huge number of people have been treated successfully within the last 25 decades.

EMDR treatment is an eight-phase treatment. The eye moves (or alternative bilateral stimulation) can be utilized during a portion of this session. After the clinician has decided which memory to aim, he requests the customer to hold unique facets of the event or idea in their mind and also to utilize their eyes to monitor the therapist's hands because it goes back and forth through the customer's area of vision. As this occurs, for reasons considered by a Harvard researcher to become correlated with all the biological mechanisms involved with Rapid Eye Movement (REM) sleep, inner relationships appear and the customers start to process the memory and also upsetting feelings. Ineffective EMDR treatment, the significance of debilitating events is changed on a psychological level. As an example, a rape victim changes from feeling dread and self-disgust into holding the firm belief, "I lived it, and I'm powerful. "Unlike talk treatment, the insights customers gain in EMDR treatment result not too much from clinician interpretation; but, by the customer's own hastened intellectual and psychological processes. The web impact is that customers conclude EMDR treatment feeling permitted from the most experiences that after debased them. Their wounds didn't only shut, rather they've transformed. As a consequence of this EMDR curative procedure, the customers' ideas, feelings, and behavior are robust indicators of psychological wellness and settlement—without talking in detail or doing assignments employed in different remedies.

EMDR treatment is really a phased, concentrated method of treating trauma along with other ailments by reconnecting the customer in a protected and quantified method into the pictures, self-thoughts, feelings, and body sensations connected with the injury, and enabling the natural healing powers of their mind to move toward elastic resolution. It's founded upon the premise that symptoms happen when injury and other harmful or challenging experiences interrupt the mind's natural ability to cure, and also that the recovery process can be eased and performed via brute stimulation while the customer is re-experiencing the injury from the context of a secure surrounding like their therapist's office (double awareness).

How Does EMDR Work?

During EMDR, people safely reprocess traumatic data until it's no longer emotionally disruptive to their own lives. There are just 8 stages of therapy, and at the Rapid Eye Movement stage, the person targets a tumultuous memory and explains the belief that they hold about themselves. When it's connected to the adverse memory (by way of instance, in handling abuse, the individual could think, "I deserved it") the person then formulates a favorable impression they would love to own ("I'm a rewarding and decent individual in charge of my own life

"). Each of the senses and feelings that move together the memory has been recognized. The person subsequently reviews the memory whilst focusing on the external stimulus that makes bilateral eye motion. Normally this is achieved by seeing the therapist precede two hands. After every pair of bilateral moves, the person is asked how they believe. This procedure proceeds until the memory is no more upsetting to the person. The person is calculating the injury.

The chosen positive view is subsequently set up, via analog motion, to substitute the negative impression.

Sessions generally last for one hour. It's speculated that EMDR works since the "uncanny stimulation" by-passes the region of the brain that processes memories, but is now becoming trapped on account of the injury and can be preventing the mind from appropriate storage and processing of their memory. During EMDR, people process the memory and that results in a peaceful resolution leading to improved consciousness regarding both formerly disturbing event as well as also negative thoughts about themselves, which have grown from the first traumatic event.

Who Replies EMDR Treatment?

EMDR treatment has been endorsed by The American Psychiatric Association and the International Society for Traumatic Stress Research. Moreover, it's used by the United States Department of Veterans Affairs, the Department of Defense, and abroad associations, such as the United Kingdom Department of Public Health, along with the Israeli National Council for Mental Health.

There are currently over 30 regular gold Studies documenting the efficacy of EMDR treatment within the last 30 years, having issues like rape and sexual abuse, combat injury, childhood trauma and failure, life-threatening injuries, and symptoms like stress, depression, and substance misuse.

Edy Nathan, MA, LCSW, is an accredited Psychotherapist with more than 20 years' experience and has been licensed as an EMDR practitioner, believes that this kind of treatment has the capability to cure individuals that suffer from all kinds of injury. "Exactly what the procedure does is to change how we process that the existence of the physiological, psychological, and mental effects related especially to some traumatic event," she explained. "The pain and feel of risk carried within oneself following a traumatic event grasp the soul with this kind of order it contributes to a feeling of being in emotional quicksand.

EMDR functions to interrogate perception systems, also called cognitions, which affects the negative cognition by means of a string of lateral eye movements, etc.

CHAPTER 13:

Trauma and PSTD—
PTSD Treatment with Hypnotherapy

Trauma is something most of us will have to deal with on our life journey at some point. Yes, it is projected that sometimes 50% to 90% of us will have to deal with it.

Psychological trauma is always a product of an experience that overwhelms the victim and does not handle or fully control the emotions produced by that experience.

The subconscious mind is disturbed by distress by an incident or a number of events, and this has profoundly affected the individual's functioning.

Essential and effective though it is certainly for the traumatized individual, the actual experience itself is less essential on a psychological level than its interpretation and reaction.

It explains why one person can very well shrug a similar event off but creates real difficulties in another. What can be a traumatic experience is not traumatic for one person.

Trauma itself can happen on a life journey at any time.

This can occur during infancy, and as a result of, for example, psychological, physical abuse, or extreme poverty and can leave the child traumatized in adulthood.

And traumas arise later in life, triggered by neglect, injuries, injury, crime, war, death, and natural disaster.

Although trauma itself is painful, about 8% are more debilitating and paralyzing effects of the Post-Traumatic Stress Disorder (PTSD) trauma.

If left untreated, PTSD can have serious consequences for the patient, serious implications, and ability to function at work or interpersonal level.

PTSD also stems from real physical damage encounters or experiences. Occasionally, however, psychological and emotional distress may cause it where no actual physical harm is involved.

Very often, though, it blends both aspects.

While a persistent and significant emotional response to trauma is essentially post-traumatic stress disorder, it differs from combat stress or traumatic stress in that it is typically much more severe and not at all transitory.

PTSD has also historically been identified as shell shock, combat tiredness, and post-traumatic stress syndrome.

Yet fighting is not sufficient to be affected by PTSD, any real trauma to the nervous system—such as a car accident or death, addiction to drugs or sexual assault—can lead to it.

However, whatever the cause, the resulting symptoms of trauma are real and distressing for a person who has to experience them.

Those with this type of trauma can experience chronic and acute anxiety, frustration, sleep disturbance, disturbing thoughts, breathtaking disorder, or nightmares. We also find it very difficult to think about trauma cases.

We find it difficult or impossible to effectively deal with and incorporate these issues on the subconscious level of the mind, owing to their upsetting nature.

And here, transformational hypnotherapy with experience can be extremely useful, offering psychological care that can lead to a full recovery from trauma.

The unconscious mind, working with a skilled and highly trained transformational hypnotherapist, can be guided to reconstitute traumatic experiences of the past in order to neutralize and reverse the damage.

The truth is that the person survived, given the frightening expectations and beliefs that were instilled during the traumatic experience. Ultimately, he or she did it through.

The details of the traumatic experience exist with the right trauma therapy, but the meaning and psychological symptoms previously induced by these facts have always been changed.

Effective trauma care allows the patient to deal with what happened so that the person can then let his or her life go and go on.

For example, leaving the traumatized person in no way means that he has to forget what has happened in the past.

Nonetheless, it very often means that an abuser or any person who has actively participated in the traumatic experience must be encouraged to forgive.

It's not for religious reasons, nor is it altruistic in any way. It's simply because failure to do so holds the person in contact with the past, retains and supports the harm the ongoing trauma pain, the continuing emotional and mental trauma.

It must be stressed that the traumatized person is encouraged to forgive. It is not necessarily the person or people who may have caused the trauma. In reality, the person or persons responsible for this very often do not know forgiveness.

But the traumatized person is released and released through real forgiveness. The patient is shown how to forgive the past with the help of transformational hypnotherapy so as to heal and move on with their lives.

If you or someone you care about has the truly debilitating and deteriorating consequences of trauma, it can really be done.

The Benefits of Hypnotherapy as PTSD Therapy

The quality of a person's life can be severely affected by post-traumatic stress disorder (PTSD). Numerous PTSD treatments with hypnosis are one of the choices. Is hypnotherapy an appropriate way to overcome PTSD, and what does it bring about?

What is Post-Treatment Stress Disorder?

Traumatized people may feel a sense of loss, anxiety, panic, and fear. Whenever these symptoms last a very long time and tend to affect the quality of life, they are referred to as post-traumatic stress disorder.

PTSD is characterized by the re-experience of traumatic incidents and hallucinations, the inability to deal with stress, and heightened fear or anxiety. Reminders such as fast breathing, intense physical reactions, and general apathy are also typical for PTSD.

Events like War, death of a loved one, natural disasters, children's problems and abuse, kidnapping, sexual abuse, domestic violence, and aviation crashes often lead to this condition. Any other life-changing and devastating incident may also contribute to PTSD.

How can PTSD sufferers Hypnosis Aid People with PTSD be recommended to try hypnotherapy because it helps in several ways?

Many of the effects experienced by PTSD are close to what happens during the hypnotherapy. Individuals with PTSD respond to hypnosis quite well and have access to the guidance of the therapist to painful memories. These memories can be restructured by hypnosis to prevent future PTSD symptoms.

Hypnosis and self-hypnosis are also great instruments for managing PTSD recurrences.

Various studies have been conducted to test these arguments. Hypnosis treatment is at least as effective as alternative treatments for PTSD, such as psychotherapy, scientific evidence on the efficacy of hypnotherapy. A study was conducted in 2005 in order to compare hypnotherapy against other therapies widely used to relieve symptoms of PTSD. The findings vary from person to person based on how suggestible the individual with PTSD is. Sixty-seven PTSD participants agreed to take part in the research. Hypnotherapy, cognitive behavioral therapy, and counseling were the approaches used for these cases.

Research showed that people diagnosed with hypnotherapy as well as cognitive behavioral therapy, had fewer signs of PTSD six months after the session. Persons receiving advice alone had a higher level of lifestyle problems related to PTSD.

Those with hypnotherapy have reported lower re-experience incidences of the traumatic event.

People with PTSD will display up to 93% recovery after six hypnotherapy sessions.

The number is 72 percent with cognitive behavioral therapy after 22 sessions and 38 percent with psychotherapy after 600 sessions.

These research and figures show that hypnosis can be used to improve the quality of life of those with past trauma and unable to heal.

Individuals with PTSD are potentially more easily hypnotized than others. It raises the value of this treatment option for people suffering from post-traumatic stress disorders.

8 Tips for Understanding Someone with PTSD

PTSD makes it difficult to communicate. Most survivors cannot find words to describe what they feel. Even when they do, it's very natural for them not to share their experience comfortably. Elements of embarrassment, terror, anger, remorse, and sorrow sometimes impede a calm, concentrated debate.

Friends and families (and anyone else who is not the PTSD trigger but stands by while someone is trying to cure) need a PTSD language translation. Through awareness, understanding, and empathy, you will have the best time to respond and connect during the healing process to your beloved PTSD. The more helpful and supportive you can be from the PTSD point of view. Now is the time for understanding, tolerance, and empathy.

#1—Power is information. Knowing the triggering mechanism, mental trauma reactions, PTSD warning signs, and symptoms, and the treatment options available to PTSD help you to understand better, maintain and direct your loved PTSD through diagnosis, care, and healing.

We need you to be straightforward, focused, and updated.

#2—Trauma affects us, trauma changes us. Upon trauma, we want to believe—as you do—that life will return like it was; that we can go on like what we were. It doesn't work like that. Trauma leaves a profound and indelible soul mark. Trauma cannot be felt, and a psychological transition cannot be witnessed.

Expect that we will be modified. Consider our evolutionary need. Join us on this trip. Help us.

#3—Our personality has been concealed by the PTSD. One of PTSD's biggest problems is that it takes over our whole view. We don't see clearly anymore. We don't see the world as we saw it before the trauma. It's dangerous, volatile, and challenging at every moment.

Remind us carefully and give us the opportunity to engage in an identity outside PTSD and trauma.

#4—We are not in our true self anymore. In the face of trauma, our true self-isolation and a healing self tend to shield us.

Believe in us, even if they are momentarily buried, our true selves still remain.

#5—How we act can't help us. We do not always monitor because we run on a kind of autopilot. PTSD is a survival mode exacerbated. We have feelings that make us nervous and overwhelmed. We behave in defense of those emotions that we are unable to control.

We often cannot avoid the frustration, tears, or other destructive habits that are so difficult for you to bear. Be patient with us.

#6—We can't make sense. Because our perspective is dominated by fear, we do not always think straight or follow the advice of those who do.

Even if your words don't seem to touch us, keep reaching out. You never know when we'll think of what you do, and it's going to ease, lead, relax, or encourage us.

#7—We can't 'get it' just. It's easy to imagine time from outside and memories fade away and pain is relegated to the past life. Unfortunately, nothing fades with PTSD. Our bodies are not going to let us forget. Due to the rising chemicals that enhance every memory, we can no longer walk away from the past than you can.

Honor our struggle with events to make peace. Do not hurry us. Do not pressure us. Trying to speed up our rehabilitation will only make us add more to it.

#8—We're not living in denial! Living with PTSD takes a tremendous effort. We know something is wrong, even if we don't admit it. When you approach us and deny that there is an issue that really codes for: "I do my best." To do what you say will need too much time, separate the emphasis from what holds us together. Sometimes just waking up and continuing our day-to-day routine is the first step in recovery. Reduce our tension by providing us with a safe place where we can find support.

CHAPTER 14:

Can Medication Help?

Medicines have long been prescribed for the treatment of PTSD; drug treatment is not as effective as trauma-focused psychotherapies in persons with this disorder. I will put here the different medications used to treat PTSD and their effectiveness based on meta-analyses of randomized clinical trials. While medication is not considered a first-line treatment for PTSD, it may sometimes be necessary to relieve symptoms to the point that people are able and willing to engage in trauma-focused psychotherapies.

Case Vignette

Richard is a 25-year old married male serving in the U.S. Army and stationed in Afghanistan. This is his third deployment to the region, and while the first two deployments went well, the present one had been very difficult. Shortly after arriving in Kabul, his armored personnel carrier drove over an IED (improvised explosive device), killing a close buddy from his previous tours, riding with him and severely wounding another member of his team (leg severely crushed, likely needing amputation). Richard suffered a mild closed head injury from the blast but was alert enough after he awoke to realize the carnage around him. Shaken by this experience, he began experiencing frequent flashbacks of the explosion during the day and nightmares where he saw the faces and wounded bodies of his comrades. Unable to continue his duties over the next two months, he was evaluated by behavioral health, who diagnosed him with PTSD. As a result, Richard was sent back home to the U.S. to recover. Since this was his third and last deployment and he was ending the period of his enlistment, plans were made for his discharge from the military. His PTSD symptoms, however, persisted after returning home, affecting his ability to work and interfering with his family relationships. At his wife's encouragement, Richard scheduled an appointment at the local Veterans Affairs hospital for treatment.

The psychologist who evaluated him at the VA confirmed the diagnosis of PTSD and recommended Prolonged Exposure Therapy (PET). After hearing about what this would entail, Richard refused. He could not imagine reliving the horrific experiences he had gone through in Afghanistan. The psychologist recommended he also see a psychiatrist, who after evaluating him, recommended a trial of paroxetine (trade name Paxil). Richard agreed and started the treatment. After four weeks, he noticed that his hyperarousal, anxiety and intrusive flashbacks were somewhat better, as was his sleep. The psychiatrist recommended he reconsider therapy with the psychologist. Now that he was feeling a bit better, Richard agreed and began a 3-month treatment program of weekly PET.

The reader is now warned. I will describe the medications used to treat PTSD and the research that has examined their effectiveness.

The various classes of medications used to treat PTSD (not all of which are recommended by current guidelines). These include antidepressants, anticonvulsants, antipsychotics, benzodiazepines, α1 adrenergic antagonists, glutaminergic agonists, and other somatic therapies

Antidepressants

The only medications for PTSD (and only if trauma-focused psychotherapies are not available or not preferred) currently recommended by the U.S. Food and Drug Administration are paroxetine and sertraline (i.e., serotonin reuptake inhibitors). These recommendations are now almost 10 years old (Stein et al., 2009). The American Psychological Association and Veterans Affairs/Department of Defense treatment guidelines have broadened the range of medications now recommended for PTSD to include paroxetine, sertraline, fluoxetine, and venlafaxine for the treatment of PTSD (and only these four medications).

Serotonin Reuptake Inhibitors (SSRIs). SSRIs inhibit the reuptake of serotonin in the space between neurons in the brain, making it more available for neuronal transmission. Defects in serotonin are thought to play an important part in the physiological abnormalities found in PTSD. In three meta-analyses involving more than 20 studies in over 3,000 patients, SSRI's overall have an ES ranging from -.23 to -.48, which indicates a small to moderate clinical effect (Watts et al., 2013; Hoskins et al., 2015; Lee et al., 2016). For individual SSRI's the ES of sertraline (Zoloft) ranges from -.13 to -.51 (again, small to moderate); for paroxetine (Paxil), the ES ranges from -.36 to -.74 (moderate); the ES of fluoxetine (Prozac) ranges from -.23 to -.43 (small to moderate); and for citalopram (Celexa), the range is +.13 to +.74 (this medication actually causes worse symptoms compared to placebo!). Note that SSRIs are the most commonly prescribed antidepressant for the treatment of Veterans with PTSD in Veterans Affairs (VA) hospitals and clinics (Bernardy et al., 2012). However, the ESs for SSRI's are dwarfed by those of trauma-focused psychotherapies that are typically -1.00 or larger, which is the basis for current recommendations.

Serotonin-Norepinephrine Reuptake Inhibitors (SNRIs). Of the two main SNRIs, venlafaxine (Effexor) and duloxetine (Cymbalta), only venlafaxine has been examined in a randomized clinical trial examining its efficacy in PTSD. Although there was an initial case report that PTSD symptom was made worse by duloxetine (Deneys & Ahearn, 2006), research since then has largely dispelled such concerns based on at least two 8-12-week open-label/naturalistic trials whose results were quite promising (Villareal et al., 2010; Walderhaug et al., 2010). With regard to venlafaxine, Watts et al (2013) and Hoskins et al (2015) reported small to moderate effect sizes

(-.20 to -.48) based on two large clinical trials. Although the FDA has not approved venlafaxine for the treatment of PTSD in the U.S., the British Association of Psychopharmacology considers venlafaxine to be a first-line medication (Baldwin et al., 2014). Venlafaxine is also one of the four antidepressants recommended by the VA/DoD (2017) and APA (2017) practice guidelines as monotherapy for PTSD in patients who choose not to engage in or are unable to access trauma-focused psychotherapy.

Other Newer Antidepressants. A number of newer antidepressants, relative to older drugs (tricyclic antidepressants and monoamine oxidase inhibitors), have been examined for their benefits in treating PTSD. These include mirtazapine, bupropion, and nefazodone. Mirtazapine (Remeron), a serotonin and norepinephrine reuptake inhibitor with antihistaminic effects, is a relatively safe antidepressant that is sedating and increases appetite in those with weight loss. Watts et al. (2013) and Lee et al. (2016) reported that a single study of 29 patients (Davidson et al., 2003) found that mirtazapine's effects on PTSD symptoms did not differ from placebo over an 8-week trial on most PTSD measures. Bupropion (Wellbutrin), a norepinephrine and dopamine reuptake inhibitor (two catecholamines involved in emotional disorders), tends to increase energy, improve concentration, and reduce appetite, and like mirtazapine, is a relatively safe drug for use in middle-aged and older adults with other medical problems. Based on a single trial of 22 patients (Becker et al., 2007), both Watts et al and Lee et al reported that the effect of bupropion on PTSD symptoms assessed by the Clinician Assessed PTSD Scale (CAPS; the standard measure of PTSD symptoms in clinical trials today) did not differ from placebo in the 8-week trial. Finally, nefazodone (Serzone)—a moderate reuptake inhibitor of both serotonin and norepinephrine—is a sedating antidepressant (although less sedating than trazodone [Desyrel], its cousin). Based on a single study of 41 patients (Davis et al., 2004), nefazodone reduced PTSD symptoms on CAPS during a 12-week trial compared to placebo with a moderate ES (-.60) that achieved statistical significance (p=0.04). However, clinicians seldom use nefazodone today due to reports of liver toxicity.

Tricyclic Antidepressants (TCAs). TCAs such as amitriptyline, imipramine, nortriptyline, and desipramine are an older class of antidepressants that have lots of side-effects, including weight gain, sedation, anticholinergic, and cardiovascular effects. They are seldom used today now that SSRIs, NSRIs, and other safer antidepressants are available. Watts et al. (2013), one of the few meta-analyses of TCA effectiveness in PTSD, indicated a small effect (ES=-0.36, not different from placebo) based on three studies involving 110 patients.

Monoamine Oxidase Inhibitors (MAOIs). MAOIs such as phenelzine, tranylcypromine, and brofaromine are another class of older antidepressants that block the degradation of monoamine neurotransmitters (norepinephrine, serotonin, etc.), and like TCAs, are very effective for treating depression but have a host of unpleasant side-effects (weight gain, hypotension, and hypertensive crisis unless careful with diet to avoid tyramine-containing foods/drinks). Interestingly, in the first randomized clinical trial to examine the effectiveness of medication for the treatment of PTSD in 1988, an MAOI (phenelzine) and a TCA (imipramine) were compared to placebo in 34 combat Veterans with PTSD. They found that the MAOI (compared to the TCA) was particularly more effective than a placebo (Frank et al., 1988). However, Hoskins et al (2015) and Lee et al (2016), who reported on the results from two clinical trials involving the MAOI brofaromine (Consonar), did not find a difference compared to placebo when treating PTSD.

Antidepressants Overall. Watts et al (2013) reported that the overall effect of antidepressants on reducing PTSD symptoms compared to placebo in 32 randomized controlled trials involving 4,276 patients was small to moderate (ES=-.43, 95% CI=-.31 to -.53), justifying their use in the treatment of PTSD (but again as a second-line treatment after psychotherapy). Nearly three-quarters (70%) of patients with PTSD seen at VA hospitals and clinics are now prescribed an antidepressant (NPEC, 2016).

Anticonvulsants

There is uniform agreement among all the meta-analyses that anticonvulsants (i.e., anti-seizures drugs that are often used as mood stabilizers in bipolar disorder, including divalproex [Depakote], topiramate, and tiagabine, etc.) have no role in the treatment of PTSD. In none of these did the effects of anticonvulsants when used along with or combined with antidepressants exceed the effects of placebo in reducing PTSD symptoms. Watts et al. (2013) reported a meta-analysis of results from 7 studies of anticonvulsants involving 388 patients and found no significant effects compared to placebo; the same conclusion was reached by a more recent review by Lee et al (2016). There is some evidence that lamotrigine (Lamictal; an anticonvulsant used in bipolar disorder specifically for bipolar depression) has been useful in treating PTSD, although the evidence is not strong and does not justify recommending it.

Antipsychotics

Antipsychotics (used to treat psychotic symptoms), even newer second-generation drugs such as risperidone (Risperdal), olanzapine (Zyprexa), quetiapine (Seroquel), and aripiprazole (Abilify), play little role in the treatment of PTSD and none of the consensus guidelines recommend them, despite their small to moderate effects that differ significantly from placebo (ESs ranging from -.39 to -.49) (Watts et al., 2013; Lee et al., 2016). The main reason for not recommending these drugs is their side effects. Those effects include significant weight gain, increased blood sugar (especially in diabetics), risk of cardiovascular effects in older adults (including heart attack, death, and stroke), and extrapyramidal symptoms. Extrapyramidal symptoms are Parkinson-like symptoms (shaking, muscle stiffness, slowed movements) that were common in first-generation antipsychotics like haloperidol (Haldol) or chlorpromazine (Thorazine), even though they are less common with second-generation antipsychotics. Combining antipsychotics with antidepressants does not help either, where benefits of doing so have been no greater than placebo.

CHAPTER 15:

PSTD Methods

Individuals with post-traumatic stress disorder (PTSD) regularly battle with visits and exceptional manifestations of nervousness. These solid side effects of nervousness frequently lead individuals with PTSD to depend on undesirable methods for adapting, for example, through medication or liquor use. Luckily, there are various solid methods for adapting to nervousness that may enable your uneasiness to go down in power, become less regular, and additionally become increasingly decent.

Profound Breathing

Profound breathing can be a significant adapting expertise to learn. It might sound senseless, however, numerous individuals don't inhale appropriately. Regular breathing includes your stomach, an enormous muscle in your belly. At the point when you take in, your gut ought to grow. At the point when you inhale out, your midsection should fall. After some time, individuals overlook how to inhale along these lines and rather utilize their chest and shoulders. This causes short and shallow breaths, which can build pressure and nervousness. Luckily, it isn't past the point where it is possible to "re-realize" how to inhale and help shield yourself from stress. Practice this straightforward exercise to improve your breathing and battle uneasiness.

Dynamic Muscle Relaxation

Utilizing unwinding activities can be a successful method to lessen your pressure and tension. One unwinding activity called dynamic muscle unwinding centers around an individual switching back and forth among straining and loosening up various muscle bunches all through the body. This unwinding strategy is like a pendulum. The complete unwinding of your muscles can be gotten by first setting off to the next outrageous (that is, by straining your muscles). Likewise, by straining your muscles (a typical manifestation of uneasiness) and quickly loosening up them, the side effect of muscle pressure may turn into a sign to unwind after some time. You can gain proficiency with a fundamental dynamic muscle unwinding exercise in this article.

Care

Utilizing care for uneasiness can be useful. Care has been around for a very long time. Nonetheless, psychological wellness experts are starting to perceive that care can have numerous advantages for individuals experiencing challenges, for example, nervousness and despondency. Basically, care is tied in with being in contact with and mindful of the present minute. So frequently in our lives, we are latched onto our subconscious minds, made up for lost time in the uneasiness and stresses of everyday life. This activity will acquaint you with care and might be useful for getting you "out of your head" and in contact with the present minute.

Self-Monitoring

Self-observing can be a useful method for understanding your tension indications. We are all "animals of propensity." We regularly approach our day without deduction, being uninformed of much that goes on around us. This might be helpful in certain circumstances, however different occasions, this absence of mindfulness may make us feel as if our considerations and feelings are totally capricious and unmanageable. We can't generally address awkward side effects of uneasiness without first monitoring what circumstances raise these sentiments. Self-observing is a basic method for expanding this mindfulness.

Social Support

Again, and again, it has been discovered that discovering support from others can be a central point in helping individuals defeat the negative impacts of a horrible mishap and PTSD. Having somebody, you believe that you can converse with can be exceptionally useful for working through upsetting circumstances or for passionate approval. Be that as it may, basically having somebody accessible to converse with may not be sufficient. There are a few significant pieces to a steady relationship that might be especially valuable in helping somebody deal with their nervousness.

Self-Soothing

At the point when you are encountering tension, it is imperative to have methods for adapting to those emotions. For instance, searching out social help can be an astounding method for improving your state of mind. Be that as it may, the uneasiness related to side effects of PTSD can here and there happen surprisingly, and social help may not be promptly accessible. In this manner, it is critical to pick up adapting procedures that you can do without anyone else. Adapting techniques concentrated on improving your mindset and decreasing the tension that you can do individually are now and again depicted as self-calming or self-care adapting procedures.

Expressive Writing

Utilizing journaling to adapt to and express your contemplations and sentiments (additionally called expressive composition) can be a decent method for adapting to tension. Expressive composing has been found to improve physical and mental wellbeing. As to PTSD specifically, expressive composing has been found to have various advantages, including improved adapting and posttraumatic development (or the capacity to discover importance in and have positive life changes following an awful mishap), just as decreased PTSD side effects, pressure, and outrage.

Interruption

Deliberate utilization of interruption strategies can really be of advantage in adapting to feelings that are solid and feel awkward, for example, tension and dread. Interruption is anything you do to briefly remove your consideration from forceful feeling. Some of the time, concentrating on a forceful feeling can make it feel significantly more grounded and progressively crazy. Subsequently, by incidentally diverting yourself, you may give the feeling some an opportunity to diminish in force, making it simpler to oversee.

Conduct Activation

Uneasiness and shirking go connected at the hip. While the shirking of uneasiness inciting circumstances may help diminish our tension right now, in the long haul, it might keep us from carrying on with an important and compensating life (particularly as this evasion becomes greater and greater). Conduct initiation is an extraordinary method for expanding your action level, just as the amount you take part in positive and remunerating exercises. Through social actuation, you can lessen your downturn and tension.

CHAPTER 16:

About PTSD & Triggers

Figuring out what sets a PTSD partner off takes work and knowledge. When you have unmanaged PTSD, almost anything prompts negative feelings and emotions. A trigger can be any situation, person, place, smell, noise, or object that elicits uncomfortable and unwelcome emotional and physical symptoms. Triggers act as the catalyst for flashbacks (reliving memories) and can negatively influence behavior and affect how the person perceives their surrounding environment.

While some triggers are obvious, others are more difficult to recognize and tackle. A military veteran might be triggered by loud sounds like gunfire, so avoiding these situations will reduce the chances of the person being triggered. A child abuse and neglect survivor might be triggered by a smell in an elevator and not immediately identify or understand the cause.

PTSD triggers can be internal or external in nature. *Internal triggers* are things the person experiences inside their own body and mind. These can include thoughts, memories, emotions, physical sensations, and the like. *External triggers* are any outside influences the person encounters throughout the day. Situations, places, people, or other things that happen outside the body are external triggers.

Identifying PTSD Triggers

It may feel as if PTSD symptoms occur spontaneously, but this is not the case. PTSD symptoms generally occur after a trigger sets them off. The best way to prevent "out of control" situations is to learn about and pinpoint triggers, and you can do this as a couple.

You must learn to become aware of them and manage them ahead of time before they disrupt the day.

To counteract the unnecessary reactivity that triggers have on the PTSD brain, the PTSD partner must learn ways to identify occurrences, situations, and behaviors that tend to trigger symptoms. Anyone can learn to anticipate these triggers, distance from them, or get in front of them and take appropriate action to prevent them from having an impact on your life and romantic relationship. Be aware that increasing awareness of triggers can bring distress, but it's important to fight through and conquer the fear to move forward.

By nature, traumatic experiences are distressing, and post-traumatic reactions of shock and distress are normal.

Most people recover naturally, helped by adequate social support.

Common External Triggers

- Trauma reminders and arguments
- Witnessing a car accident
- Certain sounds, sights, or smells
- A relationship ending
- Family, school, work, money, or relationships
- Specific dates
- Holidays
- A specific place
- A personal reminder of trauma
- Nature (weather, seasons, etc.)
- Hospitals, medical treatment, funerals

Common Internal Triggers

- Anxiety
- Anger
- Sadness

- Strong emotions (helplessness, trapped)

- Bad memories

- Frustration

- Feeling lonely

- Feeling out of control

- Feeling vulnerable

- Increased heartbeat

- Muscle tension pain

Coping with PTSD Triggers

The most effective way of coping with triggers is to avoid them, but this is nearly impossible to do because emotions, thoughts, and physical sensations cannot really be avoided. When a person with PTSD is struggling with self-regulation, their thoughts, emotions, and sensations are all over the place. While you can take steps to manage exposure to external triggers, internal triggers are more difficult to manage. Either way, without effective coping strategies, managing any triggers can be a frightening task with the potential to negatively impact the relationship. Here are some examples of coping approaches. All of them can be practiced as a couple's activity because techniques and strategies to cope with PTSD symptoms can serve to reduce anxiety and benefit both PTSD and non-PTSD people:

- Mindfulness
- Calm (Diaphragmatic) Breathing
- Progressive Muscle Relaxation
- Self-Soothing Techniques
- Grounding
- Expressive Writing (Journaling)
- Grounding
- Visualization

A variety of coping strategies will make trigger management much easier. Healthy coping strategies can also help to retrain the PTSD brain after trauma, making the PTSD partner more likely to prevent the development of unhealthy or faulty coping mechanisms.

Before practicing any techniques to identify and manage triggers, be sure you have a safety plan in place, just in case, things get too distressing.

Living with a PTSD Partner

As the life-impacting disorder that it is, PTSD can take a heavy toll on relationships. The symptoms that accompany the disorder can make it difficult for the sufferer to accommodate the intricacies of a relationship, and for the non-PTSD partner to understand the behavior of their loved one with PTSD. PTSD has a profound effect on a person's ability to provide affection and makes them more volatile. A non-PTSD partner who is not prepared or knowledgeable may feel as if they are constantly walking on eggshells or living with a stranger.

It is difficult for a non-PTSD partner not to take the accompanying symptoms of PTSD personally. It's imperative to understand that a person with PTSD is not always in control of their actions and reactions. Often, they are trapped in an uncomfortable and difficult to navigate constant state of alert that increases their feelings of vulnerability, fear, shame, guilt, and makes them feel unsafe all the time. PTSD symptoms cannot be turned off, so here are a few pointers to consider when living with a partner who has PTSD.

Remaster the Art of Listening

While people with PTSD should not be pressured into talking about their traumatic experience, they will talk when they are ready. If they choose to share their experience, it is important for a non-PTSD partner to **be a good listener** without being judgmental. Sometimes the act of listening is more valuable than any advice. Listening without expectations shows that you are interested and that you care what the other person has to say, not that you care; they listen to what you have to say.

A good, knowledgeable, and caring non-PTSD partner can be the catalyst for change in the life of their partner. If your PTSD partner feels comfortable enough to talk, because you're a good and attentive listener, they might want to **talk about the traumatic event repeatedly**.

There is nothing wrong with it, and this is part of their healing process. The non-PTSD partner should avoid telling their partner to stop revisiting the past and move on, even if the details are difficult to listen to. Respect their feelings if you want them to trust you and open to you for healing.

Provide Social Support

Often, non-PTSD partners lack a basic understanding of what life is like for a person with PTSD. The impact and far-reaching effects of the accompanying symptoms can make a person be in a constant state of anger, irritability, depression, mistrust, guilt, shame, and many other negative feelings and emotions.

A solid, loving, and caring **support system** can help the PTSD partner move away from the traumatic experience, instead of living in a constant state of anxiety that makes them want to withdraw from friends and family.

It might not always be easy to demonstrate love, support, and affection to someone suffering from PTSD, but simply being there for them can play a major role in their healing journey and process.

Don't pressure your PTSD loved one into talking about their trauma or what they might be feeling now. It can be extremely difficult for a person with PTSD to share details about their traumatic experiences and could worsen things. Be there for them when they are ready to talk or simply 'hang out' when they don't feel like a chatterbox.

Be patient with your PTSD partner. Recovery from PTSD is a long and tedious process that may involve setbacks. Don't be judgmental, be accepting, and patient about your partner's progress (or regress).

Especially during stressful times, try your best to **engage in normal activities**, those that have nothing to do with PTSD, or serve as a reminder of the trauma. It could be doing a hobby you both enjoy dancing, going for a walk, watching a movie, or hundreds of other options.

Help Rebuild Trust & Safety

PTSD fundamentally alters the way people view the world because the traumatic experience leaves the person feeling unsafe, on edge, fragile, and feeling as if, at any given moment, the trauma will repeat. These negative feelings take a toll on a person's sense of trust and safety and can become serious hurdles in romantic relationships.

As a non-PTSD partner, part of your job is to **help rebuild** your PTSD partner's surrounding world from a constantly dangerous and frightening place to a safe and trustworthy one that helps reduce anxiety. A good way to help rebuild trust and safety is to **create a solid and predictable routine** you can both follow. A structured and foreseeable world tends to reduce anxiety in people with PTSD and can help restore the lost sense of stability, security, and safety stolen by PTSD symptoms. From grocery shopping to house cleaning, to cooking, to mealtimes, anything that provides structure and organization will serve to reduce the constant feelings of lack of safety and trust.

By helping your PTSD partner rebuild, you are contributing to their ability to trust themselves and others again, a crucial component of PTSD recovery. Helping a person with PTSD rebuild trust and safety takes **work and commitment**, so make sure your partner knows you're in for the long-haul.

CHAPTER 17:

Recovery and Daily Home life Demands

Life's Normal Demands

Typically, after short or long durations of emergencies or traumatic events, individuals become disorganized in daily life tasks. Clothes are unwashed and unfolded. Trash stacks up. Dishes are unclean. Cars are filthy. Bed sheets unchanged. Bills unpaid. The grass didn't mow. Children neglected. Friendships ignored. Spouses unheeded. All daily chores or everyday relationships are pushed to the side when urgent events must take priority. Overtime work, double/triple shifts, and exhausting schedules sidetrack normal living necessities. Physical fatigue, emotional exhaustion, and mental flooding leave nothing left for daily, ordinary demands. When recovering from the demands of trauma work, we find ourselves now overwhelmed with unsolved problems at home, unfinished tasks, irritating chores, desk clutter. We have odd conflicts with loved ones who need loving attention. You are exhausted, yet ordinary demands piled up in your absence. In order to recover from your trauma work, you will need to rest and recalibrate your body's physical needs. Next, you will need to practice simple restorative inner peace exercises that help you regain mental and emotional space for recovery. Then, you will need to pay attention to the chores of daily life that you have left unattended.

We will walk you through step-by-step ways of resolving these "nagging" chores. Pick-up the pieces of your "normal" life. Reorganize daily life that has become chaotic.

Fortunately, resolving daily ordinary problems will help you 1) clear up the emotional clutter of normal life messes, 2) re-integrate you back into your daily home life and identity, and 3) repair damage created by neglect, exhaustion, and distractions associated with your work with trauma.

First Steps

Five steps below will help you deal with your home life demands:

1. Be patient with yourself.

2. Take each day and each day's tasks, one step at a time.

3. Use the procrastination tools that motivate you or help you regain your daily functions.

4. Clearly, communicate with your family and friends about your *level of stress, fatigue, or exhaustion*. This will help them comprehend what steps you are taking to recover and why you need to pace yourself.

5. Communicate with your family and friends *your plans for recovery*. Tell them your plans so they can a) help you recover, b) be patient with you, c) anticipate that their lives too will return to normalcy.

Second Steps

Now, we will give you four tools to motivate your otherwise demotivated energies to get some chores done. Daily tasks may look too big, too foreboding, or too boring. After all, work-life is horribly demanding, and the last thing you want to do is more work at home. You want home life to be a refuge.

Yet, home life has chores too. The family has desires and needs too. Frustrating isn't it, especially when you are recovering from trauma work. We will begin with the "Just-Get-It-Done" approach.

Mental Attitude Trick #1: The "Just-Get-IT-Done" Mantra

"Just-Get-IT-Done" can become your mental declaration that leads you to finish those tasks, which are staring you in the face.

"Just-Get-IT-Done" can become a mantra. Mantras are meaningful words or phrases we repeat throughout our day, which aim to steer our attitudes, emotions, and actions.

"Just-Get-IT-Done NOW!" becomes an answer to yourself any time you feel inclined to:

   a. Procrastinate

   b. Delay

   c. Avoid

   d. Pass-it-on to someone else to do

"Just-Get-IT-Done" becomes the coach on your shoulder shouting in your ears to ACT NOW.

Typically, after you begin your task, having coerced yourself with **"Just-Get-IT-Done,"** you feel less burdened, you feel more productive and organized, and you also enjoy hanging out with your new proactive self.

So, this **"Just-Get-IT-Done"** mantra is one of many tools you can use to help you resolve or finish whatever is stopping you.

Mental Attitude Trick #2: "Get Your Ass in Gear, Dude"

Some individuals wisely hassle themselves or "yell-at" themselves when they need to tackle something. Wisely hassle themselves? Yes. Sometimes. We occasionally have to become irritated with ourselves enough to kick us into action. Irritation can motivate us to finish washing dishes, pay bills, make appointments, or complete daunting projects. We wisely can use our agitated or angry feelings to motivate us when we are stalled, avoiding something, or feeling confused or indecisive.

Those people who function best "in the last-minute," use stress to wake up their brains and focus their efforts and time. Yes, procrastinators wake-up under pressure too. People with ADHD diagnoses often do their last-minute accomplishments in a harried state. When they are rushed, a task gets done. Then, they flow back to their "chill zone."

We respond quickly when we are in a crisis. Trauma work can train your body and mind to only respond when there is an emergency and be passive when nothing is urgent.

This can make ordinary home life chores harder to do because they may not seem urgent. "Get Your Ass in Gear, Dude" is a mental way of tricking your brain and body into action even when there is no emergency.

So, as you reintegrate back into your normal daily home routines, every so often, you might decide to pressure yourself with a little self-kicking such as "Get Your Ass in Gear, Dude." Chances are you will feel better after you have gotten something done that was nagging at you.

Depression and Anxiety Due to Unresolved Daily Tasks

Individuals ask me to help them stop being panicked or anxious after a traumatic event. Interestingly, one of the dimensions of their panic or anxiety can be related to unresolved aspects of their ordinary lives. A normal unresolved issue is harassing them, making them feel very demotivated, agitated, irritable, or upset. After they resolve those daily issues, a sweet calmness often settles into place. They feel internal conflicts and tensions gently soothing because they have solved the daily issues or finished the normal tasks hanging over their heads. For them, their agitation was a signal that something in their everyday life needed to get done.

Face it though, we all have unfinished projects or chores, all the time. If we live perpetually in a state of anxiety because something is not done, we will spiral into the cortisol-slaved-stress that kidnaps our body's health, our brain's clarity, and our inner peace.

Clearly, even after trauma work, we have to finish what we can in our home life. Yet, we must be patient with our progress and energy levels. Practice our Inner Peace tools. Motivate ourselves to face dreaded chores. Grow our ability to function efficiently in our normal life, one step at a time.

CHAPTER 18:

To Family and Friends

It is so very important to know and understand that your loved one is sick, lonely, unable-to-change, guilt-ridden, and shame-filled. If they could do better, they would do better. They need treatment. Good, focused professional care is required for these afflictions. Your first job is this knowledge. You also must love them in a clear, demonstrative way. And it is very important that you insist that their treatment be focused on "The Big Five" values of recovery. It is also very important that you participate in their treatment and offer consistent, ongoing support in their recovery efforts.

This stuff is not easy. You will be challenged to detach emotionally, work on yourself, and stay the course in clarity and love. Your own support system is essential. Support groups such as Al-Anon are so very helpful in this regard. They have much to offer around acceptance, understanding, and specific methods for coping and thriving in these situations. Work your own program of recovery. Getting therapy, having your own personal spiritual practice of prayer, meditation, inspirational reading, and time spent in nature are all helpful in this regard. If in Al-Anon, or another 12 Step group, actually working those steps can be a tremendous asset for your personal growth and well-being. The rewards are tremendous. To witness the benefits of long-term, full recovery from any or all of these afflictions is a great, uplifting life experience. It is happening every day, everywhere, and it can happen in the life of your loved one. Stay the course. The miracle of recovery is something not to be missed. You can allow for this to take place in your life. It is truly worth every minute spent doing the work. May you embark on this path and reap all the joy.

To Treatment Providers

I feel such a deep sense of connection to you, my brothers and sisters working in this noble profession. I know full well the challenges you face day in and day out around these difficult to treat afflictions. These work environments are so highly charged with negative emotions and human suffering, that just holding up to the barrage of it all is enough to cause doubt about your choice of careers. Yet, the upside of great reward in terms of witnessing a complete transformation in the recovery process is something that keeps you in the game, coming back each day for more.

I commend you and honor you for doing God's work. This effort is nothing short of life-saving and clearly quality-of-life enhancing. Give yourself credit for your efforts and knowledge. Know that you make a difference. Embrace the process and release the outcomes. Support your fellow team members and love the afflicted ones. Keep on keeping on, never giving in to discouragement or loss of hope for anyone. Be an enthusiastic advocate for recovery each day. Grow yourself. Know that the problem is brain-based/physical/psychological, and the solution is spiritual. Do not take anything personally while always doing your best each day. Believe!

Have clarity and focus. I remember when seeing an orthopedic specialist following a leg injury, I was told that RICE would be the best treatment. So, Rest, Ice, Compression, and Elevation is what worked. All working in that field agreed on this path. They all were on the same page.

Can we do the same? Sobriety/Stability/Safety, Love, Unity, Growth, and Spirituality (SLUGS) is the best treatment for addiction, mental illness, and PTSD. Let's get on the same page.

Note: I have addressed three afflictions together due to their common co-occurrence. It is essential that when we see any one of these, we also look for the presence of a second or third diagnosis. So many who are addicted also suffer from PTSD and/or mental illness. There is a great amount of commonality and cross-over with these disorders. Treatment can and should be designed for this consideration.

For Prevention

Prevention efforts need to focus on the truth. These afflictions are truly illnesses of the brain, a part of the body. No judgment allowed. The truth around which drugs are most addictive, who is more susceptible to these afflictions, and the real-life impact that occurs are topics worthy of focused discussion. Family-of-origin, heredity, and trauma all need attention. Adverse childhood experiences (ACE) need to be included as considerations for causation and those impacted need to be identified as high risk and helped accordingly. Most young people will not be fooled by some of the messages we have provided in the past. Be honest. For example, the truth about opiate drugs is that they are highly addictive, much more so than many of the others. The message should be "it is so good, don't even try it once." Give information about the vast and rising numbers of overdose deaths. Tell the truth about how some illegal, "street" drugs like marijuana and magic mushrooms are not so addictive, nor do they have much mortality associated, and have shown to benefit certain medical/psychiatric/addiction type conditions.

In Summary

We have to do better. The death rate for these afflictions has been on a steady increase for years. Knowledge and action must have clarity and focus. We need a firm foundation for our field and our efforts around caring for those with these afflictions. We need to know, understand, accept, embrace, and love the addicted, the mentally ill, and the traumatized in order to provide the highest level of care.

If you have one or more of these afflictions, get quality professional care, insisting on focused treatment that emphasizes complete recovery. Believe that you can experience total healing and gain long-term recovery. Life can become amazingly fulfilling and so beautiful. You can and will ascend to your highest functioning, realizing your life potential and purpose. Peace of mind is a goal that we all share. Recovery will deliver. Go for it. It is so worth it.

CHAPTER 19:

Curing PTSD with EFT, Meditation and Energy

Emotional trauma release is an intense release of a certain emotion that has been stored either in the body or the mind due to a traumatic event or repressed feelings that have accumulated over time. The emotion can be released directly through physical activity or physical therapies (such as massage) or it can be triggered by your environment or through reactions to things that others say or do. When emotions surface, you can be overwhelmed with anger, fear, sadness, hopelessness, or any other emotion, often without explanation of why you feel this way. I would experience this intense release of emotion during meditation and EFT sessions as well as from other triggers during everyday interaction and massage therapy.

Physical trauma release occurs when you release a memory of a painful experience that has been stored within a specific area in your body. The memory is released through a sequence of physical symptoms similar to the pain you experienced at the time of the trauma. The pain varies in intensity from person to person and maybe a revisit of symptoms you felt during the initial experience or a mild form of those symptoms. I would sometimes experience a few minutes of physical symptoms that were so intense it would leave me feeling disoriented for a while afterward. Sometimes it would follow with an emotional release. It would always come with a slight warning so that I could get into a safe environment before the symptoms started. I always felt so much better for the release immediately afterward, feeling a sense of less tension and more peace and present awareness. However, I was not prepared for the longest trauma release I've ever had.

During the last year, I briefly encountered an episode of post-traumatic stress. It was not a present traumatic event that set it off, but a past traumatic event that was triggered through a dream. I had no memory of it and still don't. It lasted 3 weeks, but it felt like an eternity. I had intense anxiety, constant nausea and chest pain, thoughts that seemed to stimulate my worst fears and anxieties, nightmares, night sweats, heart palpitations, a lot of physical pain during the day, and worse during the night.

Around the time before and during those weeks, I seemed to meet a lot of clients suffering from similar symptoms of PTSD that did not understand what was going on or how to get it under control. They were suffering from it for months. That scared me. I wasn't sure how I'd cope if this continued for that long! Luckily using my professional knowledge of self-healing techniques, I was able to use a combination of EFT and meditation techniques to get the symptoms under control and have periods of time (at least a few hours per day) where I had no symptoms at all and felt relatively normal). I can't say how long I would have suffered with it if I didn't have meditation tools and EFT to get through it as fast as I did. Having had this experience and trialed the same techniques on clients with PTSD I feel passionate about sharing the techniques with you so that you or someone close to you with PTSD can experience a faster road to recovery.

The combination of techniques I used included EFT (Emotional Freedom Technique, commonly known as Tapping), energy healing and meditation, and making sure I kept myself engaged in positive activities that I was passionate about as this kept my natural endorphin level at its highest. By doing this, it kept me in a positive frame of mind, which encouraged me to focus on improving my quality of life rather than focusing on the negative experience I was going through.

After reading this e-book, using the techniques described above, you will be able to:

Use EFT in 3 different ways: firstly, to reduce intense PTSD symptoms, then to manage and control your symptoms, and lastly, to fully heal from PTSD using Meditative EFT (combining meditation and EFT).

Use a short bedtime ritual to ensure that sleep is more of a sound and peaceful nature; nightmares are kept to a minimum and it becomes a productive sleep, not a traumatic one. Also, use it to go back to sleep during the night and settle yourself and your body in the morning after a difficult night to start the day feeling the best you can.

Learn the basics of meditation and use it to get better results with EFT so that you don't have to wait until your symptoms are critical before you work further on your PTSD, maintaining a better sense of control over symptoms and enabling you to take control of your own healing.

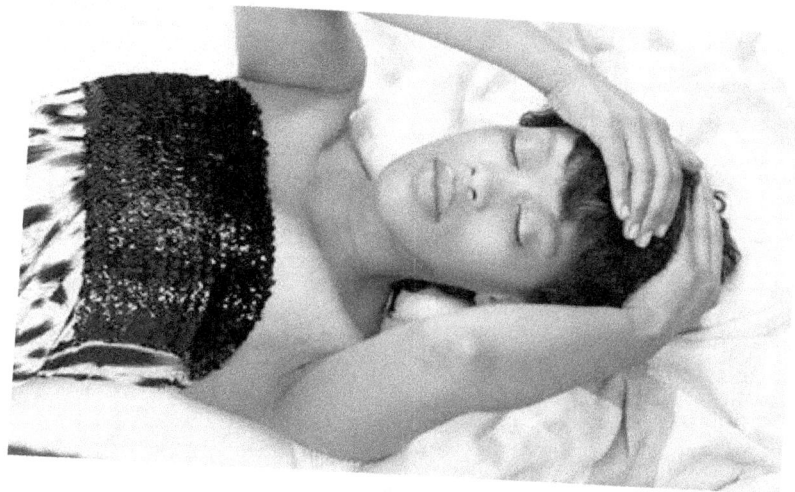

Learn the basics of energy healing through meditation. Use it on yourself to lift your mood after an EFT session enabling you to continue with your day feeling positive and uplifted.

Understand how to find your passions in life and becoming involved with them can activate your endorphins, which are your most powerful healer and steer your life into a more positive direction.

CHAPTER 20:

Trauma Treatment and Mental Health

Trauma treatment might be a rather new term to some, but too many common. Cognitive-behavioral therapy is a type of mental therapy that helps or enables one to deal with their thoughts and balance their daily mental state. This involves one's surrounding in terms of their societal constraints as well as actions and how they affect them in one way or another or their feelings. This is a study that will help you keep a profile of some of the things that trigger you emotionally as well as how to manage and contain them. Just as the name entails, it is therapy done to treat mental conditions that are caused by past experiences or situations that impacted one's wellbeing. That is conditions or ailments such as depressions or even anxiety. Yes, depression is an ailment. As we all know that when someone is depressed beyond measures, they can handle, they are prone to self-destruct or self-inflict injuries or mostly commonly abuse drugs. Trauma Treatment is not only for mental but also physical wellness as well.

This has always been a study under review and many have benefited from it in society. Its zeros in majorly on the challenges in the society or community at large that are not necessarily treatable through medicating or normal hospital appointments. Many have mental or behavioral distortions unknowingly, but when addressed and carefully decrypted, you'll find that there's always one thing that can do trigger a person not to be or act themselves. Trauma treatment help improves and uplifts one's personal emotional as well as social or even physical regulation by providing lasting and long-term solutions and strategies that add up to solving and diagnosing conditions.

The main aim of trauma treatment is to help an individual with previous problems, boost happiness as well as get rid of sadness and upgrade and treat dysfunctional and wrecked emotions one may harbor in them. As we all know, emotions affect our every move as well as influence them in one way or another. That is our behaviors, actions as well as thoughts. Trauma treatment is mainly rooted in providing and implementing effective solutions that will help an individual outgrow previous toxic habits and traits as well as uplift and encourage them to change destructive norms they take value in as well as uphold.

Conclusion

While it's up to you to do the hard work, a critical part of your success depends on the strength of support you have from the people around you. Whether you already have some of these supportive relationships or are working to develop them in the future, relying on them will help get you through the rough spots. It doesn't matter if support comes from your partner, friends, family members, clergy, coworkers, classmates, or neighbors. Just work on building a strong, supportive network of people you can count on and who can count on you in return.

It can be comforting to connect with other trauma survivors or people with similar recovery goals. The more you tell others about your experience, goals, and type of support you want, the more you'll find secure and stable sources of support.

If you've isolated yourself or used avoidance extensively, your current network may be limited. This may also be true if you've been depressed or angry and have pushed others away. Regardless, part of getting active for you will include increasing your personal contacts. It's okay to start small. Say hello to a neighbor or coworker or reach out to someone in an online forum. In-person or online support groups can also provide support when you need it most.

Take notice of the people currently in your life who already offer steady support. PTSD can be difficult to understand, even when you're the one suffering from it. Not everyone will be a good source of support. Others around you will have their own reactions to your traumatic experience or have their own personal struggles to deal with that make it difficult for them to offer the kind of help you need. Support from a loved one may come in the form of a comforting hand during Fourth of July fireworks, time spent together after a difficult day, a friend accompanying you to the doctor, or a knowing look when you seem at the end of a short fuse.

Appreciate the people who are supportive and find compassion for them when they fall short or have their own difficulties. Supporting someone with PTSD is challenging, and your loved ones are probably suffering in response to your pain and suffering. Keep in mind that there will be times that the support you need may not come in the package you expect. Support may be your 12-Step sponsor insisting you attend a meeting, or your spouse telling you to get out of bed and drive your child to school. Think about why they're asking you to do something uncomfortable and recognize that it may be the exact encouragement you need.

Asking for, and sometimes even accepting, support requires vulnerability. If someone were physically injured, you'd need to know where it hurt before you could provide first aid. PTSD is tough because there's no physical mark. You may look okay on the outside even though you're struggling. This is very confusing for everyone around you. It doesn't mean that others can't or won't rise to the occasion and offer what you need, but ultimately, it's not their job to take charge of your recovery—it's yours. Even if your trauma occurred through no fault of your own or in the service of others, your symptoms and your recovery are your responsibility.

www.ingramcontent.com/pod-product-compliance
Lightning Source LLC
Chambersburg PA
CBHW071553080526
44588CB00010B/899